Against Miserabilism

Writings 1968 – 1992

David Widgery

Edited by Juliet Ash,
Nigel Fountain & David Renton

Vagabond Voices
Glasgow

First published on 26 October 2017 by
Vagabond Voices Publishing Ltd.,
Glasgow,
Scotland.

ISBN 978-1-908251-86-2

Printed and bound in Poland

Cover design by Mark Mechan

Typeset by Park Productions

The publisher acknowledges subsidy towards this publication from the
heirs of David Widgery

For further information on Vagabond Voices, see the website,
www.vagabondvoices.co.uk

To the youth of today and tomorrow

Contents

Articles followed by an asterisk were included in Pluto
Press's 1989 collection *Preserving Disorder (Essays on
Society & Culture)*; articles without an asterisk have never
previously been anthologised.

Miscellany

End

PREFACE

Nigel Fountain

I first met David Widgery in a bar at York University, where I was then a student, in 1965. Our friendship, warts and all, lasted a generation, until his death. We had started as we would go on, since a lot of our times were played out in London bars and pubs – often, in the first decade, with the mixed pleasures of an International Socialist meeting beckoning from draughty upstairs meeting halls.

David was exciting, intellectually curious, aggressive, insecure, voracious – the only person I have known to take notes during casual conversation – and fun. He could also be stunningly rude, partly because he enjoyed it, and partly, thinking back, because he deployed it as a defence mechanism, born of vulnerability – the experience of childhood polio, *get them before they can get you*. The trick in responding was to be rude, and funny, back. And, beyond the antler-crashing displays, exhilarating vistas opened up, laughter, Marxism, Miles Davis, debate, discoveries, insights – and farce.

In the summer of 1965 David went to the United States. It was a climactic time in the civil rights movement, and he went south, got beaten up by cops in Miami, headed on to Mexico, blagged – not for the last time – his way in and out of Cuba, took in California, New York, underground papers, dope, US black and student radicalism, racism and the beginnings of anti-Vietnam war protest. That was, he said, his education, and it was a reason why, at a time when a trip to Brighton was travel, he had crashed out of the parochialism of what there was then of British youth culture.

He was born in 1947, in Barnet, Hertfordshire, the eldest of four children and only son of Jack and Margaret Widgery, respectively an interior design consultant and a primary schoolteacher. Margaret was a Christian and she cared deeply for her son. Having been expelled from the sixth form for publishing an unauthorised school magazine, David enrolled at the Royal Free Hospital medical school.

In the mid-1960s, David's addiction to print meant his interest in medicine was nearly sidelined. He cyclostyled his own inky, forever-rolling-up paper, *Snap*, raging against CIA-loving right-wingers in the National Union of Students, argued about Rhodesian racism while cutting up corpses in a Judd Street dissection hall, wrote furiously about "grown-up power" for the *New Statesman*, and fell on OZ when its Sydney founders launched the London edition in early 1967.

David was Maidenhead grammar school, part of that now extinct proud, touchy, post-war lower-middle-class tribe, and the splendidly glamorous Australians seemed classy, yet classless. They were, for a while, made for each other, giving David the chance to leap, and write, in all directions, into Beat poets and Bolshevism and Mayakovsky and capitalist crises and misspelling Che Guevara. And, *en passant*, via David did some socialists in East London and some radical bohemians in west London fleetingly "Come Together", or at least glimpse each other through that haze of the late sixties and early seventies.

In the autumn of 1967 he joined the International Socialists, an organisation whose time had come, then. IS – how initials change – possessed a world view which was relatively untainted by an embarrassing red history and mass-murdering bedfellows. It stressed self-activity and socialism from below, while grandly dismissing eastern and western blocs, capitalists, state capitalists, degenerated workers' statists, Stalinists, Fabians, Fidelistas, labourists, Pabloites, New Left reviewers, Titoists and Maoists alike.

The result, at its fleeting best, was a rarity: a relatively open, argumentative Marxist grouping.

David would remain a loyal, if oppositionally minded, member of IS (which messily metamorphosed in the late 1970s into the Socialist Workers Party) for the rest of his life. It provided him with a framework of theory, and did not impair that eclectic lively intellect. Indeed, it obligingly offered him, occasionally, the ammunition to berate – from that somewhat hazardous higher ground – those he considered in error, or fallen by the wayside.

In 1972 he graduated from medical school and began working at Bethnal Green Hospital. In 1976 his first book, the anthology *The Left in Britain, 1956-68* which he edited and narrated, was published.[1] By then the rise of the National Front, the casual racism of some rock stars, and the rightward tide led David to become a co-founder of Rock against Racism. He feasted on music, of almost all kinds, and was ideally suited to the turmoil and movement that was RAR. A decade later his book on RAR, *Beating Time*, was published.[2]

David would for the rest of his life be a doctor in the East End and, after working in two other medical practices, finally joined the Gill Street Health Centre in Limehouse in 1985, where he remained until his death in 1992. Three years earlier he had married Juliet Ash – one of that small group of remarkable women who majorly impacted his politics and his feminism. There would be several other books, but most notably – and out of his Gill Street experience – there was the superb *Some Lives!: A GP's East End* which, unsentimental, funny and true, has become one of the classic works on London: a portrait created in the late twentieth century that transcends its time.[3]

---

1 David Widgery, *The Left in Britain, 1956-68* (Penguin, 1976)
2 David Widgery, *Beating Time* (Chatto & Windus, 1986)
3 David Widgery, *Some Lives!: A GP's East End* (Sinclair-Stevenson, 1991)

This anthology contains some of the early polemics, burning with a youthful exhilaration, some agitprop, but also the works of his maturity. Some of the pieces included are from the anthology of articles that David collected and published under the title *Preserving Disorder* that is now out of print.[4] We include his comments in italics at the beginning of these pieces as a rationale for their republication, whereas the pieces we've selected that have not been previously republished do not contain David's comments.

As the years have passed since his death, his experience of life – and life in the East End – makes his combination of reportage, humour and a belief in a better society, exceptional. His Marxism was always a tool, rarely a club, and that early flamboyance, while never lost, yielded over the years to a greater subtlety, texture and nuance. But, of course, David never lost his wit – or his anger.

4　David Widgery, *Preserving Disorder* (Pluto Press, 1989)

Against Miserabilism

Writings 1968 – 1992

INTRODUCTION

Juliet Ash

The other side of the destruction of traditional working-class communities is what has replaced them,
which is a Conservative Legoland ... Which is not
about making anything, even making people better
who are ill, but a vast exercise in making money out
of money itself, a kind of twentieth-century South
Sea Bubble ... There is a real danger of getting too
depressed about the apparent triumph of a particularly tawdry and irresponsible sort of finance capitalism and the state of the labour movement and the
cowardice and lack of vision of its leadership. But
I'm very against miserabilism.[5]

David Widgery wrote those words in 1984 and he died a
quarter of a century ago. The only way to introduce, or
indeed think about his writing is to hold it up to the light
and ask, Are his thoughts still relevant?

In 1989 Pluto Press published an anthology of Widgery's
writing, *Preserving Disorder*, which is now out of print.
The anthology you now hold in your hands includes some
extracts from that book, but much more besides; it is effectively a sequel and provides clear evidence that his words
do travel. Despite big bangs and bigger crashes finance
capitalism still holds sway. Left-wing politics are often still
enfeebled despite the occasional successes. Those of us

---

5 David Widgery, Unpublished biographical piece, 1984. See
Bishopsgate Archives for original.

who want social and political change still need cheering up – but we, and the generations that have followed remain, of course, resolute against miserabilism.

Dave was the sort of person who threw himself into all aspects of his life, whether it was his writing, his medicine or his leisure time. At weekends we would go out with the children on adventurous excursions scrupulously planned by Dave, but once home he would often return to writing. It was the same routine after a day at work, a childcare shift, night-time duties as an on-call general practitioner, political events and meetings at the Hackney Empire theatre – he was on its board. He wrote fast and furiously, up in his bedroom where the walls were plastered with posters, newspaper clippings of strikes and sit-ins and amusing local headlines from the *Hackney Gazette*. His noticeboards were crowded collages that cut between photographs of cultural, socialist and medical heroes and heroines, and snaps of his children, their drawings, their school events, their escapades and their lives.

It was as though Dave was aware he had limited time. He wrote, with recourse only to notes he had jotted down in his spidery, utterly distinctive handwriting, with his dark green stylo fountain pen, in large hard-backed Daler-Rowney sketchbooks. He didn't do much new research, since his politics, medicine and prose were all informed by copious reading. And then there were his enthusiasms, for history, literature, art – even if he didn't always understand the latter in any depth! – jazz, punk, and rock and roll. All of that creativity was shaped by the personal encounters with patients and their lives in the impoverished part of the East End that comprised his medical practice and was the core of his life.

From 1967 until his death in 1992, Dave was a member of the International Socialists (IS) which, in 1977, became the Socialist Workers Party (SWP). Such a commitment to the far left has been known to lead on to pedantry. Dave was too contrary and original to suffer such a fate, and he also chose to learn from splendid writers and theorists. One was Victor Serge, the Russian revolutionary socialist, libertarian and sometime anarchist. Another was Peter Sedgwick, the leading English translator and writer on Serge.

Sedgwick had quit the Communist Party of Great Britain in 1956 over the Soviet suppression of the Hungarian revolution, and became a notable IS intellectual in the 1960s, which is when Dave met him. The older man quit the group in disgust when it became the SWP, but he and Dave remained close friends. Sedgwick was a brilliant scourge of the "anti-psychiatry" movement and its promoters like RD Laing and Michel Foucault, which, in its turn, fed into Dave's politics and journalism.

Dave, as this book demonstrates, developed his own form of reportage, illuminated by asides and perceptions that flash across the text. This also allows for one of his more endearing, albeit sometimes infuriating traits: the magpie syndrome. When worsted in an argument – or sometimes just for the hell of it – he took to shoehorning other people's well-expressed sallies into his own repertoire. "Sampling" is one contemporary term for it. There are others, less polite. But the prose became *almost* that of his own making, and often – moulded with his own imagery – it soon was, and often more illuminating than the original.

We only think we are living in the present. Because those moments when you do beat time are the important ones and they can let you glimpse something that has potential for a different future. And when our children and grandchildren look back from the early twenty-first century, from hopefully a much better sort of society across the world, I would imagine their main feeling would be, Why on earth did you put up with it so long, with exactly the same

5

tone of amazement we now look back on children
down the mines or women without the vote![6]

Well, Dave erred in the above instance on the side of
optimism, and we are, it seems, still putting up with it. But
the "present" that Dave inhabited spanned back into the
nineteenth century and forward to a future of possibilities. His was a peculiarly eccentric, bloody-minded sort of
Marxism, but it provided a crucial sense of history.

We have asked some of the people with whom he attempted to frame and contest that world between the 1960s and
the 1990s, and who are still challenging the status quo,
to introduce various sections of Dave's writings from that
period. In addition, some of the explanatory pieces written
by Dave for *Preserving Disorder* are included. We end the
book looking forward to better worlds, and this is introduced by a younger generation of Dave's family.

Dave would've been appalled by the tragedies of the
opening years of the twenty-first century. Yet he would also
have been transported by moments of lived magic – as we
are – by, say, a Chinese lighted lantern floating into the
future of the night sky. It is partially these fluctuations of
despair and elation that make his writing so dynamic and
honest. We feel that his words are still prescient today and
worth republishing for future generations.

---

6 David Widgery, Unpublished biographical piece, 1984. See
   Bishopsgate Archives for original.

POLITICS

An introduction by Anthony Barnett

Aged only twenty-one David Widgery emerged like a boyish
Venus from the waves of '68, his politics, prose and sexuality perfectly prepared for the revolutionary currents of that
moment while scorning the surrounding foam. In so far as
any one person can, he embodied the revolution attempted
in Britain in the sixties that my generation fought and lost.

My first memory of him dates from before 1968. He
must have just joined the International Socialists, later
the Socialist Workers Party (SWP). I got to work with him
much later in 1984, when I commissioned *Beating Time:
Riot 'n' Race 'n' Rock 'n' Roll* for the short-lived Tigerstripe
imprint of Chatto & Windus. Widgery created the book
jointly with Ruth Gregory and Andy Dark, who laid it out
in the spirit of *Temporary Hoardings*, the broadsheet of Rock
Against Racism (RAR) that Widgery and others launched
in 1976.

Any introduction to his political writing must start with
this moment when his sweeping cultural radicalism and
political loyalty, so often in tension, found a joint home
in RAR. It drew on the SWP to help turn the energy of
punk into a mobilisation against fascism. Defying the reactionary "downturn" of mid-1970s Britain, Widgery wove a
revolutionary's dream of working-class youth, new music,
defiant *lèse-majesté*, graphic invention, confrontation and
celebration. Defying police lines they smashed the UK's
incipient far right thanks to RAR's contemporary, the
Anti-Nazi League. The experience meant that unlike most
of the colourful radicals who became youthful Trotskyists,

Widgery made a creative alliance with his grouping and never left it.

Also, the tension attracted him. You can feel it in his effort to politicise the readers of OZ in his piece on Harrods and his interest in non-Marxists like Bertrand Russell. His reflection of the 1970 Pilkington strike shows his realistic sensitivity when he describes it as a victory for dignity and self-respect. His hope that its future will be ownership by "the rank and file" is unfulfilled: today, Pilkington is owned by Nippon Sheet Glass. The defeat was ordained in the corruptions of labourism and the rise of Thatcherism that Widgery lucidly responded to at the time in the two great pieces collected here.

In the eighties his task was not to persuade readers of OZ of the need for political action but, as his appreciation of Allen Ginsberg shows, to convince political comrades to be open to other energies: "It is also worth reminding ourselves that movements of popular revolt against long periods of reaction, such as we have been enduring for the last decade, often come in unpredictable, impetuous, and in infuriatingly subjective idioms."

Given he died so young, what would his politics be now? In his introduction to *The Left in Britain* Widgery wrote, "Because such a small group of people actually find written words convincing, I half wish that it wasn't a book at all but some species of talking poster..." Today, what else is the Web but talking posters? It would have been a home from home for someone as fast, opinionated, engaged and knowledgeable as Widgery, who, as he writes in "Whatever Did Happen to the Revolution", intended "to grow more dangerous as we grow old."

When Harrods Is Looted

David Widgery comments: *This was for the post-May events OZ, an Agit-OZ production with a cover of detachable sticky slogans in Day-Glo which in those days caused appalling production as well as political problems. I was trying to be serious and the effort rather shows: the mass conversion of a legion of hippies to my rather ill-understood notion of Bolshevism was, in retrospect, improbable. It was printed in violet on green, except for several passages reversed out into oblivion and accompanied by a complicated political diagram which indicated William Morris's affinity with Rosa Luxemburg and Mao's with Stalin. It was overprinted with a cartoon of Herbert Marcuse with a thought bubble containing a diagram of a brain – a hippy witticism.*

1968 would be as good a year as any for the liberal intelligentsia to start taking politics seriously. Let's, for example, pretend that the Metropolitan Police are the Wehrmacht and the dockers are breaking the windows of all the Chinese restaurants in Gerrard Street. Or we could make-believe in the National Conservative administration of 1971, the first-shot striker and the Student Problem. Or perhaps the meat porters do find out that it's the bankers and not the blacks. Either way the elaborate parlour games of most of our political intellectuals could be broken up very fast by the realities of a world recession, concentrated economic and political power, and eroded democratic institutions.

Fleet Street's chain of fools and their allies in the university have told us for years that the class struggle didn't exist or wasn't needed any more or that it was our business to be on the other side of the barricades anyway. When the students in Germany talked about overturning capitalism, they patronised them and put the rebels on the front of their glossies like cavemen-painted mastodons to show their mastery. When it happened in France, they talked of its "style" and how we have a middle tier of oppression so it can't happen here. And when it does happen here and maybe it's no longer chic but brutal and muddy and the rubbish is burning and Harrods is looted, they will not still see it's about revolution and socialism and that for us all else is folly. The nice people will have to choose then between those who honked their horns around the Champs-Elysées and shouted "Cohn Bendit to Dachau" and accurately "Liberate our factories," and the workers marching in the Place de la Bastille with the clothes they have stood besides machines in all their life. And if that's already too much like cliché, then you've already chosen your side. As for us, we should have chosen long ago. For until this struggle against capitalism and for popular power is finished, we remain in this logjam at the middle of the century – slung, as Matthew Arnold wrote, "between one world dead and the other still powerless to be born".

At least while the Labour Party is in opposition the myths of Fabianism might be maintained; for the intellectual that increased parliamentary representation of the Labour Party means the increase and then the achievement of popular power, for the worker that if there was a Labour government as well as a Labour council then rents would not still go up and houses would get built. But the vulnerability of the British economy to international capital movement and "confidence" has revealed yet again the marked and unjustified optimism that social democrats have always had about economic and political power. The independent foreign policy, as beloved of CND as Sir Alec Douglas-Home, is so many sweepings before the broom of American Power. The "export-led boom" depends simply on for how long and how low working-class living standards can be forced, and the science of 1964 means the productivity of 1966 means the exploitation of 1968. Labour has simply been taking its pleasure too often on the bed of capital for us still to be crying rape. But the rewards of collaboration with capital have not been adequate to buy mass support with wages and domestic booms, and Labour has been without mass support for four years now. But over the last two years even those party activists who remained have been finally sickened away from politics and gone back to *Gardeners' Question Time* and mild and bitter. Increasingly suitable undemocratic professionals of Labour's central office at Transport House are wielding the dead weight of a party defined by the absence of militants or real strength from the class socialism is all about. In fact the students' emphasis on opposition outside Parliament is a precise expression of the options open to serious socialists in the face of the shift to the right which social democracy and European communism has made over the last twenty years. Coalition social democracy has abandoned even its verbal claims to equality and social reform; the rhetoric of European social democrats like Harold Wilson, Willy Brandt, Guy Mollet and Pietro Nenni (and for that matter the Eastern bloc economists the Czech Ota Šik and the Soviet Evsei Liberman) is now thoroughly state plannist, elitist, technical and manipulative.

The communist parties have in turn occupied the reformist parliamentary programmes which social democracy has vacated. The drive towards respectability and the attempt to strip the tiger, ballot box by ballot box, has meant the isolation and frequent suppression of the CP's militants so that its functionaries could achieve the plush comforts of the parliament. The Marxism they practise is for the most part the ruling-class ideology of the Soviet Union: national and conservative and forced to express the most authoritarian elements of European socialism. The responsible CPers appealing for moderation at tenants' meetings are as fundamentally reformist as the French Stalinists who shopped the students and workers of Paris, just less successful. They are no more de-Stalinised than the West German politicians Hans Globke and Theodor Oberländer are de-Nazified. The cameos are plain; the leaders of the Confederation of British Industries (CBI) welcomed to the leather chair of the Kremlin to complain about their workers over vodka aperitifs; the cautious and "responsible" behaviour of the Moscow Narodny Bank Ltd in tiding over the last two gold crises.

But because there is no visible political institution which can be seen to represent student socialists and because loyalty to Eastern Europe is no longer an accurate litmus to the far left, the political trainspotters and student affairs "experts" whose ideology is end of ideology have assumed that students are no longer interested in theory and analysis but are just in it for the punch-ups. If only lines of communication could be opened for full and free dialogue and the troublemakers eliminated, the universities could get back to the real and superbly harmless works of scholarship. Whereas in fact political students spend their waking, thinking, drinking life utterly bound up in politics and analysis. Those who are fond of asking why we don't join the National Liberation Front should not suppose that the workers and intellectuals of the Spanish Civil War are the only people who meant what they said when they declared they would die for what they believed. Indeed, the very franticness of students, their capacity for outrage and hope, is an affront to the play ethic of late capitalism for which a flayed self-awareness wears so much better than conviction.

What is at the back of this urgency, what makes the anger last and deepen is the horror which must happen every day to maintain the US occupation of South Vietnam and the final horror which comes from the realisation that the

Vietnams will be repeated until the US is either a fortress in mutiny or so overextended that the final reckoning comes. But students' response is not just the contempt that any person with a sense of meaning must feel over the mouth disease of Lyndon B Johnson, Labour Foreign Secretary George Brown's righteous hypocrisy and Wilson's diatribes written in the Pentagon. It is not only the well-chronicled, familiar, glutinous lies, the genocide to save a civilisation, humanity's Incendergel, the fragmentation bomb of freedom. The mirror Vietnam holds up to the West illuminates precisely those myths that are at the centre of the status quo: the absence of class struggle, the inevitability of economic growth and thus increase in living standards, the postcolonial powers' benign international intentions.

International capitalism has obliged the triple anniversary of Marx with a life-scale demonstration of precisely why it cannot make the world liveable for its people. It is not just the war in Vietnam, but the needs of an economy which makes Vietnam the rule rather than the exception, an economy "stabilised" only by high unemployment and massive defence-related expenditure, a system required to police the neocolonial empire that it has, at least for a few more years yet, to expropriate economically and supervise politically. America, that fine citadel of democracy, needs its guns and buttresses; to get them Tom Paine must be bound naked to the stake of militarism. As the late Isaac Deutscher, whose magnificent witness against the new barbarism alongside Jean-Paul Sartre and Bertrand Russell was an initial inspiration to the movement which has grown up across Europe to defeat the Americans in Vietnam, wrote: "About sixty years ago Rosa Luxemburg predicted that one day militarism would become the driving force of the capitalist economy but even her forecast pales before the facts."

The helplessness of Wilson even to make a formal diplomatic break with America (and thus the helplessness of those on the left whose sole aim was to pressure him into dissociation) illuminated the nature of our satellitism to the needs of imperialism as clearly as the bankers' budget, the gratuitous cuts say in the NHS for the foreign audience, and the shows of "toughness" indicate the helplessness of national capitalist planning with capital international and irrational.

The world's on fire; all Wilson can offer is the nudging and anticipation of backward British capitalism into mergers, investment and what is known as technological advance. The carrot is his grim dedication to the task of depressing living standards to a level at which even British business cannot help but become more competitive in the bitter conflict over dwindling growth (perhaps even an absolute decrease in 1968) margin of world trade. The political drive towards state capitalism makes sense to the Conservative Reginald Maudling and Labour's Peter Shore as well as the economist Lord Robbins and is resisted mainly by small CBI firms. Its main political implication is the increased induction of the higher levels of the trade union bureaucracy into the state planning machinery and then the use of the unions themselves to discipline their own rank and file. The TUC leaders find themselves wandering the corridors of power without entry to any of the doors of control and having abandoned even the notion of a militant rank and file on their journey to the top.

In the 1950s, it proved easier for much of British business to pay wage drift rather than fight it, and union officialdom was able to acclimatise to relatively automatic reformism from above. But the conditions which underlie the gold crisis mark the end of this era; wage increase must be fought and won in conditions which inevitably link the industrial to the political. It is in this promising situation, and in the opportunities it provides for attacking the fact and the politics of freezism, that student socialists have tried to find a footing. But as the aprons and boots in St Stephen's Yard suggest, there is no guarantee provided that the turbulence and disillusionment within the union rank and file will turn to the left, although similar vacuums in Germany, France and the US have led to important achievements for the revolutionary left. What is clear is that the Labour Party's roots in the working class are withered in the air; the MPs and intellectuals who remain must feel as far away from the young people who proudly carry NLF flags, as they do from the workers who are no longer ashamed to shout "Keep Britain white."

The Sunday press waxes or rather wanes eloquent, the svelte left cries into its whisky and the parliamentary left continues to flog its dead horses in the Augean stables of Westminster, but not one of them notice there's no one listening and nothing is revealed. Of course the taste for revolution is nothing new to the young middle class. Acid hippies, progressive school bohemians and bored pop entrepreneurs all like the language of liberation and the look of Che Guevara (and some can even spell his name right). But as for theory, history and ways of understanding these are all brain diseases. Indeed, the more the underground loons on about the revolution, the more obvious it becomes that pot serves roughly the same role that gin did in the 1920s: to enable the enlightened to sit around talking about their enlightenment. The club called "Revolution" where youthful members of the ruling class whinny under the portraits of Mao and Che is typical. The hippies in Britain are about as much of a threat to the state as people who put foreign coins in gas metres.

As the traffic to Xanadu thins, it ought to become clearer which of the new orientalists are moved to ask or answer any serious political questions. But in the USA the generous dreamings of the acid left have been overtaken by reality. Hippies give away food but Negroes take refrigerators and will hopefully leave the induction centres, police stations and tenements in ashes. Ginsberg did drink the water of the Ganges and he did have dysentery for a month afterwards. The intelligentsia seem happy enough treading the water of the Mall palaces, content in the knowledge that we live in a world of violently interacting bourgeois bric-a-brac. The whole thing makes you realise how much more important is a single busman on strike than five thousand critics campaigning to legalise pubic hair.

What, on the other hand, characterises the political militants is a strong sense of the impotence of seminar socialism, Marxist hash evenings and all the complicated rationalisations of the liberal intelligentsia which ultimately serve to limit all activity to discussion and contain all discussion within the magic circles of the academic middle class. It has made them wary even of the photogenic struggles within the university. For the result of such militancy is usually the collaboration within a few committees on the herbaceous border of power where a large amount of time is spent comparing the students' white with the administration's black and settling on a negotiated charcoal.

Those who are serious are increasingly aware that the universities and the technical wing of the binary system are essentially there, enlarged or otherwise, to provide specified amounts of predictable skills at the medium levels, to a given industrial system. It is this system and the ways of changing it which finally concern us; the JCRs are voting their money to the picket line not the pantomime, students spend as much time with tenants' associations as with their tutors, the spectre is still haunting Europe but its banners this time read "Today the students, tomorrow the workers". Unnoticed by the whispering gallery of the London left, students and workers are making growing contacts, gaining mutual self-respect and through their activity and their experience of it retrieving something from the husks of Wilsonism.

For without these roots into and connections with working-class life, the most scintillating critique of bourgeois ideology, the fullest of blueprints for student power, and the grooviest of anti-universities could all be paid for by the Arts Council for all the danger they present.

To wait for revolution by Mao or Che or comprehensive schools or BBC 2 is to play the violin while the Titanic goes down, for if socialists don't take their theory back into the working class there are others who will.

Similarly the solidarity with our German and French comrades was not just a vicarious gesture, but because we know our struggle is integrally linked to theirs and that we both face and are overcoming very similar problems. The spirit in which the students of Europe increasingly collaborate and meet politically is specifically one of socialist internationalism, not the remnants of the Fourth International nor the furniture of international Stalinism or the dining clubs of European social democracy but rather the invisible international which the great revolutionary Victor Serge wrote of.

It represents the beginning of a recovery of the tradition of European revolutionary socialism and the activist heart of Marxism within it. It is no accident that Luxemburg and Karl Liebknecht were the faces paraded in the German streets and Trotsky's face that the students pinned across the courtyards of the Sorbonne. The rifle butt and the canal for Luxemburg in 1919, the ice axe for Trotsky in 1940 and the pistol for Rudi Dutschke in 1968 – these are different weapons of different ruling classes.

The message of this last year is that their imperatives are being taken up again in the cockpit of Europe.

OZ, 1968

Bertrand Russell

The bourgeoisie's recent discovery that some of us want a revolution has led them to a certain indulgence towards mere rebelliousness. "The great rebel", they said of Russell, as if somehow to consign him to a specialised inhuman world of principle, honour and ineffectuality. But what should matter to us is the stamina of his politics and the quality of his indignation. More than any other man, he could speak to and was treasured by the rising generation of the post-war left. This was not just because of his rationality, his mental apparatus and intellectual achievement, but for his vehemence, his ability to speak plain truths, his icy contempt for the fawners, the liars and the hypocrites who pass for public life. If he was the last of the great liberals, he was, too, the first of a new generation of revolutionaries.

He was a rebel, too, of course. His popularisations of irreligiosity, sexual and marital candour, atomic physics and educational reform may now read somewhat over-argued and unshocking. Those brightly coloured Allen & Unwin paperbacks which aroused and fortified our schoolday iconoclasms may now seem tame. But when he wrote those books he incurred the absolute wrath of an academic and social world who rightly felt themselves deeply threatened by his ideas. Of those many hands which bore away the coffin of Edwardian ideology, he had the tightest grasp.

The politics of his early life were defined by his studious avoidance of affiliation or activity in political groups; for the champion of the free and disinterested inquiry, personal activity was a remote prospect. "An intellectual", he wrongly believed, "should remain independent of political parties since they are prone to dogmatism." At a time when the Liberal Party was collapsing inwards and militant trade unionism had split into the semi-skilled manual trades, Russell remained a political aristocrat, temperamentally still a liberal and entirely aloof from the fissiparous socialist parties growing within the working class, the women's movement and the Irish struggle. His disgust with the First World War was as much an intellectual one as the emotional revulsion recorded by Siegfried Sassoon and Robert Graves. He thought the brutality and injustice of war so obvious and the official pro-war idealism (whether that of HG Wells or the Oxford Faculty of Modern History) utterly transparent. The absolute clarity of his moral reflexes and his contempt for those who failed to share them was, here, first displayed. It was as if he alone could visualise the real forces that worked within politics, operating with the same fearful symmetry as the geometry which he had embraced as a child "as a first love".

The war had made him a socialist by belief, if not by activity. But his attitude to the Bolshevik revolution and to the infant Communist Party in Britain was again a lurching blend of fastidiousness and sloppiness. His views on Russia were gained when he attached himself as an unofficial guest to a Labour Party tour of Russia where he was treated like a prince, "made guest of honour at splendid banquets, quartered in historic places and found the only evidence of the proletarian revolution was the constant playing of 'The Internationale' by military brass bands." Russell seemed deprived by his very logicality of the ability to identify the actual struggle which had brought the working class to power in Russia and whose example was transforming the world labour movement. Instead he attempted a cool equation, applied a political calculus to the deprivation and suffering the Revolution was passing through and found such a basis was quite unsuitable for the realisation of the high aims of communism. Some part of him was baffled and excluded from any actual struggle.

But because he still talked of "Mankind" with a straight face and because his "passion for liberty" was not simply a euphemism for the Cold War, Russell never fitted into Cold Wardom. His insistence on the perfection of the socialist future effectively debarred him from sympathy with either of the conservative and irrational social systems which locked the post-war political strongbox. It was with the nuclear bomb that his vision of the future and his voice in the present could come together to inspire CND and its direct-action wing. Russell could quite literally hear the H-bomb's thunder; his sense of indignation, his hatred of waste and ruin, his inviolate vision of rational man gave the anti-bomb movement its special quality of desperation and affirmation alongside it. As he wrote from Brixton Prison in 1961, "There are supposed to be two sides, each professing to stand for a great cause. This is a delusion – Kennedy and Khrushchev, Adenauer and De Gaulle, Macmillan and Gaitskell, are pursuing a common aim: the ending of human life. You, your families, your friends, and your country are to be exterminated by the common decision of a few brutal but powerful men. To please these men, all the private affections, all the public hopes, all that has been achieved in art and knowledge and thought and all that might be achieved hereafter is to be wiped out forever."

Russell's concerns and the political assumptions behind them indicate that, perhaps under the influence of the young men he chose to surround him, his outlook was heading into a kind of Marxism. Towards the very end, Russell seemed to be renouncing the attempts at international statesmanship and the efforts to press rational ideas on influential men (say the Pugwash scientific conference which met under his auspices). Rather he seemed to recognise that the fight against imperialism is in the present tense and that his role was to support and advise those forces of liberation within the working class, the student and the national movements.

Above all, the richness of his last years was crowned by the Russell War Crimes Tribunal. Before the Tet Offensive of 1968, before Pinkville – the My Lai massacre – or Eugene McCarthy's run as the anti-Vietnam War Democratic presidential candidate, Russell summoned those few men of international repute whose sight was as clear as his to sit in judgement on the war crimes of the mightiest empire in man's history. Isaac Deutscher laid aside his *Life of Lenin*, Sartre and Simone de Beauvoir went to Stockholm and Dave Dellinger, the American delegate, was to leave it to end up in another trial – the Chicago Eight – in Chicago.[7] Russell's *Appeal to the American Conscience*, perhaps his finest piece of political writing, was to display again that wonderful old indignation: "There is no dignity without the courage to examine this evil and oppose it. President Johnson, Dean Rusk, Robert McNamara, Henry Cabot Lodge, General Westmoreland and their fellow criminals will be brought before a wider justice than they recognise and a more profound condemnation than they are equipped to understand."[8]

Idiot International, 1970

---

7 Eventually reduced to, and better known as, the Chicago Seven.
8 Bertrand Russell, *Appeal to the American Conscience* (Bertrand Russell Peace Foundation, 1966)

The Pilkington Strike

Review of Jim Allen's TV play "The Rank and File"[9]

David Widgery comments: *In Britain student activism of 1968 fed into a rising arc of working-class struggle which was, in the early 1970s, to produce the highest level of strikes since the 1920s. This included long national strikes by unions like the builders who had never taken coordinated action before, the miners' strike which produced the Three-Day Week and the Battle of Saltley Gate, the dockers' triumphant rescue of their imprisoned members from Pentonville Jail, and the UCS work-in on the Upper Clyde. Factory occupations against closure and job loss sprouted and developed national networks of support. Women workers were prominent. Even hospital workers, with hardly any trade union experience, started answering back. And rank-and-file workers developed their own newspapers, industry by industry, in which the International Socialists, which I had joined in 1967, had a genuine and creative influence. Ex-students, either as white-collar trade unionists themselves or as socialist organisers, had produced a revolutionary leavening in British trade unionism which heartened the existing militants and which the bureaucrats found impossible to contain. And many artists, especially in theatre and TV, added their impetus to the industrial movement. The Pilkington strike, with its almost accidental origins, its anti-bureaucratic character and in the marvellous film Allen and Loach made about it, embodies many of these elements.*

---

9   "The Rank and File", *Play for Today*, dir. Kenneth Loach, 1971

The road to St Helens in April 1970, to the explosion of working-class anger they said didn't happen any more, is a long and narrow one. Until the late 1960s, post-war labour history amounted to short, small and successful strikes. Their essence was cash, their impact was local, their conflict muted. Broadly it was the politics of Brother Kite in the Boulting Brothers' classic of Ealing snobbery *I'm All Right Jack* – among the militants a half-remembered loyalty to Russia, among the rank and file a political agnosticism.[10] But across this period were superimposed a series of violent upsurges of class revolt, disputes which, for an instant, reached insurrectionary level only to burn out in their isolation. The 1958 bus strike, St Pancras rent strike, ENV closure, the Shell lockout, the Barbican strike, the Roberts-Arundel dispute formed a litany for the left, a series of proofs of the revolutionary equation before the May Events proved the whole theorem yet again.

These disputes, recorded only by the pamphlets of the far left and the court reports of the local press, were the dragon's teeth. "The Rank and File", Jim Allen and Ken Loach's magnificent TV dramatisation of the Pilkington strike, examined what has grown out of them. It shows such a local conflict but now against the background of an open and declared war of attrition between the working class and the state, a battle which can only end in one side breaking the other's back. It lifts the smirk off the face of the world of "industrial relations", where all claims are "inflationary" and all strikes "damaging". It showed us a glimpse of the real world which smoulders behind TV "reality". As a film, its political effect, perhaps "invisible to a superficial glance", will be far more than that of *The War Game*, Peter Watkins's H-bomb film which single-handedly extended CND's life by four years.[11]

---

10 *I'm All Right Jack*, dir. John Boulting, 1959
11 *The War Game*, dir. Peter Watkins, 1965

We live in a time dizzy with statistics. But we know that prices increased more in a month this year than they increased in an entire year in the 1960s, that we have already had more strike hours than any other year since 1926, and that rickets is being reported again after twenty years among the children of Liverpool and Nottingham. We know that British capitalism remains unable to grow at anything more than a quarter the rate of its main trading rivals. And that means, in the cool appraisal of one professor of industrial relations, "more and more managements seem to me to be becoming aware that the labour situation has drifted dangerously far and that they are faced with the need to re-establish control over their workers" (Allan Flanders).[12] "Re-establishing control" means a battery of attacks from productivity dealing through legislation and welfare cuts to that most successful incomes policy of all, one and a half million unemployed. And as each sortie by the state is driven off, the next one is more extreme. Conversely, every victory of the working class strengthens its confidence ("If the militants succeed in imposing their will on this government, they would be in a stronger position to frustrate a reforming Conservative government", the *Sunday Times* fretted three years ago).

The features of the struggle may alter. Yesterday's union lord with his eyes on a Bank of England governorship is replaced on the "left" by the "aggressive" union leader less liable to let his contempt for his men show. Beer, butties and midnight negotiations with Harold Wilson are replaced by Edward Heath's deliberate seeking out of set-piece confrontations with ill-led unions. Old-style Labour Party "modernisation" of the social services is replaced by the Tories' flamboyant assaults on health and welfare rights. But the essence of class struggle over the last five years is its

---

12 Allan Flanders, *Steel Review* (July 1966)

continuity and the break with the traditions of the preceding fifteen years' hibernation.

It is against this background that Jim Allen's remarkable transcription of the Pilkington strike has such political value. It is a primal drama where a company whose profits rose in 1969 from £13 million to £120 million, and which boasts it's in the top twenty-five per cent of the big three hundred companies in Britain, meets its town – one of the thirty most socially deprived areas in the country with ten per cent of its occupied houses classified as slums. A town where, as a striker put it, "People are always on about providing us with facilities for extra leisure. I can tell them where OUR leisure is spent – AT PILKINGTONS."

Allen's life as an active trade unionist (he came to write for *Coronation Street* after coming to Granada's notice as a trade union journalist and before writing *The Lump* (1967) and *The Big Flame* (1969)) gave the detail of the outbreak of the strike its uncanny realism. He had demonstrated his quite unique skill at scripting the dialectics of negotiation in the opening scenes of *Big Flame* where dockers put the case against Devlin Stage Two. The speed of the outbreak from the flat-drawn department's complaints over payslips to a full strike for £25 for forty hours was brilliantly developed. The snowball of self-confidence as the glassmen tasted their own power: "It was fantastic, the atmosphere that afternoon. We could have done anything. We could have stopped the world. We didn't give a monkey's for the rain, the bobbies, the union. It was ... bloody great."

Allen and Loach never allowed themselves to be trapped in the heavy-handedness which so often beckons left-wing dramatisers of strikes. Rather it was the delicate understatement which gave the film its power. The brutality of a strike in such a tight community was shown as it must have been: muffled, ugly and nearly incomprehensible. The imprisoning web of TUC telegrams, TV cameras and phone calls showed how the committee was enveloped as the strike became a national issue. The tattered march and the ancient silk banner and the singing of "The Red Flag" explained so well the deep roots and instincts which give shape to the joyous spontaneity. The faces chosen by the director actually looked like the real people who inhabit mass meetings, with motorbike helmet kept on so no one will pinch it, long untidy hair, careful ears and the lines of age and work.

Some of the actors deliberately echoed faces from the actual strike – Gerry Caughey, the slight and intense strike spokesman, and Bill Bradburn, one of the old-time GMWU stewards. The national officer, modelled on David Basnett ("probably one of the finest negotiators in the country"), had the Robin Hood bat and boardroom manner of the species, strongly reminiscent of the Ford trade-union whizz-kid Moss Evans.

The impact of the strike on the old, the children and the strike leaders' wives, their incomprehension and their loyalty, was honestly if not optimistically stated. The agonised row between the ignored and excluded wife and her husband exhaustedly jabbing out a strike bulletin on an old typewriter was bitterly unsentimental. There was no happy resolution as in Biberman's comparable *Salt of the Earth* where the women fight equally on the picket line.[13] In Lancashire that didn't happen. And even the comedy which seems to rise in the most austere political situations was there, the Laurel and Hardy scenes which arise when sticking up posters and the old gag to pinch the ticket on the bus to London.

Much had to be omitted, although if you want to see the "management's point of view", it can in fact be seen twenty-four hours a day. Allen's insistence in spelling out the role of trade union officialdom in carefully stamping out the flames of a hundred years' anger and his determination not

---

13 *Salt of the Earth*, dir. Herbert J. Biberman, 1954

to let the scourge of the stockbroker belt, Hugh Scanlon, off the hook seemed an excellent decision. Post-Pilkington events, notably the collapse of any real TUC opposition to the Industrial Relations Bill and the defeat of the postal strike, vindicate Allen's politics. For the Tories are not out to smash the unions, they need their bureaucracy and want to strengthen it to work against the membership. The Vic Feather-Jack Cooper right wing and the Jack Jones-Hugh Scanlon left wing both accept the indefinite continuance of capitalism and are arguing about their role within it. Cooper, leader of the GMWU, the Pilks union, has already broken ranks on the Croydon TUC decision and announced his intention to register with the Tory Industrial Relations Bill.

After a decent interval, and unless the militants hold them to the non-cooperation policy which they themselves have advocated, the lefts will register too. As Scanlon's "settlement" of the Ford's strike, condemned by the Ford stewards, showed, he is prepared not only to damage the fight for parity but to obey the Tory laws before they are even passed. The Communist Party are so short of excuses they had to hold down an IS car worker from Glasgow who wanted to propose defiance of the bill by a strike on the day of its introduction and for his pains denounced him in the *Morning Star* as a playboy Trotskyist. It is in this situation that the rank and file, not as a hopelessly romanticised bunch of Spartacuses but as men often out of their depth and not unfrightened, are left with the obligation to give shape to factory struggle.

The Tories would much rather frighten the rank and file than jail them. Like the criminal who robs the bank with an empty gun, they would rather not pull the trigger: they prefer the union officials to do their work for them with some talk of voting Labour next time. It is in the rank and file and their own experience that the only real answer to the Tories lies. In answer to the question, "What have we won so far?", the Rank and File Committee bulletin issued at the end of the strike said, "First and foremost SELF-RESPECT – and the respect of the people of St Helens and the rest of the country. We have received an EDUCATION that money could not buy. We have seen the real face of Pilkington Brothers and the NUGMW."

Plays like this have reached an audience some millions of times greater than the early morning salesman of the *Workers' Press* and *Socialist Worker* could ever hope to address. If a previous generation of industrial militants looked back on Jack London, Upton Sinclair and Robert Tressell as the writers whose vision of socialism captured their imagination, perhaps the young workers of today will find their images of the future and the suffering through which it comes in "Cathy Come Home", "The Big Flame" and "The Rank and File".[14]

For those who still imagine the working class is a bribed, bamboozled and bewildered force, Loach and Allen's film has painstakingly traced how the creativity and solidarities of class struggle are constantly exploding out of the constrictions which surround it. Most of all their film points to the possibility of a future when St Helens is run, not by the Lord Pilkington, but by the rank and file.

Ink, 1970

---

14 "Cathy Come Home", *The Wednesday Play*, dir. Kenneth Loach, 1969
   "The Big Flame", *The Wednesday Play*, dir. Kenneth Loach, 1969

Whatever *Did* Happen to the Revolution?: Memoirs of an Inner-City Marxist

Although the leading authorities assure us that the system is, once again, on the verge of collapse, the winter of '79 is proving poignant as well as exhilarating for us lefties. The workers are out on the streets again, thank God, from Tehran to Tottenham Court Road, and the plump smile of the Stock Exchange has gone noticeably ashen. But are we really witnessing the birth of a new society, or merely a further instalment in the disintegration of the old? For even we, the benighted bootboys of the SWP, the rent-a-mobsters, the mindless extremists, tertiary pickets and habitual holders-of-the-nation-to-ransom, sometimes fall to pondering, "Are we getting anywhere?"

It is a decade on from the Tet Offensive and the heady days when 100,000 marched in London in solidarity with the Viet Cong. Ten years since Danny Cohn-Bendit's infectious grin and Alexander Dubček's wan smile seemed to be signalling, from Paris and Prague, new revolutionary possibilities. Only ten years ago since Bernadette Devlin and the young civil rights campaigners first raised their banners on the Bogside. And only five since a Tory government, hell-bent on high unemployment and stern wage restraint, was overthrown by wave after wave of industrial action – by builders, dockers, engineers and miners – on a scale which hadn't been seen since the days of the General Strike. Revolution did seem in the air, somewhere.

"Now what have we got?" inquires Sham 69's Jimmy Pursey of his motley followers. "Fuck-all" we roar in self-mocking delight.[15] Tom Robinson is more precise: "Consternation in Mayfair | Riot in Notting Hill Gate | Fascists marching up the high street | Smashing up the welfare state".[16] And don't write those lines off as rock and roll melodrama ... they could have come straight off the telex tapes. One doesn't have to be punk or gay to feel that the UK in 1979 has turned out rather less appetising than the menu promised in 1974 of Social Contract flambéed in "the red flame of socialist courage". Our new Jerusalem has turned out a harsher, meaner, poorer Britain.

This Is Madness

Since 1974 the most radical post-war election manifesto and a cabinet studded with Tribunite heavies has succeeded in bringing back mass unemployment as a permanent feature of the economy. The only thing that changes is the length of the adjectives ministers use to deplore it. Whole regions of Britain are slipping quietly off the industrial map. Not just the Toy Town cooperatives so cynically set up by Citizen Benn but, over the last few months, household names like British Leyland, Dunlop, Tri-ang, Massey Ferguson, Singer, British Shipbuilding have announced major closures. Go to Liverpool or Wigan and Skelmersdale and see the bleakness in the streets and the despair on the faces. Jobs gone for good, skills made useless, redundancy pay that melts away. Town, community, way of life crumpled like a cardboard cup. "I've heard of homicide and suicide," goes a current Liverpool joke about a girl in primary school, "but can you tell me, Miss, what Merseyside means?"

The only thing we can manufacture and sell is our past: Agatha Christie movies, stately homes and the cheapest

---

15 "Song of the Streets (What Have We Got)", *Song of the Streets* (single), Sham 69, 1977

16 "Up Against the Wall", *Power in the Darkness*, Tom Robinson Band, 1978

tourism in Europe. In a weird double take on nineteenth-century imperialism, Arab sheikhs shoplift C&A, black-locked prophets call hypnotically for the downfall of Babylon, and the Tories demand we arm the Maoist millions for a holy war against the Russian Bear.[17]

The welfare state and the "Beveridge assumptions" of full employment and adequate social services were the political outcome of the Second World War and the high point of humane planning in Britain this century. Their inverse, the public expenditure cuts enforced so strictly over the last three years in everything from nursery schools to road repairs, are no longer just an exercise in budgeting within the welfare state way of life. The cuts are a code word for a social counter-revolution, the replacement of the very idea of public provision for those in social need with the philosophy of self-help, because I'm damned if anyone else will. The ideals of Clement Attlee and Aneurin Bevan are being replaced by those of Samuel Smiles and Mr Gradgrind.

It isn't just the closure of comprehensives and teacher training colleges and art schools – the very character of education is being altered to fit the needs of industry more precisely. The nationalised industries, conceived as public utilities able to produce and distribute essential services efficiently and cheaply, are now run and judged on the same profit ethic as Woolworths. Nursery closures are justified not just for the immediate cash saving but because, it is hinted, women shouldn't really be out at work in the first place. The National Health Service, the jewel in Labour's 1945 crown, is not just being neglected and starved of resources, it is being forced into mediocrity, often by administrators who talk of medical care but who have the mentality of asset strippers. David Ennals will be seen in relation to Britain's hospitals much as Henry VIII is seen in relation to Britain's monasteries.

---

17 By "black-locked" Widgery means dreadlocked black people.

The scale of the retreat is difficult to measure with the eye. It isn't socialism but a species of cost-benefit accountancy. As the late Anthony Crosland, theorist of the social-democratic consensus, is reported to have remarked at the end of the cabinet meeting which accepted the full terms of the 1976 IMF loan, "This is madness. But we must do it." It is against this mentality, as well as their own meagre wages, that the public sector strikers protest.

Decline and Fall

Nor can any reasonably free-spirited person hold much confidence in the present government's commitment to civil liberties. We have in Merlyn Rees the most reactionary Home Secretary since Henry Brooke – a Methodist junta-man obsessed with official secrecy and deportations. Silkin is a standing joke and the Special Patrol Group (SPG) grows in its audacity every year, an elite force apparently encouraged to regard itself above the normal limits of the law.

"No thanks darlin', that's not our style," an SPGer told a friend when she offered him the key to a front door he was about to batter in first with a sledgehammer. Their performance at the Huntley Street squat and the Reclaim the Night demo made *The Sweeney* look like *Dixon of Dock Green*.[18] Oh yes, and in these radical days such old friends as Judge Michael Argyle, who starred in the fabulous freaky OZ trial, are still alive and well. Last July four Asian brothers (the Virks) were given a total of twelve years, despite claiming self-defence against racist attack. The jails cram, Largactil doses go up, the police crack down and the Chief Constable of Greater Manchester who organised the National Front's Martin Webster's £250,000 walkabout, confers on the Decline of Family Life (yes it's declined so far, they've had to send for the police). Of

18 *The Sweeney*, creator Ian Kennedy Martin, 1975–1978
   Dixon of Dock Green, creator Ted Willis, 1955–1976

course Britain isn't a police state, but there are one or two police cities all right.

In some senses we've witnessed a 1931 in slow motion. Labour is the National Government and sod the Conference and the backbenchers. After all, the parliamentary alternative is indeed grim: Margaret Thatcher, the crazed prophet Sir Keith Joseph, and Paul Johnson as Poet Laureate. Watching the assemblage of hunt-ball drunks, high-street proprietors and bondage freaks who seem to constitute the Tory Party Conference baying at John Davis, it seemed indeed enough to give one a brain tumour. And what of that last white-hope-turned-black-sheep, the Liberal Party, marching, as Jeremy Thorpe once rather unwisely put it, "in the direction of the gunfire"? It is hard to see the Minehead cast of incompetent hitmen, unlikely millionaires and unstable company directors as the stuff of the "New Politics". The aroma is distinctly nineteenth century.

Apolitical

So life goes on. Those with money spend it; business is booming at Harrods and the White Tower and Jack Barclays. A slightly sinister apoliticism is fashionable, the reactionary chic of cocaine and art nouveau and surplus value games. No one, it must be said, has yet opened a boutique called "Biko". But one must view with some alarm a civilisation whose leading intellectuals combine vanity and reaction in quite such an overblown concoction as Messrs Levin, Johnson, Stoppard and Waugh. Left-wing trendies were indeed rather distasteful but right-wing trendies are a very great deal worse.

Meanwhile the long-suffering general public attempt to get on with life if only the bus hadn't frozen up and the ambulances weren't on strike and a loaf of bread didn't cost 8/6 and *Any Questions* hadn't got lost on the dial. "It's a disgrace" is offered up so often, it's almost become a universal *pietas*. Everything is a disgrace: the SWP and the

NF, Labour and the Tories, Thorpe and Andrew Newton, unions and bosses. Punks think their parents are a disgrace and skins think Teds are a disgrace. I think *Time Out* is a disgrace.

This is the real fruit of the three years of the Social Contract: somnambulance, a universal sense of resentful passivity, a nation of Basil Fawlties, barely suppressing hysteria. We're doing what we're told, so it must be someone else's fault things still go wrong: the blacks, the reds, the queers, the strikers.

Those who stand out against the tide of national obedience; the Right to Work marchers with their valiant orange jackets and blistered feet, the firefighters in their strike huts last Christmas, the Fightback Committee at the gutted Hounslow Hospital, they are blamed, held responsible for the very conditions they protest against.

Indeed in the past few weeks we have endured a bourgeois version of the May Events, an enthusiastic pageant of reaction, aimed at the honourable, dignified and reluctant strikers who seek to raise their appalling images by withdrawing their labour, and have the temerity to make their action effective. From all sides we are told National Salvation depends on an irreversible transfer of wealth and power to the wealthy and the powerful. Although it will require an explosive agent more potent than hot air to demolish the architecture of post-war working-class organisation, the experience has been ugly.

One needs to be forcibly reminded that in '75 and '76 the level of strikes in Britain fell so low that it almost seemed that the great British institution, the striker, was becoming an endangered species. Indeed for three years we have been lectured so frequently on the virtues of sacrifice and moderation, it has been like living in a Calvinist seminary. Avuncularily by James Callaghan, belligerently by Denis Healey, worriedly by David Ennals, hypnotically and hypocritically by the unfortunate Michael Foot. The barefaced lie that wage rises are the main cause of price inflation was repeated so incessantly that it sunk in by sheer habit. The bosses took the hint dropped so heavily by Healey's pronouncements at City banquets. "The employers united shall never be defeated" became their watchword, and the tactics of Grunwick's George Ward of Willesden were soon taken up by Duke Hussey in Fleet Street.

There is, however, one problem about this great exercise in national belt-tightening. The cuts, the wage restraints and the government fiscal policy have been operated in the name of a transfer of resources to private manufacturing. But, despite the oil and one or two special exceptions, British industry has shown its customary reluctance to invest and expand, despite all the hospitals and schools being closed *pour encourager les autres*. There is nothing more galling than a pointless sacrifice. The exuberant rank-and-file industrial action of the last few weeks, seen by bourgeois commentators as unpredictable as an explosion, is the absolutely predictable fruit of three long years of severe wage control.

Contradiction

So what of the revolutionary left, apparently so well placed in 1974? And the women's movement's permanent revolution against patriarchy and capitalism? It would be betraying no great secret to admit that there has been a certain faltering of impetus here. The revolutionary left in the '74-'77 period became very prone to purging and splitting and, as usual, quite a lot of people who couldn't see what it was all about anyway pushed off to have kids, or lick their wounds or do their horoscopes.

The SWP has now in fact nearly 4400 members, roughly twice the figure of 1974. But their standing in the labour movement and their experience on the left has probably declined in those years. The Communist Party was preoccupied for much of this period with a rediscussion of its own programme which has ejected formal Stalinism and replaced it with a species of chummy left reformism which is masterfully ambiguous on several key matters. What strikes an outsider is that now that the Great Debate is over, the party seems at a loss to know what to *do*, and the level of its political initiative seems lower than for years. The small Trotskyist groups, and one should here say post-Trotskyist, neo-Trotskyist and in most cases sub-Trotskyist, divide and multiply, mostly in the fertile mould to be found in constituency Labour parties and student union bars. The libertarians seem unable to get beyond the status of a circle of friends, intellectually fertile but organisationally feeble.

One suspects that the great majority of ex-members of left groups, monogamous feminists, browned-off trade unionists and retired avenging angels of the student barricades are biding their time rather than selling out their beliefs. One does not live by politics alone, especially in a period of pronounced rightward swing. Indeed one is taunted daily by the apparent irrelevance of one's vision.

Revolutionaries in such times tend to elaborate their belief systems ("theory") or opt for something, however reformist, which does at least group a few people together who will make a stand ("practice"). The two ends of the equation waltz away from each other like separated ballroom dancing partners. This bifurcation is all too obvious in the bookshops, which quake with unspeakable tomes of Marxist studies, alcoves of surplus value debate and corridors of deviancy. I look with pity on the poor students stocking up on their pricey set books of Louis Althusser and Perry Anderson. For them the red base turned out to be a grey rectangle.

But despite the hilarious contradictions presented by academic Marxism and careerist feminism, the growth of the independent socialist publishers and the collectives of sexual, philosophical and scientific radicals who meet and argue and publish in idioms and formats of such diversity is wholly healthy. The Publications Distribution Co-op busily parcel out journals, from *Gay Left* to *The Radical*

Ornithologist, to a national network of radical bookshops whose audience must well exceed the fifty thousand the Left Book Club had achieved by 1937. And the left still does, however feebly, uphold the international solidarities incumbent on citizens of one of the oldest colonial powers.

For only when viewed internationally do we see the full starkness of the decade. Most disastrously the military overthrow of Chile's Popular Unity government was an upheaval as decisive as Franco's seizure of power in '30s Spain. Then there were the massacres of JVP youth and students in Ceylon in 1971, the barbarous military coup in Thailand in 1976, the Lebanese Phalange's murderous bombardment of the Beirut Palestinians.

Such acts of bizarrely efficient bloodletting inspire a certain dizziness. It is hard to retain a sense of moral perspective in a world where the strapping soldiers of the South African security police literally gun down schoolchildren who simply ask to be taught in English, not Afrikaans. Week after week for nearly eighteen months until there are over 1200 officially reported dead. And we march to Trafalgar Square one Sunday and think we've done something.

A White Problem

As for Ireland, one sometimes despairingly wonders if there wouldn't be more response if it was happening in South East Asia instead of thirty miles over the water. Leaving aside the issues of nationalism and self-determination, we are quite literally digging our own grave if we don't realise the technology of control being perfected in the streets of Belfast and Derry is intended, if and when required, for local application. "The British Army are waiting out there" wails Joe Strummer in "(White Man) In Hammersmith Palais", the single of the decade.[19] And he's dead right.

---

19 "(White Man) In Hammersmith Palais", *(White Man) In Hammersmith Palais (single)*, The Clash, 1978

But it's when internationalism comes home to roost, in opposition to racism and fascism, that the far left can be proud of its success in turning what was becoming in the mid-seventies a very ugly tide. Remember when it was thought intellectually devastating to argue that the SWP was, in fact, identical to the National Front – a philosophical proposition which as Orwell put it "is like saying rat poison is the same as rats".[20] The effort put into identifying the fascist cadres of the Front, the attempts to block their unwelcome passage with the ominous drum beat and the spiked Union Jacks through migrant communities, the public stance against any resurgence of Nazism made by the Anti-Nazi League have met with an overwhelming response from people who felt too that it was time for a stand to be taken. The problem here is whether the left can take the vehemence and passion of the initial anti-Nazi stand towards some deeper understanding of how respectable racism operates in the courts and the customs offices, and how racism is a *white* problem at heart.

But here, and in the still more intimate field of sexual politics, battles, debates, squabbles, anger and misunderstanding still entangle, enflame and pain the left's responses. Feminism's discoveries and questions can't just be "fitted in" to an already existing, finished Marxism, and Lenin certainly doesn't tell you much about gay liberation. New forms, new definitions of socialism are needed which see resistance to sexual and racial oppression as part of the making of socialism. Such definitions are unlikely to be possessed *in toto* by any one party, group or creed. But the way in which sexual, racial and industrial issues are now intertwined in modern capitalism was exemplified by the Grunwick strike. Though the day was lost, it was about time British Labour went on the line for a dispute led by black women. The performance of the TUC, Roy Grantham and

---

20 George Orwell, *The Road to Wigan Pier* (Victor Gollancz, 1937)

Tom Jackson in snatching defeat from the jaws of victory will be recorded in another, less hallowed annal.

Still Infants

So this is the winter of '79 and what have we done? Well I and I survive, like the badge says. The student visions of '68, the working-class insurgency of '72 and '74, the socialist parties which tried to fuse them – all three hit an impasse in the late seventies. We had to hang on for our very existence against a swing to the right which was almost audible some nights.

Yet the system we oppose is itself in grave condition: its economics unstable, its products poisonous, its subjects rebellious. Perhaps the fascination with which the fate of the shah is viewed, not least by our Foreign Secretary, is the evidence events in Iran give of quite how dependent modern bureaucracies are on the loyalties of functionaries which can change politics overnight. And how the ideas of the extreme left can suddenly become the property of the mainstream. Poor Mr Pahlavi – last year the most powerful man between Tel Aviv and Tokyo – now deserted even by his dog handlers and with the loyalty of his dogs in question, is truly an omen of our time.

As for our left, bedraggled but alive, we are still infants. We have not yet come of age and are far from the height of our powers. But we survived and, in Tom Mann's words, intend to grow more dangerous as we grow old.

The New Left of '56 vintage used to have a slogan – "It moves" – meaning that there was at last a shift in the monolithic, frozen political structures of the Cold War. We can perhaps alter it to "It grows." In the grim faces of the striking ambulance drivers, in the amateur anti-cuts committees, grinding out another abortion petition against yet another attempt at restrictive legislation, in the heroism of Lewisham and the harmony of Victoria Park, in the hospitals and the mines, something is stirring again, coming out of the Social Contract anaesthesia. Orwell put it bluntly as ever: "The struggle of the working class is like the growth of a plant. The plant is blind and stupid, but it knows enough to keep pushing upwards towards the light, and it will do this in the face of endless discouragements."[21]

Time Out, 1979

---

21 George Orwell, "Looking Back on the Spanish War" (est. 1942)

I'm Not Going to Work on Maggie's Farm

David Widgery comments: *This was written for the 1979 election issue of* Socialist Worker. *It was apparent before she entered office that Mrs Thatcher represented a more traditional and class-conscious conservatism than the consensus Tories we had grown up with. It was also clear that she would provide severe problems for the ineffectual and ill-officered Labour Party. So don't say we didn't warn you.*

General elections are not enjoyable times for socialists. Their purpose, said Nye Bevan – who should know – "is to beguile democracy to voting wealth back into power".

The Labour government's record in office has been so numbingly mediocre, and the lip service paid to socialism in the new manifesto is perhaps the most feeble and grudging since the Labour Party became officially socialist in 1918.

But we should not draw the facile conclusion that it is indistinguishable from Toryism.

Because a Tory government, led by Mrs Thatcher, would be even worse than this government.

Mrs Thatcher is, even by Tory standards, lacking in human rapport. She seems to have an uncanny inability to appear relaxed, to "fit in" or transmit the merest scrap of genuine compassion.

The fact is that Thatcher is out of place; the Tory Party are suffering badly from exclusion from the parliamentary power they once took for granted and both are desperate to fling Labour out. However, they hide that desperation. The most coherent and stable capitalist party in Europe, born out of the most successful empire and expansive industry of the eighteenth century, finds its automatic right to govern gone.

The High Tory ring, bounded by Anglican piety, public school decency, Oxbridge loyalty, Stock Exchange insights and safe seats, is disintegrating. The first-class carriages still pull into Paddington, but there's no *Times* crossword to hide behind and a season ticket costs a fortune.

The village green is dwarfed by a motorway, the chaps on the Rhine don't have enough spare parts for their second-rate tanks, the vicar has put up a petition for Medical Aid to Zimbabwe, and the Tory son and heir has gone off to be a punk rocker.

The British Medical Association (not unfairly known as the Tory Party at the bedside) still end their chapter on "ethics" with the advice that "when all is said and done, a chap knows what's cricket." But that was before Kerry Packer's exercise in free enterprise.

The old school has gone to the jumble sale, the newsagent's been taken over by an Asian couple ("terribly nice people though") and the lovely little man at the garage is now a Toyota spares dealer.

The lights are going out all over the Home Counties: being a Tory is plain going out of fashion. There are complicated causes: stagnation in world trade, demographic movement into cities, secularisation, female integration into productive labour, the extending role of the state and most important, too many years in opposition. But that doesn't explain to the man on the Brighton Belle why "Made in Britain" is a joke, or why his wife and children answer back, and school doesn't seem to teach either good handwriting or good discipline any more and costs a fortune into the bargain. Or why that man Callaghan looks so damned smug all the damned time.

The Tory Party rank and file are a long-suffering body and this decade has been a particularly hard one. They have come to learn that when their leaders achieve office, they "go pink" ... make their peace *with* the multinationals and Home Office liberals and Yorkshire miners. They are numbed to their leaders' "flexibility".

But the rise of Mrs Thatcher and her Philosopher King Sir Keith Joseph, over the utter disarray of the humane wing of the party, marks a new course. We face a new Toryism, frankly elitist, not just making racialism respectable but reaction itself fashionable.

By announcing an official end to Tory compassion towards the "undeserving" and by her avowed intention of "putting the unions in their proper place", Thatcher moves the Tory Party away from its traditional claim to mediate, rather like the Church of England, between all class interests.

Something called "freedom" is the battle cry. "Freedom", it soon becomes apparent, is closely connected, if not identical with, money. Mrs T will grant us the freedom not to have any obligation towards fellow humans who are ill, out of work or incapable so that *we can* have the freedom to select *whichever* private ward, public school dorm, restaurant or town house we wish for ourselves.

Dazzling avenues of freedom will become apparent in the very same supermarket you naively thought you were doing the shopping in. With all the promised tax reductions, you might well be able to make a successful bid for the British National Oil Corporation, the British Aerospace and Shipbuilding Industry, or a slice of the local casualty department.

This morally squalid equation of freedom with the thickness of your wallet is still more horrible a formula when you consider that it can only be achieved by a deliberate campaign to make the poor poorer.

Mrs T's much-loved "scroungers", who are at present hanging on to their dignity by their teeth and fingernails, will be formally and legally kicked over the edge. For their own good, of course, because Mrs Thatcher's new brand of Toryism knows that misfortune is but the evidence of vice, weakness or error, and that it is therefore kind to be cruel.

Ask Mrs Thatcher if there must not be ninety-nine failures for every success and she will agree; the socialists, as she insists on calling them, only produce disappointment by asking for equality.

In this brave new barbarism, public spending cuts, which Callaghan and Co. at least *pretend* to regret, turn into positive virtues. The virtual halt on public housing is an emancipating act for the poor, the overcrowded and unhoused since it will protect them from morally destructive dependence on the state. Further rundown of the National Health Service will be a tonic of great efficiency; those without money will no longer be able to afford to fall ill.

Strikers' children will learn about life, too. Going hungry alongside their parents will teach them a robust respect for their future employers. It will indeed be the Sale of the Century, and what remains of the Conservative Party's sense of social decency will be one of the items to get knocked down.

It is *The Archers* meets *Mrs Dale's Diary* with a touch of *Toytown*, introduced by David Jacobs.[22] It is how the Queen might carry on if she lived at *Crossroads* Motel.[23] It is not reality and never was.

Nor is the rapacious bustle of the Stock Exchange the peal of Liberty's Bell and should not be so confused.

Hitting the poor may be expedient, but it is pushing it a bit to claim it as some kind of moral crusade to bring back the age of personal service. Mrs T reminds us that the gnawing of poverty is a better instrument of discipline than the policeman's truncheon. Not that truncheons are out of favour.

The proposals which will receive the hurrahs at Tory hustings will be for more corporal punishment, longer,

22 "Mrs Dale's Diary", *Light Programme* (BBC radio), 1967–1969
  "Toytown", *Children's Hour* (BBC radio), creator Sydney
  Beaman, 1929–1960s; adapted for TV (ITV) in the 1970s
23 *Crossroads*, creators Hazel Adair & Peter Ling, 1964–1988

harder jail sentences, more police, bigger borstals and prisons, and the job creation of a public hangman, that hooded creature of the barbaric days when torture was public sport.

And how do you get respect for law and order when respect for its agents does not exist? You teach people fear, that's how. You tell people that "they are afraid of being swamped" or "scared to go out at night" or go to Tesco without being captured by the Baader-Meinhof Gang often enough and they start to believe it. You announce, as one prominent London Thatcherite did last week, that "Lambeth has become the first Marxist state in the city of London." You imply, in the pretend "shocked" but-suspected-all-along voice of the corner shop gossip, that crossing the average city street at night is only slightly less hazardous than the parachute drop on Arnhem. You garner your scared votes, you extend and improve state security, and brutalise more effectively people who can, roughly speaking, be made to appear culprits.

"A short, sharp shock", promises the Tory Manifesto, licking its lips.

As for the unions, one can say with conviction that there will be a great deal of dishonest verbiage in all possible directions until 3 May. Everyone claims to think that the unions have too much power but also knows most strikes this year have been isolated and defeated with precision and tactical skill by Mr Callaghan. The Thatcher philosophy is clearly to keep off the whole subject and leave Mr Prior to say unfrightening sensible-chap things.

But given her philosophy of Freedom as Obedience and her barely concealed distaste for the gentlemen of the General Council, it would seem likely a Thatcher government would seek to call the bluff of the TUC rather than indulging in the rather weary Old Pals Act that Jim, Leo and David act out so gawkily.

While appearing to accept the Congress House end of the unions as something as essentially British as the Crown Jewels, she will simply dispense with the bone-trading, announce her plans and tell them to like it or lump it. There will be a sudden fall in the number of Len Murray TV interviews outside No. 10. As always in Thatcherland, you are free to be ineffective.

And with pickets licensed and labelled rather like pet dogs, solidarity action illegal and social security denied to strikers' families, industrial action which accepts those terms will actually be a declaration of weakness. This ground is already half-conceded in the Concordat, that appropriate amalgam of concord and diktat. Then watch unemployment take a quantum leap.

A maliciously minded person might almost think the TUC deserved such a deflation after its quite grotesque accommodation to every whim of the present cabinet. But passage of a Thatcher Industrial Relations Act would be a serious blow.

Once again. Freedom would rule. Those who employ labour could then be gently relieved of all that tiresome red tape about safety and unfair dismissal and maternity leave. The present isn't much, but we have to hold on to it.

Over the last ten years, trade unionism has come to mean something more challenging than just bartering up the price of labour. Not the Gen Secs on *News at Ten* but the solid, unglamorous improvements in the condition and nature of work and the level of humanity between fellow workers. The muscle-bound drags of the Tories' imagination are just that ... imagination.

Now Thatcher's trying to steal back our lines and our confidence:

"Say it loud, I'm capitalist and proud..."

"Profit makers come out – you have nothing to lose but your shame."

"Two, four, six, eight, We don't want a Marxist state."

Her borrowed idiom is a curious tribute to us. Us, who are rendered invisible on the swingometer but who have done more than we realise to shift the heavy pendulum of British politics over the past years.

We have clashed more and more openly with the powers that be, usually the police, about issues that are as real as our lives, not out in Hanoi or even Aldermaston.

We witness official Labour's shrinking of moral concern, the narrowing of its political eyes, the deadened reflexes. The unwillingness to really challenge the harsh new moral philosophy of Thatcher, except when it was convenient to drum LP members into activity they had otherwise long lost stomach for.

Yes, we will vote Labour this time too, and try to convince others to overcome their queasiness at the thought. Every working-class Tory vote is a tug of the political forelock.

But our business is to offer a perspective to workers, not an analysis about them. Our vision is becoming less and less far-fetched as the facts catch up with our predictions. "Ours is no dream," wrote William Morris in 1883. "Men and women have died for it, not in the ancient days, but in our own time; they lie in prisons for it, work in mines, are exiled, are ruined for it; believe me, when such things are suffered for dreams, the dreams come true at last."[24]

Socialist Worker, 1979

---

24 From an 1883 lecture in which William Morris considered the question, "Is Socialism a dream?"; can be found in E.P. Thompson and Peter Linebaugh's *William Morris: Romantic to Revolutionary* (PM Press, 2011)

Our Ken

If you were brought up on Danny Cohn-Bendit, it's impossible not to have a soft spot for Ken Livingstone. Underneath the C&A safari suit and that odd moustache glimmers sufficient honesty, insubordination and post-electronic political showbiz to identify a post-'68 socialist.

For if punks were the revenge of the hippies, so Livingstone's pre-eminence is an ironic tribute to the style of the May events. Not only is he wonderfully rude about such great British institutions as the House of Lords ("It's pointless trying to count heads ... because they die before you finish the head count"), the Northern Irish state ("Such things done to black people in a more distant colony would cause uproar") and Clause Four ("It's unpopular both in the nationalised industries and among the tenants of Tower Hamlets housing department"). But he's also scathing about that diagram of ineffectuality, the modern Labour Party ("The only difference between us and the Mafia is that we've stopped killing each other," and "The party leadership needs to be driven out of Parliament, if necessary with cattle prods") and therefore himself ("Life is a flurry of paper, much of which I don't have time to read").

Against the lardy self-congratulation of Roy Hattersley and the calculated spontaneity of Neil Kinnock, our Ken has a streak of plebeian London candour which will no doubt be his downfall in the Labour Party but is a refreshing contrast to the upper-crust, Oxbridge pomposities oozed by so much of the left.

Livingstone's intellectual brush with the revolutionary left was superficial; reflected not, as supposed, in his skill with the Labour Party machine or his pluralist approach to interest group funding and the salaried career structure for otherwise unemployable ex-revolutionaries now established at county hall (Marxists would be incapable of the former and hostile to the latter), but in an occasional weakness for mid-period *Red Mole* Spart-talk ("Capital is prepared for this strike in a way it hasn't been since the General Strike").[25] But despite the period jargon, Livingstone's administration isn't markedly different from many modern European municipalities and he is much nearer New York mayor Ed Koch than Friedrich Engels in his views on the urban crisis.

Much of his appearance of extreme radicalism lies in the favourable contrast to the undistinguished record and personnel of post-war Labour local government and the extreme provincialism of London Tories ("GLC Are Bats: Official" – this *Evening Standard* headline is not untypical of the intellectual level).

Livingstone's administration has made me proud to be a Londoner in a period when there was little else to be cheerful about. But then I happen to prefer reggae-and-Rowbotham-on-the-rates to office blocks and Horace Cutler. For the mass of London workers, it is a matter of style rather than serious political reform: the GLC couldn't get to grips with the fundamentals even if it wanted to. Local government is local government: not the last resting place of the epicentre of world revolution.

The cheap fares policy is probably Livingstone's single biggest practical reform, but London Transport has been offed with virtually no action by the transport workers' union while Ken and Co. were busy head-counting at the Palace of Westminster and auditioning admen.

Meanwhile, the ideological functionaries inside county hall somehow imagine themselves part of the Paris Commune without appearing to notice that, unless it was

---

25 *Red Mole* was a 1970s revolutionary paper that carried a broad range of left-wing opinions in its pages, aligned to the International Marxist Group. Its editor was Tariq Ali.

very discreet, there has been no proletarian revolution in London yet. The left getting its hands on the chequebooks for a while is exhilarating, especially for those in receipt, but it is no substitute for real political change from below.

New Society, 1984

Operation Bookbust

Last Thursday, the bailiffs arrived at Goldsmiths Row, Somerford Grove and Howard Road. Not to evict people, but books. At 3 a.m., protestors who had been occupying the three small Hackney libraries all summer waited nervously behind barricade-sized shelves of Barbara Cartlands, rows of early learning kids' books and racks of reference tomes, large-print thrillers and multilingual accounts of young East Enders' visits to the family back in Bangladesh. Outside, the council mustered its lorries and rolls of corrugated iron to board up the library windows and crates to confiscate the books. A fortnight ago, the threat of strike action by NALGO town hall members and the refusal of council building workers to assist the eviction had temporarily scotched the effort. But Hackney Council remained set on Operation Bookbust.

By Friday, Goldsmiths Row was already reoccupied. Early Monday morning, the same was true of Somerford Grove. All three libraries had been occupied by volunteers who had kept them cleaner, busier and better used than under council administration. Even now, two are bravely attempting to stay open for business. Over the last six months, Goldsmiths Row has continued to offer information (an impressive range of leaflets on everything from AIDS to old-time dancing), literary classes and homework facilities. NALGO have paid for the electricity and light. "We've even repaired the skylight," says cartoonist and local resident Phil Evans ruefully. "A library in a place like this isn't just an optional extra," says another stalwart of the occupation, Jane Kelly. "They may well have less libraries per head in Harlow or Milton Keynes, but it isn't a fair comparison. They've got more jobs, more money, more cars to get to libraries and more room to read their books at home."

To Londoners shell-shocked with cuts stories, the boarding up of three East End libraries may just be another sign of the times. But viewed in a historical perspective, the closures mark a new chapter in the decline of municipal socialism. In the late twentieth century, in an amenity-stripped pocket of a working-class borough where illiteracy is rising, migrants are struggling to learn English, and the video shop and the *Sun* provide the extramural education, a Labour council is boarding up libraries. That the party which did so much to build up London's public libraries is now closing them down surpasses the imagination of even those hardened by the volte faces of "left" local government.

For the left and the socialist movement is the home of the pedagogue, the autodidact and the bookworm. It was for the possession of books and pamphlets that the Covent Garden shoemaker Thomas Hardy, secretary of the London Corresponding Society, the first working-class political organisation in Britain, was arrested and sentenced to death in 1794. The Chartist movement depended on secret libraries of radical papers and books (most famously Tom Paine's *Rights of Man*).[26] In the London of the 1880s, possession of books was the *sine qua non* of the radical movement and in Bethnal Green and later Poplar there was fierce working-class agitation for public libraries, which the Tories always opposed on the grounds that they were unnecessary and frivolous luxuries. What would a socialist like the radical bookbinder Joseph Emes, who would have stayed "lost in the great Forest of Ignorance" had it not been for contact with books, have thought of councillors who closed rather than opened libraries? Or Thomas Okey, the Whitechapel basketmaker who joined the socialist movement via

---

26 Thomas Paine, *Rights of Man: Answer to Mr Burke's Attack on the French Revolution* (J.S. Jordan, 1791)

University Extension and went on to write the delightful *A Basketful of Memories?*[27]

Books and libraries are not part of a leisure directorate package, sandwiched somewhere between squash courts and swimming pools. They are a means to emancipation, not less now than a century ago. Aneurin Bevan, as chairman of the Library Committee of the Tredegar Workingmen's Institute, insisted that "however great the shortage of cash, expenditure on books must never be skimped." Bevan's reason was hard-headed: "We have discovered that nearly all the successes at secondary school are children who use our library." Through University Extension, then the Workers' Educational Association and National Labour Colleges, the labour movement has fought to provide itself with education. And education, notwithstanding Marshall McLuhan's electronic village, means books. In South Wales, miners saved to build their own lending libraries, in Red Clyde the Glasgow Imps (short for impossibilists), published Marx's *Value, Price and Profit* and Engels's *Origin of the Family* in Britain for the first time.[28] And so it goes on through the Communist Party of the twenties, the Left Book Club, the New Left, and the socialist and feminist publishing boom which crowned the sixties.

People who already possess a rich book culture seem able to shrug off the trio of libraries as rather insignificant. "I'm afraid I'm depressingly right-wing on the subject," a Hackney veteran told me. "The political machine at the town hall has decided and there it is." I am reminded of

27 Thomas Okey, *A Basketful of Memories: An Autobiographical Sketch* (Dent, 1930)

28 Karl Marx, *Value, Price and Profit* (speech, 1865; book (German), S. Sonnenschein & Co., 1898)
    Friedrich Engels, *The Origin of the Family, Private Property and the State: In Light of the Researches of Lewis H. Morgan* (Verlag der Schweizerischen Volksbuchhandlung (German), 1884)

George Gissing's comments a hundred years ago when William Morris was arrested in defence of free speech: "Keep apart, keep apart, and preserve one's soul alive – that is the teaching for the day. It is ill to have been born in these times, but one can make a world within a world." With the decline of London's public education system, public libraries are needed more than ever, as an entry to the imaginative world. Hackney Council should, even at this late stage, think again. It is not only damaging its best traditions, but intellectually maiming its citizens.

Time Out, 1987

HEALTH

Wonderful Pictures in Words

An introduction by Anna Livingstone & Kambiz Boomla

Anna Livingstone writes: It was mid-October 2015, and even the *Daily Mail* had to admit that at least twenty thousand junior doctors were on the march to Westminster. They were demonstrating for fair, safe National Health Service job contracts and, recalling the spirit of Aneurin Bevan, its founder, rejecting privatisation, cutbacks, low pay, bullying and the Conservative government's mortal threat to the service. We, East End general practitioners, were there on the streets with them, just as we had been with David on many campaigns of the eighties and early nineties. We had been part of the campaign for the reinstatement of the radical obstetrician, Wendy Savage. We opposed NHS cuts, closures and marketisation, protesting on the steps of the Royal London Hospital in Whitechapel.

Now we are bereft of his eloquence as tribune for patients, GPs and the NHS. After David's death, the consultants at the Royal London Hospital stood in respect at the joint medical committee he attended, but a new generation rises to take on the fight.

David joined our practice in Limehouse in 1985, taking over from the eighty-year-old Dr Moss. In this fascinating and deprived environment we worked as a team. We were all ground down by the same things, under-resourcing, hard work, and patients with hard lives. Racism and the chaos of docklands development added to their problems. Sometimes we doctors were jealous that David could finish his surgeries faster than us. He would rush off, sometimes irritably – and then create wonderful pictures in words. His writings were enriched by the captured words and anecdotes of patients and co-workers, recorded in his spiky black Rotring pen script or, cheekily, and unthinkably now, with the hidden tape recorder in the consulting room drawer. Confidentiality was not an issue when a photograph of names in the appointment book appeared in an article in the *Sunday Correspondent*.

David harnessed his experience of the NHS, together with his political understanding, into an intensely radical perspective, and one that looked at the service in its totality. "I have heard more compassion ... and more sense," as he writes below in "The National Health Service – The Great Pyramid", "in five minutes from a Scots laundry steward than in five hours from some administrative whizz-kids. And I would take the media's enthusiasm for patient care more seriously if it didn't depend on the proximity of a strike." His words were inspiring, a weapon to defend a great institution under attack. Now the attack has intensified, and down a generation his words resonate – and they are louder than ever.

Kambiz Boomla writes: It was the end of June 1978 and, at a mass meeting, staff at Bethnal Green Hospital voted to oppose the closure of their accident and emergency department. Six other local hospitals staged a twenty-four-hour strike in support. The occupation of Bethnal Green A&E had begun and David Widgery, a young GP, was elected chair of the Keep Bethnal Green Hospital Campaign. GPs, the emergency bed service and ambulances cooperated in continuing to send patients into Bethnal Green Hospital. After thirty days a partial victory was won and, for a short while, a limited casualty service was conceded by the area health authority.

Those were exciting times. David and I were both members of the East London hospital workers' branch of the

Socialist Workers Party. Indeed, I was a young, just-qualified doctor and he was amongst the people who had persuaded me to join. We spread our message of solidarity through our rank-and-file paper Hospital Worker. It was very amateurish. David taught me how to make headlines from sheets of rub-on Letraset artwork. We had fundraising jumble sales to keep the paper going. But that paper was exciting. David's flair and prose style, coupled with the reportage and comment from health workers made it so. Between us all we had wired imagination into a solid network.

So I have a debt to David from those earlier days of hope. He possessed a combination of organisation, imagination and flair. It is as important now as it was then.

The Death of a Hospital

David Widgery comments: *The impact of the cuts on the NHS, which were already apparent in East London in the 1970s, has become so marked in the Thatcher years that now none of the smaller East End hospitals exists, one having been converted to a luxury private hospital. But in 1974 the closure of Poplar Hospital was a momentous sign of things to come. My introduction to the Isle of Dogs, where I now practise, was by two of the women shop stewards campaigning against Poplar Hospital's closure. They took me into every workplace on the five-mile road which curves round the island: arguing with Sikh pattern checkers, making speeches in ship-repair canteens plastered with pin-ups, marching inside the fortifications of the West India Docks and round the back of the gasworks. There were leaflets, flyposting and motions passed everywhere from the local darts team right up to the South East region of the TUC. There were Saturday high-street marches with the kids, and the paper carnations and the "Save Our Hospital" signs, handwritten and heart-rending. Finally, an audience with Barbara Castle herself. None of it worked. They closed Poplar forever, knocked it down brick by brick, and are now driving out the population it once served so well to build a shambolic mixture of post-industrial estates and yuppy ziggurats sans planning restrictions, sans planning, sans everything.*

Among the many lights switched off by Edward Heath this week is one in the heart of East London's dockland which may never go on again. It belongs to the casualty and admissions department of Poplar Hospital, a black, brick-built tower off the East India Dock Road.

It was never a very fancy hospital, no East London hospitals are. But for more than a hundred years it has served the dockers, factory workers and seamen and their wives and kids who live and work on the Isle of Dogs, in Poplar and down towards Newham.

For a year now, the hospital administrators have been playing bureaucratic games with a strong local campaign to save the eighty-one-bed hospital. The official local campaign, which consisted mainly of press statements by the local Labour MPs, was confident that their protests had registered, and had in writing a promise that Poplar would stay open at least until April 1974.

Then, two days before Christmas, the bureaucrats struck. "The staffing difficulties in Poplar Hospital have now reached a point where it is considered that the level of care that can be given to the patients is below that required for safety and in the best interests of the patients it has been decided that there is no alternative but to suspend admissions to Poplar from 31 December 1973. ... Arrangements will be made to divert ambulances. ... As and when it is found that staff are no longer required at Poplar Hospital they will, if they wish, be transferred to other hospitals," wrote L.C. Phipps, the hospital secretary, who had promised exactly the reverse only two months before.

The Labour MPs have issued another hurt statement, but the nurses, technicians, porters, telephonists and cleaners at the hospital, many of whom live themselves on the vast, isolated estates which surround the hospital, had no time for indignation.

Extreme

On the morning of 21 December, they were simply herded into a meeting, of which no warning was given, and told the hospital was to cease admitting patients. When nurses and doctors demanded to know who had decided "the medical standards" had fallen, they were told there was "a panel of impartial medical advisers".

When NUPE stewards wanted to know why management were suddenly concerned about "staff shortages", the secretary could offer "no details".[29]

And details of the promised alternative jobs in "other hospitals" were vague in the extreme. As a NUPE steward at Poplar told me, "At the rate the regional board is going, it doesn't look like there will be any hospitals left to transfer ourselves to. And after this shambles, I don't think any of us will ever believe another word from hospital management."

For the people of the area, the news was broken still more brutally. Early on New Year's morning, a docker who arrived with a child with a badly scalded hand took a swing at the gate porter who had to tell him that the Casualty had been closed at midnight that night, for good.

Handful

When your kid is screaming with pain, you can't cope with "shadow regional health authorities" and "formal recommendations to the Secretary of State". You just know that one more of the handful of amenities provided for East London workers has gone. And you lash out.

For anyone in a workshop accident, a pub fight or a late-night overdose on the Isle of Dogs, that vast floating housing estate circled by cranes, will now have another quarter of an hour added to their emergency journey. If they are on foot, and many casualties walk into hospital, the journey to the nearest, already overloaded casualty department at Bow could mean another half hour.

---

29 NUPE stands for the National Union of Public Employees, a UK trade union that was in operation (under different names) from roughly 1877 to 1993. Not to be confused with New Zealand's trade union (formed in 1992) of the same name.

And the loss of Poplar Hospital, which during the Blitz became something of a symbol in the East End and which has provided medical care for more than a hundred years to four generations of East Londoners, shows quite how severely the cuts in social spending are biting.

A man outside the closed Casualty with a hand dripping with blood who, surprisingly good-naturedly, offered to sign a protest petition in his own haemoglobin, said, "Well, unless they start knocking downhill the estates and selling them for firewood, there's nothing much else down this way they can close, is there?"

For the implications of the Thames Group Management's apparent success in outmanoeuvring the protesters and disregarding one of the strongest Labour councils in Britain, MPs and all, are frightening. Plans to close the German Hospital, a fine old Lutheran charity hospital in Dalston, and the Metropolitan Hospital in Shoreditch have already been announced.

The London Jewish Hospital in Whitechapel is under the axe. Each East End hospital closure meets with a storm of local protest, packed town hall meetings, furious letters to the papers. People who have seen death and birth of those close to them in their local hospitals don't like them suddenly vanishing or being turned into old folks' homes.

Closure

On paper there are ambitious new plans to build regional superhospitals, all piped music and waitress service. The Board of Governors of the London Hospital quietly announced last month they intend razing to the ground the East End's most famous hospital with, of course, plans to replace it with a medical skyscraper some time early in 1980.

But given the overall economic situation, the continuously unrelenting cuts in health expenditure and the almost inevitable delays in all hospital building, East Enders are doubtful about the closure of existing facilities in the name of future medical promises.

A meeting of NUPE stewards in the Thames Group last Friday at St Clement's Hospital took a hard line against any loss in jobs or medical facilities until satisfactory alternatives are actually in existence. Hospital workers in the remaining open hospitals are learning the hard way quite how ruthless the new-style cost-conscious NHS administrators are.

Nobody, least of all the patients and staff of the threatened hospitals in East London, or the many other parts of Britain where the same battles are in the offing, is arguing that these old hospitals are the answer. However hard you try to overcome it, they are grim and still bear the stamp of the Poor Law.

If healthcare really was developing in Britain, these hospitals would probably be best developed as local community hospitals, run mainly by GPs, and housing day centres for the old, nurseries and antenatal and childcare centres which fitted what is needed for the continuous good health of the working class and not the emergencies of accidents and acute illness.

Until hospital workers and hospital patients can assert some control over the mysterious forces which govern the present health service and thwart their plans to dispose of existing medical services, this is so much pie in the sky. Ask the man with the scalded baby.

Socialist Worker, 1974

Blood on the Lino: Twenty-Four Hours in Casualty

David Widgery comments: *During the 1970s, that political transition zone which delivered us to the mercies of Mrs Thatcher, I was working as a doctor in acute hospital medicine while attempting to write while on call or early in the morning. For over a year I was involved in a particularly gruelling Casualty rota at St Mary's Hospital, Paddington, which included one stretch of twenty-four hours without a break as the only Casualty officer in the hospital. This is an account of one such twenty-four-hour stint, written up at 9 a.m. the following morning in the tea bar on Paddington Station.*

8 a.m.

The morning starts slowly enough: sprains, twists and tears; lumps, spots and abscesses. The daily influx of patients returning to have their stitches cut out, their wounds dabbed and redressed, their tetanus jabs, their certificates and their reassurance.

Not that the mornings don't bring real emergencies. It is almost impossible to imagine quite the things that can fall upon, hit, crush and cut the human body. The world of Casualty is like a gravity-less lunar capsule where limbs and surfaces are continually colliding and objects constantly tumble and drop. Heads are bombarded by falling saucepans, dropped cans, abandoned half-bricks and unexpected beams. Fingers are minced with an awful regularity on tin tops and chopping knives, scraped on potato knives and corkscrews – accidents of an awful banality and a great deal of blood and trouble.

Industrial work injuries are always on a bigger scale with flesh crashed instead of bruised, eyes bright red instead of pink and watery, fingers chopped clean off instead of sliced, hands burnt down to the wrist instead of scalded at their tips. A screwdriver falling from scaffolding unprotected by toeboards reaches a velocity lethal even to a helmeted building worker after one hundred feet. What is chilling is not the wounds but the victims' stoicism. Manual workers still take damage to their bodies at work as part of the deal and express an infuriating lack of anger over missing fingertips and sliced tendons.

And there are the morning regulars, those people mortgaged to illness and harnessed to pills, the dicky hearts continually dissolving tablets under their tongues to push away heart pain from hardening arteries, the diabetics for whom a single spot may grow to an infected boil and threaten life, the old with blocked and baffled circulation whose blood only just forces its way to toes and fingers continually threatened by gangrene. For them, Casualty is part of life and they will expound briskly on diagnosis and treatment, having overheard and memorised the seminars held for years over their faulty limbs. Regular, too, are certain medical emergencies, asthmatics who arrive panting on stretchers, blue and wrestling for breath, and epileptics raging with themselves.

It is a demanding kind of medicine and yet all the Casualty officer is required to do with the urgent cases is to admit them to the care of another doctor as swiftly as possible. The job is therefore exhausting, bewildering and, since it places paramount importance on diagnosis and little on treatment, curiously unsatisfactory. Shift work, low pay and lower prestige, generally poor facilities and lack of career structure has made Casualty a dead end.

1 p.m.

Lunchtime brings its small crop of violence. A warm morning in the pub which goes wrong by lunchtime and ends with somebody's boyfriend bottling somebody on the next table in a fog of drunkenness; the first of the traffic accidents; falls and black eyes with unconvincing stories attached. Heads are strong but bleed a good deal. Casualty starts to look like Casualty. Much of the lunchtime punching takes place inside the home, within the family. Frustration which ranges from a plate thrown accurately in anger to the systematic battering of a wife beyond unconsciousness. Those who uphold the sanctity of the family as a solution to all our problems might care to spend a few hours in a Casualty, to face the debris, when all the sugary ideals explode, when babies are bounced against the bedroom wall to make them stop crying and wives are loved and honoured and beaten up so thoroughly that they can't talk because their teeth are still chattering with terror. By afternoon there is already an hour-long queue to be seen and thirty pairs of eyes pierce any attempted emergency with the particular malice that the English reserve for queue-jumpers.

4 p.m.

Just as the queue is thinning down and you think there may be time for a cup of tea, pandemonium arrives. An ambulance team pound through the doors with a corpse they have kept alive by thumping his chest and puffing and sucking into his lungs. A cardiac bleep summons anaesthetists clumping in theatre boots and surgical greens, a worried medical registrar who has to interpret the electronic squiggles of the ECO into decisions about drugs which must be shot straight into heart muscle, and other floating doctors and nurses who connect up leads and position electrodes, draw up syringes and slice off clothes.[30] One anaesthetist

---

30 ECO, short for echocardiogram.

threads a plastic airway through the bluish throat while another plunges the needle of a drip into a neck vein and pumps in replacement fluids. The cardiac man brandishes two electrodes the size of dinner plates and, dripping with salty grease, claps them on the chest and throws a two-hundred-volt current through the patient, jerking him momentarily clean off the table. They banter all the while in measured tones about golf, their last cardiac arrest, and hospital gossip. A nurse drops a bottle and everyone glares at her. Only the doctors are allowed to make mistakes. Someone is dispatched to find out, in the nicest possible way, the patient's age from his wife, sobbing outside. Then, to everyone's surprise, the patient starts to revive, achieves a row of perfect cardiac complexes so that his pupils shrink, and goes a seedy pink again. "Oh, God, I was hoping to go over to the boozer this evening," says the registrar, glum at his success.

Another try at tea but you can't get away from the noise reverberating over the institutional surfaces: the groans of inpatients, the noisy sobbing, the overloud conversations, the abandoned lung-bursting scream of kids in pain which echoes on long after it has actually stopped. But as night rises, a swath of drunkenness seems to sweep across the outside world, as single bemused and fallen creatures, couples propping each other up right, and the wounded dragged away from street-corner arguments and pub affrays by friends, lurch in.

With the booze comes violence. Between drinks and after closing time sober patrols of muggers round up the staggerers and relieve them of their valuables. The violence is bewildering, inexplicable, random.

1 a.m.

Fortunately, alcohol solves the problem of anaesthesia. Little lignocaine is used after closing time. The police breeze in and out, squawking like upright birds. Their vital weapon is now their radio, not their truncheon. But it can order them away in the middle of trying to piece together a case against the person they end up arresting. Police vans shuttle drunks between the cells and the Casualty ward. The smell of stale alcohol and the tongue-tiedness of the drunk fill the rooms, and the once prim and orderly department is reduced to a wash of plaster of Paris footprints and bloody bandages. With the drunks come the suicides, midnight's other staple.

2 a.m.

The mentally ill who do come into Casualty are often curiously sane, just unacceptably honest about the lack of love in the heart of the city. A lab technician is lugged in screaming with terror, his whole appearance scatty, as if something inside has slipped sideways. He is terrified that he is dying from chest pain. In a quarter of an hour he has quietened down and desperately wants to talk, to show the family photos he sleeps with under his pillow. A young wife collapses, convinced she is unable to breathe, panting and screaming and shaking. When she pulls herself together she's worried that her husband will beat her up for breaking down. It's mental, all right: an acute anxiety state. But it's only just the other side of the Radio One phone-in and the Lonely Hearts ads and the sex shop.

4 a.m.

A tramp with magnificent eyebrows and a mane of silver hair describes the biblical proportions of his diarrhoea in language he has learnt to use to shut officials up. He says he is a shepherd by profession. Under the trolley his paper bag contains a large furry gorilla. "Well, I am also a street entertainer," he says with dignity. When he realises he is not going to get a bed for the night, he becomes wrathful. "You're a Londoner, I suppose. Once London was a city. Now it is a mess."

6 a.m.

It's almost morning. Still, unbelievably, people wander in with toothache and constipation exhausted by a night spent wrestling with pain. The night staff, alert but exhausted, having paced their weariness through the small hours with phone calls, fags and cups of coffee, are now anxious to stumble home to a morning bedtime. In comes a Belfast man shattered with drink but somehow totally in control. We sit in the corner of the waiting room while a Portuguese ancillary cleans the blood off the floor with an electric scrubber. "I'm on these pills, you see, Doc, Valium. I started taking them in Belfast and now have them sent over to me. Without them I just couldn't get myself across the front door. I take about thirty a day. You know I can only talk to you like this because I'm drunk." He wants to go into a hospital where he can get off his tranquillisers. He wants a doctor to talk to about the terror in his head. The floor is almost finished now. "Well, I can get you an urgent appointment with our psychiatric clinic?" I offer. He smiles without warmth. "Well, I'm sorry to have wasted your time, Doc. I just thought maybe you could help me."

Time Out, 1976

The National Health Service
– The Great Pyramid

In the chaos-capital of the strike-torn NHS, today was a busy day for me as a family doctor. Forty-eight patients in the surgery, three home visits, two drug company salesmen. And two possible emergencies ... the sort of patients who would make the front page of tomorrow's *Daily Mail* if they died and it could be blamed on pickets rather than physical causes.

It's exhausting, difficult and not very well paid. But there is a considerable consolation. The patients thank *me* for what is done for them.

In fact it's not me at all. The doctor is a coordinator of many other skilled, underpaid and underappreciated health service workers. I automatically rely on district nurses, pharmacists, physiotherapists, X-ray photographers and laboratory technicians as well as an invisible host of clerks, telephonists, porters and laundry workers. Hospital consultants depend even more on the low-paid legions of ancillary workers to achieve their clinical miracles.

When that surgical Sir Galahad of Reading refused to treat trade unionists, he was depriving sick patients not only of his own good offices but those of many lesser mortals, many of whom are hospital trade unionists themselves. The NHS as a whole *depends* on the joint efforts of many skills. As Bevan put it, "It is a triumphant example of the superiority of collective effort and public initiative applied to a segment of society where commercial principles are seen at their worst."

In a more honest society, the title "doctor" would be expanded to include those who built and designed housing, provided hygienic water, air and transport, and brought up and educated healthy, sane children. But doctors and health administrators are often afflicted with a mixture of megalomania and ignorance which leads them to acknowledge the assistance of lesser non-clinical mortals only when it suits them. Indeed the health service is itself a pyramid of privilege and power with white, male university-groomed specialists at the top and immigrant, female, drudge labourers, taught only to read, write and obey orders, at the bottom. The pyramid contains a complicated pecking order of class, race and sex. One hospital I know has eight separate dining rooms to make sure the different grades don't meet each other.

Laundry worker speaks only to cook, porter to State Enrolled Nurse, staff nurse to Sister and the senior nursing officer, and the consultant only to his conscience. Men give orders and women carry them out. Anglo-Saxons fill in forms, Celts and Caribbeans dispatch and Asians and Mediterraneans execute them.

It's not just the money. United Kingdom consultants are in fact rather badly off by international standards. The difference between Sir Lancelot Spratt and Mrs Mopp is one of power and prestige too.[31] He has the right to be unpunctual, arrogant and almost sadistic to the patients he dislikes. If she dares to be late or answer back or, as at the Westminster Hospital last week, withdraw services to private patients who aren't supposed to be there anyway, it's the sack. If he complains, it's a matter of clinical judgement. If she seeks to increase her wages, it's antisocial greed. And if she protests about the cuts, she just doesn't understand

31 Sir Lancelot Spratt (James Robertson Justice) was the chief surgeon in the comedic film *Doctor in the House* (dir. Ralph Thomas, 1954). Mrs Mopp (Dorothy Summers) was the office charlady in the BBC radio wartime comedy programme *It's That Man Again* (creator Ted Kavanagh, 1939–1949).

the medical issues and is sneered at by those who write the cuts-crazy district plans.

As for the patient's position in the pyramid, all health workers learn that the patient is always wrong. Indeed to judge from films like *Hospital* and *Coma*, the patient's true location is in the pyramid's funeral vault.[32]

So in some ways Colin Barnett, the NUPE full-timer in the North-East, is right to call the last two weeks' action by public servants "a peasants revolt". Because the low-paid, like the unemployed and the housewives, can't even sell their labour at a decent price. The work of compassion isn't even worth exploiting.

The low-paid are gnawed by the knowledge that, judged by wages, their work is worthless.

But if a striking ambulance driver dares to say "So be it" or a hospital porter states that "if society can't pay us, we can't go on doing the job", hark at the indignation. There is a rush of high-minded candidates to do the job "never mind the wages", although I rather doubt how long the patriotic volunteers would last tending the incontinent at 4 a.m. when they want to heave at the smell and their eyes ache with the neon light – and there's no public transport on the way home to get the kids up in the morning.

For the last two weeks a moral mixture of sudden concern for the sick and still more passionate attacks on the hospital strikers has had a queasy and dishonest quality. It is as if in their hearts, the well-off and self-righteous guardians of "public opinion" know the "bless them (but don't pay them)" approach won't wash – that workers in the public sector simply can't afford to be noble any longer.

Perhaps even the hardened hearts at the *Sun's* subs desk and *News at Ten* (who wouldn't know a Pott's fracture from a pink gin) have noticed a certain contrast between

---

32 *The Hospital*, dir. Arthur Hiller, 1971
   Coma, dir. Michael Crichton, 1978

the worlds of Sir Eric Miller, Peachey Properties, with the £65,000 necklaces, gift-wrapped champagne and free helicopter hops, and the hospital workers' rather modest claim for a £60 weekly wage.

"Pity," said William Blake, "would be no more, if we did not make somebody poor."[33] For here we get to the heart of the moral matter. It's not about clinical judgement of emergencies or the ethics of terminal cancer care. It's about the right of the ancillaries and nurses (whose wage claim is being busily forgotten) to have an opinion about the NHS and an ability to feel compassion.

Steerforth, a medical student, if I remember my Dickens, explained in *David Copperfield* the educated opinion of the lower orders' moral sensibility: "Why, there's a pretty wide separation between them and us. They are not expected to be as sensitive as we are ... they have not very fine natures, and they may be thankful that, like their coarse rough skins, they are not easily wounded."[34]

Or as a modern Steerforth, who thought he was a socialist, informed me about January 22nd's great carnival of resistance: "It's a pity the women are so backward" – because he had discovered a hokey-cokey formation dance team of NUPE Manchester cleaners shrieking "Make love, not war" instead of the politically correct but emotionally bald chant of £60, thirty-five hours.

For the present uprising in the public sector is not fury at Mickey Mouse wages, moronic administrators and the futile sacrifices of four years' wage controls, but at the whole mentality of the cuts, the servile state of "ancillaries" and the future direction of the Health Service. The handwritten banner of Hanwell Branch 635 of COHSE put the feelings of thousands: "We appeal to the public to help us

---

33 William Blake, "The Human Abstract", *Songs of Innocence and of Experience* (Self-published, 1789)

34 Charles Dickens, *David Copperfield* (Bradbury & Evans, 1850)

so we can help you in sickness. We *want* to work, but with low pay there's *no way*."[35]

Cuts and wages are married. Bill Geddes and Bill Tizard, of Hammersmith Hospital NUPE, have spent four years organising resistance to the cuts in West London while they persuaded their members they had a right to fight on their own wages too. But there were no Shock-Horror-Terror headlines in the *Sun* when the administrators literally smashed apart West London's Hounslow Hospital in October 1977. James Morris, of Westminster Hospital NUPE, battled away to save Bethnal Green as his local general hospital for nearly a year. But did the *Daily Telegraph* put him on the front page when the work-in and industrial action at the Green *saved* the lives of patients who were treated in a work-in casualty department that the authorities had officially closed?

I have heard more compassion ... and more sense, in five minutes from a Scots laundry steward than in five hours from some administrative whizz-kids. And I would take the media's enthusiasm for patient care more seriously if it didn't depend on the proximity of a strike.

For years the large subnormality and psychiatric hospitals in this country have been an open scandal; harsh, forbidding, understaffed, overcrowded, isolated. Repeated preventable outrages are reported ... and promptly forgotten. One of the most diligent medical inquiries, that of the Hospital Advisory Service, of Dr H.A. Baker, has reported a "very considerable gap between generally accepted policies and the realities of the service as the patients find it". In psychogeriatric hospitals, subnormality and psychiatric hospitals all over Britain, every day of the year, there is tragic evidence that, although psychology has found ways

---

35 COHSE stands for the Confederation of Health Service Employees, a UK trade union in operation from 1946 to 1993 that primarily represented NHS workers.

of teaching independence, few hospitals have enough staff to implement theory. But then, that's "not news", not unless there are some trade unionists to pillory anyway. A suitable cause for concern five years ago, for outrage now. But Fleet Street isn't interested because there are no trade unionists to victimise. Only the victims of a society which seems solely interested in the NHS when someone's on strike.

So the fate of the public sector strike in this bitter winter of 1979 isn't just about percentages and prod deals. For as Will Crooks, the nineteenth-century workhouse reformer, said, "The first lesson one learns in Parliament is the two great parties generally forget their political differences when the just claims of the people threaten their pocket." Despite the political Punch and Judy show, Labour and Tory privately agree that "we" must cut back spending on health, both wages and capital, until that long-awaited day when manufacturing makes a profit so splendid that we can once more afford a decently paid, staffed and equipped health service. The Tories would be more blatant about it: inferior doctors for an inferior class, and far more openly commercial medicine where the motive is greed and the marketplace the final arbiter ... an Anglo-Saxon Argentina.

But Labour has already got away with forcing the NHS into mediocrity by a thousand cuts and a million petty meannesses. What Labour's Secretary of State for Social Services David Ennals has done scares me more than what his Conservative successor Patrick Jenkin plans. If a Tory government does dusk the day, it's but the finish of what Labour slay. And those stalwarts of the Labour Party who still, four years on, promise alternative policies and left resolutions are only deceiving themselves and history.

Labour is no longer a crusade, it's a £3,300 champagne party. It was that old social-democratic sage Bevan who said: "No government that attempts to destroy the NHS can hope to command the support of the British people." Thirty years on it is clear that to save the NHS-as-we-know-it, a decision must be taken to transfer major financial resources into the service, either from revenue presently committed to industrial investment, arms or interest, or confiscated from the commercial concerns, from bedpan suppliers to tranquilliser manufacturers, who have done so well out of the NHS.

And it's even clearer that neither Callaghan nor Thatcher intends to do so, unless forced by immense popular pressure, of the sort the health unions have begun.

So support for the public sector workers is not only about low pay and wage control. As Mr Callaghan said (though he meant something quite different), it's about the kind of society you want to live in.

Don't wait, because it might just be too late.

Socialist Worker, 1979

Meeting Molly

David Widgery comments: *My first daughter died of rhesus haemolytic disease in 1982 in the middle of the industrial action by nurses and ancillaries and the national stoppages which, although unsuccessful, were the biggest solidarity strikes since 1926.*

I first met my daughter Molly in an operating theatre. She had been delivered by emergency Caesarian section, two months early, suffering from rhesus haemolytic disease. She lay panting on the back of an anaesthetic machine: tiny, mahogany-jaundiced and with the gleaming, near-porous skin of the very premature.

I have worked enough in theatre to know from the air of controlled pandemonium, the litter of hurriedly discarded catheters and that particular scampering noise that theatre shoes make when things are going wrong, that it had been a close thing. She must have required immediate artificial ventilation to resuscitate her.

In the adjacent room, her mother Juliet was still unconscious and having a hasty blood transfusion. For a moment it looked as if I might be losing both of them. Molly and I were the only people in the crowded, harshly lit room not wearing theatre greens, and I felt as naked and almost as helpless as she looked. I hardly noticed how beautiful she was or realised how brave she was going to be.

Doctors, and their kin, make notoriously bad patients; men are famous for finding that birth unlocks unexpectedly powerful emotions. As a doctor, I recognised the euphemisms consultants use in these circumstances: "Long, uphill road"; "Sicker babies have survived." I have used them myself. But as a father I just longed for them to say the one

76

thing they couldn't guarantee: that Molly would make it.

As a doctor, I wanted the most intensive medical care possible and wanted to know about it down to the last platelet count and percentage of her conjugated bilirubin. But looking at her, hoist on the special baby unit operating table, grilled by overhead lamps, continuously exchange transfused, trussed by tubes and swaddled by machinery, it was impossible not to want to snatch her and hear human sounds instead of the electronic sighs and blips and flickers which came to signify her life.

Since rhesus haemolytic disease had been diagnosed, I had been haunted by the drawing in the first available textbook of the stillborn "hydrops" baby in the untreated cases, with its abdomen distended and ribs splayed by the enlarged liver and characteristically turgid skin. And those clinical signs and the problems of their neonatal management were what my medical mind first registered. But my father's eyes simultaneously saw her long, delicate fingers and fathomless brown eyes. And felt that if only we hoped hard enough, her spirit would pull her through.

Rhesus disease is an essentially prosaic incompatibility between the blood group of the mother and her baby which leads the parent blood system to generate antibodies defensive to itself but potentially hostile to a developing child, like Molly, who had the misfortune to adopt her father's blood characteristics. Its consequences have been described, under various names, for centuries and its prevention is a major achievement of immunological theory and modern obstetric practice. I was examined on it for my obstetric viva in finals and have lectured medical students on its implications for perinatal mortality and health service policy.

Nonetheless, a mother can still acquire antibodies whose effect becomes more destructive with each pregnancy. And then an academic, diagrammatic matter becomes a harrowing drama with mother and unborn child doomed – thanks to the father's genetic contribution – to

immunological war. Meanwhile, medical effort uses prodigious technology to protect the growing child from the
maternal antibodies and the anaemia, jaundice and brain
damage they will engender if not controlled.

So, long before the drama of Molly's birth, Juliet's pregnancy had been turned into a high-technology obstacle
race which, without the thoughtfulness of the hospital
staff, the solidarity of other mothers and her own courage,
would have been an unendurable ordeal. Plasmapheresis, a
transfusion technique which can separate out the destructive maternal antibodies, had to continue, twice weekly,
through holidays, heartburn and heartache. When it went
smoothly, it was an uncomfortable and exhausting procedure, but when veins collapsed or tubes blocked or the
machine went wrong, it was agonising.

A Hair-Raising Manoeuvre

Over the last two months, the plasma antibody levels need
to be supplemented by examination of the optical characteristics of the amniotic fluid. So amniocentesis, which even
as a one-off screening procedure can be traumatic and not
without hazard, became a weekly ritual. And in the final
weeks, when the haemolytic process can unpredictably
accelerate, blood transfusion has to be made direct into the
abdominal cavity of the baby as it bobs about in the womb.

This hair-raising manoeuvre, done under local anaesthetic, requires passing a fine catheter through the uterine
wall and easing its tip into a safe position within the baby
itself. Juliet and Molly had it and survived it three times
while I sat on the end of the bed feeling the pregnant
father's normal turbulent mixture of pride, passivity and
irrelevance, magnified tenfold.

Summer had turned into autumn and the banners of the
hospital strikers smudged and misted outside the hospital
front gates. Over syringes and biscuits, the nurses discussed
how they would be voting in the ballot and whether the

hospital would ever get the money to purchase the plasmapheresis machine now on loan. As Arthur Scargill toured the coalfields, Molly kicked and Juliet retched. The world shrank, against our will, to that little pattern of lines glimpsed on the ultrasound. Illness shrinks and birth privatises, and to experience both processes working against each other within someone you love is most confusing.

But, after such a dramatic birth, the first week of Molly's life was even more terrifying. Juliet chain-smoked two floors beneath the special baby unit awaiting the knock that meant another exchange transfusion and forcing herself upstairs to express breast milk and glimpse her daughter. I wept at home over the Polaroid photo the hospital provided and wondered if anything was real. Worry became a way of life: every advance had to be undercut with reservations, every hope guarded with doubt and clothed with caution.

Days of Hope

When the crises of the first weeks seemed over, I registered her birth but stuffed a leaflet about death grants into my pocket. Not that I thought it likely, but just to demonstrate that it was still a possibility. Besides crying a lot, I did other uncharacteristic things like reading Lucretius and trying to assemble a two-hundred-part cardboard model of the Tower of London which was the halfway point on the now numbingly familiar bus ride to the hospital. One day, I thought, I'll take Molly over the Tower Bridge gallery and we'll look down at the No. 47 buses and laugh about her turbulent transpontine birth and my clumsiness with cardboard models.

As the weeks passed and we grew to be on more equal terms, her mother and I peered through the plastic incubator and took turns to answer the phone and will each other up the stairs to the unit. Encouraged by the hospital to visit whenever possible, we watched her shape come back as the oedema eased, saw the jaundice fade and delighted as she took food into her stomach and began to put on weight.

Her five-year-old brother visited: bemused and confused until through the porthole he had his finger squeezed by Molly's tiny hand. She grew strong enough to fight the nurses, tug at her drips and smile the most melting of smiles. After seven weeks she came off the respirator and at last breathed for herself. No celebration yet but we allowed ourselves to collect the baby bath the neighbours had been holding for us. It was the weekend of the big Greenham Common demonstration and, a little ashamed of our self-absorption, we thought quite seriously of making the first trip out of London for months.

We were right not to risk it. We were phoned unexpectedly by the registrar whose quizzical smile we had come to rely upon. Molly had had "a setback" and needed to go back on to the ventilator. At first we were confident; she had survived the prematurity and the haemolysis as well as necrotising endocolitis and a septal heart defect. But Juliet caught Molly's eyes rolling. And by the third visit it was clear that something was badly wrong.

Molly seemed to have lost her way, her ability to concentrate on survival. We drove backwards and forwards through the Blackwall Tunnel, unwilling to leave the unit but finding it unbearable to stay. By 3 a.m., it was clear that she had no more strength to resist an overwhelming infection. The doctors were taking it in shifts to "bag" her but when manual resuscitation was stopped, the heart rate on the monitor fell back remorselessly: ninety, seventy, fifty.

"She's dying, isn't she?" we asked, unnecessarily. And once the ventilator and the other tubes were removed and the traces went flat and silent, Molly passed away in moments with one last gentle wave of her right hand. The nurse wrapped her body and put it into our arms. It was the first time we had been able to hold her properly. We had never heard her cry or laugh. And now we never would.

The shock of losing her after such effort and with success

so near is overwhelming. The knowledge that the death of a baby is still a frequent experience in modern Britain and a commonplace in much of the world is no consolation. We tried to write letters of thanks to the staff but, as other parents agreed, there is no way words can express one's gratitude and admiration both for particular individuals and the system of healthcare which makes their work possible.

Words Are Not Enough

Nor is it easy to express the sadness. "There aren't words really," wrote one friend, rightly. Words are not enough and an attempt like this to externalise a private grief is infuriatingly unable to convey more than the surfaces of the experience. Nor is it possible to obtain the comfort of "accepting" Molly's death as ordained or inevitable or after all for the best; she wanted to live too much. And I hope I will always feel about any such death like a close colleague who wrote, in condolence, but also defiance, "Thirty years of practising medicine have still not reconciled me to these tragedies." But within the misery there is something politically inspiring.

Molly was born and so nearly lived only because of a chain of organised and unselfish human beings which stretched from the unknown blood donors whose gift sustained her in the womb to the nurses who got Molly and us through so many nights and still spared a thought to tuck a white carnation in her death wraps. In the 1980s, politically dominated by the philosophy of possessive individualism, the NHS still allows a different set of values to flourish. And it makes manifest the spirit of human solidarity which is at the core of socialism, and which our present rulers are so concerned to eradicate. While Molly's death is a tragedy, her life was something brave and marvellous.

New Society, 14 April 1983

Unemployment and Health

Review of *Unemployment and Health*, by Richard Smith[36]

Unemployment comes in many guises: structural, frictional, cyclical. It is presented to us as the consequence of folly or inflexibility, the cost of technical advance, even a kind of retribution for the wage militancy of the 1970s. But to be denied work is a devastating personal blow. This is not because of loss of money alone (although unemployed people promptly become poor) or because work is inherently noble (it is not). It is because the discipline involved in membership of a productive group engenders a kind of torque and meaning to one's own life. This is not something abstract like "status", as if one's job was the equivalent of a pair of designer jeans. It is very practical. Work allows the exertion of collective power, first over work, then through organisation and finally by the ability to withdraw labour.

This is why mass unemployment is such an effective weapon in lowering working-class self-confidence and militancy. Not only are those still in work less powerful ("If you don't want the job there are a thousand others who do"); those out of work find it impossible to organise effectively. As Marie Jahoda's seminal work on the Austrian town of Marienthal showed in the 1930s, unemployed workers did not read the magazines they were offered free nor attend the political and social clubs set up for them. They did not become angry and effective but introspective and disorganised, easy prey to Nazism's warm greatcoats

---

36 Richard Smith, *Unemployment and Health: A Disaster and a Challenge* (Oxford UP, 1987)

and war economy jobs. Or as Richard Smith puts it, the modern image of the unemployed is a workless man staring day after day at his untended garden. Without the cruel but necessary collectivity of the work process, the capacity for intellectual and political activity withers fast.

This excellent and challenging book therefore raises even more important issues than its author realises. Firstly, how does prolonged unemployment change people to make them more vulnerable to mental and physical ill health? But second, and surely connected, how does unemployment make people more vulnerable to the appeal of right-wing politics, whether Hitler in the period Jahoda first studied, or Thatcher, Princess Di and the soaraway *Sun* today? Answers would help both our medical practice and our political understanding, and link political economy to psychology, that holy grail of twentieth-century Marxism.

Smith does not provide that answer and it is a strength of his approach that he recognises one must call on many disciplines, including literature, to get a true feeling of the experience of unemployment, let alone to analyse it. He guides his readers with deceptive skill through the complicated statistical issues of aggregate studies, associated most notably with M.H. Brenner; he looks in depth at the Office of Population Censuses and Surveys' longitudinal study and the work of the British Regional Heart Study, and with affection at the work of the Wiltshire GP Norman Beale, whose studies of consultation rates before, during and after the closure of a large sausage factory in Calne, Wiltshire are neat, unequivocal and an example of real GP research. He also quotes from journalistic and fictional accounts of the experience of unemployment, both in the 1930s and now.

His survey of the psychiatric literature is particularly effective, and the relationship between mental illness and unemployment is clearly proven. This is most clear and tragic in suicide and parasuicide, but also registers in the intractable depression and anxiety of the unemployed family simply getting on each others' nerves.

Perhaps the most alarming section is on the health of the children of the unemployed. There seems to be consistent evidence of unemployment pushing up the birth rate, most of all among the unskilled working class. In Bea Campbell's words, "Unemployed girls who've never experienced economic independence are doing the only thing they can – having babies." But the families are poor, often disorganised, demoralised, and sometimes drunk: a new lumpenproletariat of video and Special Brew rather than music hall and gin. Not only is the neonatal health of the babies markedly less good, but their chance to lead a normal child's life is eroded and they become scared, manipulative and distrustful when they should be open and adventurous. Their chance in life, like their parents', is forfeited before school has started. It is no accident that domestic violence and child sexual abuse have been reported more often in the present period of mass unemployment. In the old inner cities, this new workless underclass is immediately adjacent to those whose wealth has soared through the financial process made possible by mass unemployment: the health divide squared.

Smith recognises this possibility, "a nightmare in which the unemployed will grow in numbers and in poverty while those with employment resort increasingly to armies and policemen to keep them safe." But he also sees a different future, almost along the dreamy lines of William Morris's News from Nowhere, where much shorter hours of work are shared, and art and creative leisure are more highly valued.[37] He is, however, poor on how we get there, apart from citing a few interesting but tiny initiatives. And he is insufficiently interested in the not always unsuccessful

---

37 William Morris, *News from Nowhere or, An Epoch of Rest, Being Some Chapters from a Utopian Romance* (Reeves & Turner, 1890)

attempts of the unemployed to organise themselves and make common cause with those in work. He never fully accepts that mass unemployment is a conscious tactic rather than a natural accident which renders real benefits to those who run society in the present wasteful, unhealthy but profitable way. No wonder they refuse to consider the misery, poverty and injustice ... or even the extra work for the NHS they are also creating. They wouldn't, would they?

Radical Community Medicine, 1988

A Doctor's Week

Monday: St Vincent's, "the Forgotten Estate"

Start the week irritable and embedded in the semi-permanent traffic jam which is the Commercial Road. I live only two and a half miles from the Limehouse Health Centre where my two female partners and I practise, so the journey would be quick but for the traffic generated by the massive Docklands building projects whose cranes hover and peck over the Isle of Dogs like giant flamingos.

We work in the most deprived part of a deprived borough, adjacent to a sprawling housing complex recently designated "the forgotten estate". St Vincent's House on St Saviours Estate was built for dockers and their families, but more recent occupants have been immigrants from Bangladesh and Vietnam. So many of the patients I will see this morning are ill-fed, ill-housed and ill-clad, as well as plain ill. The three of us are responsible for a list of 5400, with a high proportion of under-fives and young mothers, often single parents. Many of the new registrations are homeless people in temporary hostel and hotel accommodation.

Monday is always busy. Emergencies which have occurred over the weekend need reviewing, besides the booked appointments, the sick-note brigade and the inevitable urgent "extras". I see twenty-two patients, including three with cancer and two more who have undergone recent surgery.

One, an Irish building worker, is having practical and emotional problems with his colostomy bag; a lady who survived skin cancer now has a cervical malignancy and a third, an emaciated ex-docker, probably has carcinoma of the bronchus or the lungs and has to be told the diagnosis. It's impossible to do this in a painless way, especially as his devoted spouse is crippled and physically dependent on him. But it's also impossible and insulting to lie about the situation. We talk and exchange looks. He abruptly changes the subject back to his wife. There has been a moment of mutual recognition.

A late extra is a waiflike Italian heroin addict who is supposed to be on methadone, but whose forearm has a recent injection site. Apparently she was owed money, but the debtor could only repay her in heroin. I've usually got about a dozen patients with declared heroin problems, but it fluctuates wildly, and it's hard work – apart from the medical problems, they demand instant attention. Indeed the "routine" work is harder than it used to be, not least because the end of the era of hospital expansion and the increase of vocational training for general practice mean that a great deal of clinical work, which would in the past have been performed in the outpatients department of the local hospital, is now carried out at GP level. But then it is the humdrum aspect of medical life which provides the real satisfaction: that which life demands is as important as what it offers.

The first home visit of the day is to a grim barracks of an estate to see a child who, with the east-end taste for habitual hyperbole, has been both "spewing up" and "burning up" since 6 a.m.

The child, who is actually fairly cheerful, is wheeled out of a fuggy front room full of cigarette smoke, lunchtime television and cans of Special Brew. She blinks at the light. Her eardrums and chest are fine, and her coughing is as much to do with the cigarettes as her coryza (the medical term for a cold).

By the end of evening surgery, which stretches from 3.30 to 7 p.m., and includes another nineteen patients, I still haven't managed to eat a sandwich. I take a long deep breath when a seventy-two-year-old temporary visitor from Pakistan sits down firmly and her son unfurls a list of "several things we need to speak about". There is never enough time. It's a long day's night, and I get home after eight, good for nothing.

Tuesday: Stress in GPs

The receptionists are infinitely skilful at persuading people who can wait to come back for a proper, booked appointment, but there are still those who insist. In fact, today all my "urgent extras" are bona fide: a little girl whose mother has been coping all night with an asthmatic wheeze which needs nebulising on an inhaling machine, a male model with VD, en route from Barcelona to Manhattan, and post-coital contraception for a condom failure.

One of my "heartsink" patients (the ones with immense notes, endless complications and obdurate resistance to cure – in other words, hypochondriacs) turns out to have a genuine new problem: cancer of the spine. The telltale symptom is "foot drop", an inability to curl up your toes because of cancer invading the nerve-ends. In general practice, experience is often an unreliable adviser. A colleague on the night rota which we operate with an adjacent health centre phones to tell me, not without a slight edge of relish, that a lady with upper abdominal pain whom I had visited on his behalf and, after a lot of humming and hawing, thought dyspeptic, was later that day admitted with a suspected heart attack.

Before I can escape to do visits, I am collared by the district nurse to look at a heavily tattooed skinhead discharged from hospital to the Salvation Army hostel with a stab wound to his chest. She is rightly worried: it's forming an abscess. After his swab dressing and antibiotic prescription, he lopes off to rejoin a trio of fellow drinkers at the back of the waiting room, all identifiable by the ill-matching, second-hand clothing the Sally Army has provided them with.

The East End remains London's main skid row, and a considerable proportion of newly registering single men has past or current alcohol problems. Two years ago I discovered, to my discomfort, that the anti-tremor tablets which I was prescribing to some of these men, allegedly to help them dry out, were in fact mixed with cider as an aid to intoxication. As I come through the churchyard to work each morning, the first Special Brews and Tennent's Extras are already being hoisted. The paths are strewn with empties and the four-leaf-clover patterns of their plastic holding straps.

The antenatal clinic goes smoothly for once, although I have major language problems with a newly registered Ethiopian girl of sixteen who is five months' pregnant and giggles non-stop, a rather effective way of disorientating male doctors. I also have difficulty in getting her to disrobe for a physical examination, but when she does I note, with a little surprise, that she has been surgically circumcised. The practice has a number of North Africans on its list, especially Somalis, but I seldom come across female circumcision.

Among today's lunchtime paperwork is a postal questionnaire researching "Stress in GPs". I race through the fifty-two questions while waiting for the London Hospital switchboard to reply (two minutes and thirty-two seconds: I now use a stopwatch as well as a remote phone). Later, rereading my replies, I get an unflatteringly candid picture of my current feelings from the underlinings I have made. Yes, the White Paper will make work more stressful. Yes, I do have language problems with patients. Yes (treble underlined), I often feel "torn between" family and work. I see I have answered "no" to the question, "Would you do GP again?" Is this an aberration or a moment of truth? Am I really cut out to work in these anorectal junctions of the planet?

To add insult to injury, one of the health centre's very alert health visitors hands me a cutting from someone called "the *Sun* Doctor" who states that "most of Britain's GPs earn on average more than £65,000 a year". My pre-tax income and that of my partners, as stated in our certified accounts, was precisely a third of that sum, for an average working week which, including hours on call, is fifty-nine hours and twenty minutes. When I am on call out of hours, I have sole responsibility for the domiciliary primary care of over twelve thousand patients. London GPs don't even get the London Weighting Allowance, which is now such an important element in salary scales, and which both our hospital colleagues and our own staff get paid! The levels are different, but the problem is exactly that of ambulance drivers, nurses and midwives.

The government is spendthrift with praise but, judging by the more revealing criterion of actual cash expenditure, values its health service even less. In the sits vac columns, there are city and computing professionals at starting salaries considerably in excess of my salary, achieved after a gruelling six years as a student and seventeen years of experience as a doctor.

Tonight is the monthly East London meeting of the Medical Practitioners' Union which, in inner-city areas, more and more young GPs are joining instead of the BMA. However, there is widespread admiration at this meeting for Tavistock Square's feisty advertising campaign. Even the dear old BMA, not unfairly regarded as the Tory Party at the bedside, and initially so suspicious of the NHS, has been driven by our beloved government into opposition, though no doubt at a later stage deals will be struck, as doctors also have highly partisan interests.

What worries me as co-chair is that we are getting punch-drunk with repeated service cuts which began back in 1974 when Poplar Hospital went. Is the diagnosis indignation fatigue? It certainly isn't – I fume as I get home at 10.15 – too much time spent on the golf links.

Wednesday: The Domino System

For the last ten days, I have been carrying a radio pager awaiting a primip domino. Primip is medical slang for a woman having her first baby, and domino is the code for our local scheme of community obstetrics (short for "domiciliary in and out").

In the early seventies, antenatal care, delivery and post-natals were largely hospital events, but, increasingly, GPs and midwives attend the birth in hospital. I would calculate that at least a quarter of the normal live births in this area have now had a greater part of their care in the community, which ought to make considerable savings in medical and clerical costs. The problem, however, is that there is no such thing as a "normal" delivery: obstetrics, especially intrapartum, is a high-risk area of medicine and no one wants to put at risk the tremendous improvement in outcome for mothers and newborn babies which has been achieved in post-war East London. Even experienced GP obstetricians will have limits on their clinical ability and knowledge, not least because nowadays we are also expected to be experts on child development, diabetes, asthma, drug addiction and so on.

Partly because of working closely with the consultant Mrs Wendy Savage, who is keen on community obstetrics, and partly because of the high calibre and morale of the local midwives, I have found myself giving community-based antenatal care to such distinctly un-"normal" mothers as an intravenous heroin addict whom we helped kick the habit during her second trimester (three-month period), a Bangladeshi woman of thirty-six, three of whose previous pregnancies had ended in stillbirths, and several diabetics, asthmatics and under-sixteen-year-olds, all so far with good results. None of this is out of bravado; obstetrically I'm very much in favour of a quiet life. But many of these women have such serious social problems that they would probably default from hospital care entirely and then end up presenting themselves unbooked and in labour in Casualty.

The community midwife tells me that Pat, today's domino, went into labour at 9.30 a.m. She is a well-motivated, socially secure woman with a solid husband. But it is her first baby and though she is only twenty-nine, by obstetrics' peculiar standards she is no longer young.

She was nearly fully dilated by the time I could get through my surgery appointments and up to the labour ward at the London Hospital, but things appeared to be progressing well. Feeling happily irrelevant, I was chatting with the student midwife when suddenly the foetal heart rate began to dip dramatically during contractions and failed to recover promptly: a classic sign of foetal distress.

Within minutes, and without the midwife's voice faltering a semitone, the bed was repositioned, stirrups were set in place, an incubator for the baby was wheeled in by a paediatric senior house officer, and the obstetric registrar, whom I had hauled in from the coffee room, was scrubbing up.

The husband, twitching like all fathers during first deliveries, blanched as the once empty and informal delivery room filled with equipment and doctors.

Pat herself was getting exhausted and losing momentum, but with the foetal heart rate now electronically monitored by the electrode the midwife had hooked to the baby's head, the registrar held off with his forceps for almost a quarter of an hour in order to allow her, with a final burst of pushing, to deliver spontaneously.

By the time I returned to the labour ward after evening surgery to check the baby, everyone was dressed and ready to go home: the crisis had evaporated. But on my way home down the familiar backstreets of Bethnal Green, I find my hands shaking and have to stop for a moment. Relief partly, and also suppressed anxiety about the delivery. But the story was not yet over. The following day, my half-day, one of my partners was called out urgently about a possible fit in the new baby.

Thursday: Mugged in Hackney

On Thursday evenings I am the only doctor in surgery, which at least has the virtue of clarity: I have to sort out everything medical alone. The problems include a manic-depressive engineer on a high, a new alcoholic patient with pneumonia, a miscarriage and a distressed, feverish child. My brain starts to scramble. I take the bus home, hoping to read the biography of Nora Joyce, and walk the few hundred yards from the bus stop to my home, marvelling at the sunsets Hackney sometimes throws up.

Then thump, bang and I'm full-length on the pavement, the plastic bag in my left hand torn away and a young but strong Afro-Caribbean lad, one of four, hauling me by my briefcase along the gutter. The briefcase, which contained drugs, held together, and the bag they did take only had a bottle of cheap wine and a dirty shirt in it, but I had been mugged good and proper; upper incisors adrift, forearm lacerated, and bruised and grazed all down my right side.

My emotions? Well, exactly what I have so often advised assaulted patients to expect: fear, anger and guilt for about seventy-two hours, and then three months of looking over your shoulder. Interestingly, although I get much sympathy, no one – colleagues, patients, even the children – seems particularly surprised and many, unknown to me, have themselves had similar experiences. In a rather repulsive way, I feel I've somehow lost my criminological virginity and got away fairly lightly.

After all, I've had a grand total of nine cycles stolen, the car broken into three times and the health centre is quite regularly burgled. One of my partners even had her telephone nicked.

What is annoying is the siege mentality one has to adopt to prevent crime – that and uncooperative insurers, one of which, Lloyd's of London no less, had the gall to write and allege that I had faked a break-in of my own vehicle in order to upgrade my car stereo.

Friday: Baby Clinic Day

Language problems in the practice are acute: the recent immigrants, women more than men, tend to have minimal English but high fertility. Tower Hamlets contains about a fifth of all Britain's Bangladeshis, and probably over fifty per cent of new births in the district are to women of Bangladeshi origin.

The average number of children in Bangladeshi families is seven, compared to 1.8 across the UK, although this is changing rapidly as British-born women, better educated and less male-dominated, choose to limit their families.

The Vietnamese, the other main ethnic minority who, by surname analysis, comprise about eight per cent of our patient list, also have large families, which means they, too, are often grossly overcrowded in their two- and three-bedroom council accommodation.

This great outburst of fecundity (the general fertility rate of our area is forty per cent above the national average) makes baby clinics like today's a crowded cacophony.

I give the jabs. Another of the partners checks the children's development against national yardsticks in order to identify problems like deafness or spasticity. The clinic clerk weighs and measures, and the health visitors deal with the babies' progress and the problems that the mothers bring.

On paper, it sounds wonderfully rational. In practice, it is both intellectually difficult (assessment of small babies is one of the technically most demanding areas of clinical examination) and physically uncomfortable (imagine trying to assess hearing when in the adjacent room a vaccinated child is bellowing its lungs out). Sometimes the newly born children coming for their six-week check haven't been properly registered or even named. Like using dental floss, one knows it makes sense but wishes there were an easier way of doing it.

The post-clinic meetings also review the progress of children on the "at risk" register. The sort of problems we refer to paediatricians include temper tantrums at home and school, sexual precociousness when the parents are separated and the father violent, persistent sniffing of lighter fuel, bed-wetting, delay in bladder control, insomnia, a mixed-race child who "wants to be white", and extreme learning difficulties. There is also child sexual abuse – a minefield of allegations, disclosures and legalities, not to mention inter-professional difficulties.

Monday: A Riot on My Doorstep

Thank goodness for a more restful unstructured weekend making picture books of Verdi libretti with the kids and ill-tempered attempts at DIY. My body bruising has stopped hurting now, but the forearm injury, which the district nurses at the health centre have been kindly dressing, although shallow, is quite extensive and painful. I must have left a goodish sample of epidermis on the pavement of Richmond Road.

I have, however, now had time to think up a jaunty rejoinder to colleagues' condolences: "I don't have to read *London Fields*, I've just been mugged in it."[38] But I don't feel all that jaunty inside. I am on call again tonight, for the first time since the attack. I catch sight of myself looking distinctly grim as I don the radio pager. *Allons, commençons la dance.*

Our practice is still fairly unusual in that we still do all our own out-of-hours visits and, probably because of high deprivation and our high percentage of under-fives

---

38 Martin Amis, *London Fields* (J. Cape, 1989)

and single elderly, the call-out rate is high. It's a kind of mental equivalent to lumbago. Even if you are not called out, you tend to sleep badly. In this respect, and much as we oppose its overall philosophy of marketplace medicine, our earnings will improve somewhat under the proposed new contract, which introduces a lower rate of payment for visits made by deputies from the commercial answering services. Still, one fears for colleagues who, for perfectly genuine reasons, want to use the deputising service which is bound to become more expensive.

Thank goodness it's a reasonable night, reasonable in the literal sense that I am able to give telephone advice which is useful to two callers and make two visits to ill-numbered council estates without getting too lost.

The second, in fact, is for a true pustular tonsillitis (relatively rare: most sore throats are viral and don't need antibiotic treatment). This one gets an immediate injection of penicillin.

Just before midnight, back at the health centre to check the patient's case notes (I suddenly half-fantasised that the child's father, who is "away", had a penicillin allergy), the tremendous din of a low-flying helicopter rumbles overhead, shaking the building. From the child guidance unit upstairs, I get a ringside view of an intensive police operation on the estate where we work. A police helicopter with searchlight is trying to trace fugitives, while all over the estate policemen leap in and out of riot vans and make rather random-looking arrests. I can see others like myself offering noisy advice, abuse and in some cases, arming themselves with makeshift weapons, including a spade, for self-defence. I have promised my wife to be careful but, quite honestly, I would have been very hesitant to go on to the estate without a police escort which, under the circumstances, would not have endeared me much to the patients.

The next morning, the surgery is given over to a post-mortem and an action replay for residents who slept through the real thing but saw the major police operation reported on the news on television that morning.

It seems that a long-standing feud between two semi-criminal families has erupted, with the Isle of Dogs contingent accusing the Limehouse lot of being police informers. The second gang had simply turned up at a meeting called by the police to help arbitrate problems on the estate, but, as far as the Isle of Dogs boys were concerned, this was grassing. They issued their challenge on a nearby wall, using (appropriately) green spray paint.

Involved in the quarrel is a serious case of child neglect by a teenage mum, who for a joke had given her infant a can of Special Brew. This had been discussed with the police at the original meeting, as had the intimidation of Bangladeshi residents, who had burning newspapers pushed through their letter boxes. According to the locals, the police had overreacted and arrested the wrong people, so the culprits got away. Who knows? The real cause of the social instability is that the council block at the centre of the fighting has been half-emptied before being demolished to allow for the new Limehouse Link motorway to Canary Wharf – at £150 million for just over a mile and a half, it is one of the most expensive roads in history.

Even if the people get properly rehoused, they will have lost that sense of neighbourhood which is one of our most valuable possessions. And Limehouse, one of East London's oldest coherent communities, will be decimated. As the patients never tire of telling me, "People don't count for anything any more." But I still treasure the human warmth with which our most experienced receptionist, an ex-bus-conductress and cockney of the old school, takes a newborn Bangladeshi or Vietnamese baby into her strong arms and congratulates the mother. I pray the immigrants remember this in thirty years' time, and not the roadworks and the racist bastards. One of our clerical workers, whose parents were from Bangladesh but was herself born in Bancroft

Road, has the last word on the riot. With an immaculate cockney shrug, she just says, "Well, you take it as it comes, dontcha?"

"True speech", as the East End kids put it. And as true of GPs, I expect, as everyone else.

The Sunday Correspondent, 1989

The Doctor Is Sick

It's midnight in the back streets of the East End, hard rain is sluicing down, and I am trying to locate the abdo pain's front door. This medical day started at 8.30 a.m. with forty-five patients, many with no English, in two surgeries and an antenatal clinic. This is the fifth home visit, and on-call duty doesn't finish for eight more hours. Carcinoma, methadone, diabetes, depression, miscarriage and angina have poured down as unremittingly as the weather. Tonight I'm the rota doctor on call for thirteen thousand people, all potential patients, and the strain is beginning to produce its familiar bi-temporal headache.

There is at last a dimly lit porch, the number twenty-one just visible. Bent double, nipping to the car boot to get the drug bag, I see the car's rear window has been bashed in, broken glass shards cover the back seat. Five minutes spent at the health centre looking at the patients' notes and someone has removed my medical bag with all my portable diagnostic equipment inside. The Sikh pattern-cutter's abdomen is examined with a distinctly shaky hand that tries to elicit the signs of a possible perforated ulcer as his family of six stare on with fixed incomprehension. There are previous laparotomy scars, and a certain amount of overacting going on too. Still, he'd better go into hospital. One of his daughters takes me to borrow the telephone of a surly neighbour, who insists I pay for the call. The hospital telephonist eventually gets hold of the surgical registrar. He's keeping his last remaining beds for acute admissions and asks, not unreasonably, for the patient's blood pressure. "Can't help you I'm afraid, I've just had my sphygmomanometer stolen."

If there is a last straw, this is it. The newly opted-out hospital trust is trying to close Casualty and is running down the wards of the Mile End branch of the Royal London Hospital, which has been serving the East End since 1858. Waiting lists are longer than ever, yet the day-surgery wards designed to cut them have been padlocked until the end of the financial year. Prolonged NHS underfunding causes daily problems, and GPs have had the worst year most of us can remember, trying diligently to make some sense of their government-imposed contracts.

Versatility is all very well but we are now expected to be accountants, personnel managers and lawyers as well as dermatologists, psychiatrists, obstetricians and general physicians. And the prospect of yet another massive reorganisation of the NHS has made 1 April, 1991 a date in very poor taste. The morale of British doctors is severely eroded, particularly in general practice, which throughout the eighties, was expansive, innovatory and, increasingly, the most popular career choice for newly qualified young doctors.

All this is grim enough. But stealing the tools of your trade when you are out in the middle of the night is macabre. I drive home, the rain pelting through the window, depressed and angry: musing on what other professional would be doing emergency night work without uniform, cover, radio or specialist vehicle. And be expected to do a full day's work the next day? Yet I know the hours of the junior hospital doctors are even worse.

In the space of four weeks, not only has my car been broken into, but the health centre has been robbed of computer hardware for our new cardiovascular screening programme, I have been threatened with violence in my consulting room for refusing to prescribe opiates, and my home has been burgled at 5 a.m. by a seventeen-year-old wielding a club hammer. Small beer to the police, but it makes you feel a fraction unwanted. At breakfast my seven-year-old daughter enquires, quite seriously, "Daddy, do you like being a doctor?" Slightly shocked, I hear myself say, "No."

Since Asclepius, doctors have enjoyed complaining. About the hours, the stress, the inadequate resources, the uncomprehending bureaucrats and, most of all, about the incessant and insatiable demands of patients. Occasionally there have been eruptions, most famously when mass pressure by GPs forced the 1966 reforms in primary care – the first substantial public investment into what had been a backwater of general practice. More recently, junior hospital doctors took to the streets over their appallingly long hours, up to ninety in a single week. In general, though, post-war morale amongst British doctors has been high. We don't earn much by international standards, conditions of work are arduous, and chronic underfunding often makes them more so. It is seldom possible, however many hours worked, to provide the quality of care we have been trained to deliver, except at the expense of the non-acute patients on the ever-extending waiting lists.

The paradox exemplified: next day, I'm at Mile End Hospital with a patient who arrived with a pleural effusion, desperately short of breath, the previous night. Lucy Wedderburn, the young medical registrar, has been up all night inserting drains and carefully drawing out bloodstained fluid, and she's still on duty, witty and vivacious through the exhaustion. She finds time to sit down with the patient before she's wheeled off to X-ray, explaining exactly how the lung will be sealed off, that pain is inevitable and how it will be controlled. She then shows me the various x-rays, and we discuss the discharge arrangements. There is real gratitude in the eyes of the lady whose life has probably been saved that night. But Wedderburn is less thankful. Over coffee and NHS apple crumble in the staff canteen, watching the West Indian cooks quietly stir the carbohydrates, she describes the staff's attitude to the opted-out hospital trust as "bitter indifference": "A lot of people are just worried about having a job or getting their required training experience.

We don't even know if the new rules on juniors' hours will apply to trusts."

The new head of the hospital trust is an avuncular ex-admiral brimming with ill-justified optimism who told his first meeting with bewildered staff that "there is a lot in common between the NHS and the Navy". "Sinking ships?" Dr Wedderburn suggests as she dashes off to answer her bleep. On my way out, I pass sealed-off wards, underused equipment and dingy staff accommodation, the shameful – because unnecessary – stigmata of the nineties NHS. This hospital is being forced to transfer its acute services to its overcrowded sister hospital in Whitechapel because of underfunding. But, ironically, it has recently opened a wing for old people, one of the most modern in Europe. Unfortunately, instead of being integrated in a general hospital as planned, the wing will now be left high and dry. There is a state-of-the-art cardiac resuscitation unit, much better than the one on the general medical wards. But most of the patients' notes are marked "Not for resus"!

We went through all this in the late seventies with Bethnal Green Hospital – a much-loved general hospital that was first geriatrified and then closed completely. It used to provide a first-rate local casualty service and routine operating sessions that, especially in hip replacement, really sliced through the waiting lists. The campaign waged by both public and hospital staff was one of the biggest in East London's political history: over seven hundred people at the York Hall, the old boxing venue, twenty thousand signed petitions, a two-hour protest strike and the first-ever hospital work-in, which kept the hospital running for a month and treated 1100 emergencies after its official date of closure. In the eventual settlement, fine promises were made about equivalent facilities becoming available at Mile End Hospital. And about geriatrics never again being isolated from general medicine and surgery. But now they're doing the whole thing all over again. Would you buy a used hospital off people like this?

It's the patients who suffer, stranded on the waiting lists, nursing their pain and their justified anxiety till they get to see the specialist. Inevitably, some will have diseases that go undiagnosed and therefore untreated. The culprit is not, on the whole, inefficiency, indolence or excessive private work by hospital consultants. Indeed, small miracles have been achieved in improving efficiency, shortening inpatient stay and improving facilities for day-surgery. The problem is that we as a nation continue to expect a clinical quart out of an economic pint. By all valid international comparisons, the NHS is underfunded by at least two per cent of gross national product. Medicine is highly labour intensive, and the NHS simply does not have the money to hold its own with the sheer weight of clinical traffic at present, let alone cope as the population gets older, the drug costs escalate and research brings exciting but expensive treatments.

This prolonged underfunding strikes the GP most dramatically when he tries to admit an acutely ill patient. The London Emergency Bed Service reports that this winter things have been four times as hard as last year, and my experience confirms this. For six months I looked after a valiant clerical worker with cancer of the colon, which had spread to her liver before her condition was diagnosed.

When she became too ill and breathless to come to the surgery, I visited her once a week. She was single, had no close relatives and didn't want the neighbours to know the diagnosis. Her massively enlarged liver splinted her diaphragm, making her permanently breathless, and pressed on to her abdominal veins so that her legs became horribly swollen. Yet despite the pain and dyspnoea, she would fuss over me and make tea for me with her best crockery.

For a long time she managed to keep up her little flat herself, maintaining careful arrangements of dried flowers, folding newspapers into tidy piles, even sewing a teddy bear for a local charity raffle. But in the final weeks she began to fall, and I organised a home help and district nurse. I put her name down for the local hospice without her permission, because although she definitely insisted she didn't want anything to do with it, I thought things might change as she deteriorated.

When I was finally called one wintry Monday by the neighbours, she looked quite dreadful: her face was bruised from several falls the previous night, she was struggling for her breath, her legs and thighs were very painful and swollen. She was incoherent and incapable of unassisted movement. I heard myself saying the line that had been waiting ready for months, "I think the time has come when you *must* go in." She nodded.

It then took me an hour as she lay there sobbing to find her a bed. She was nowhere near the top of the hospice waiting list (a bed was finally offered six days after her death). The general wards were packed with acute cases and, although I received a sympathetic ear, no one really wanted to know. Eventually, I found a young hospital registrar who said, not entirely as a joke: "I expect we'll find a cupboard for her." As I hung on the phone, I ingested the sad evidence of a service which, although well intentioned, simply hadn't coped. The promised home help hadn't turned up despite several letters, and there'd been no sign of the district nurse over the weekend. The normally immaculate room was a dirty mess, and pus was oozing through a leg ulceration into a bandage that looked several days old. I couldn't be certain how much painkilling medication she had taken, but it was almost certainly not enough. The neighbours, once in the picture, were kindness itself – though the woman who had rung me, standing smoking on the steps, shouted after me: "Took your bloody time, didn't you?"

Next day, as soon as I'd finished giving a police statement about a drug addict who had threatened me and attempted to steal syringes and prescriptions, I went to see her in hospital. The ward, packed with seriously ill patients, was in a state of controlled pandemonium. I eventually tracked down the ward sister, who was wrestling with an intravenous drip that had collapsed. The nurses seemed overwhelmed, and when I did find one with a moment to spare, she told me my patient had died half an hour earlier. Her body had already been removed. "We need the space, I'm afraid." I wanted to ask if she had died peacefully, whether they had used a syringe driver, if there'd been anyone to comfort her. I refrained because the evidence suggested the answers would all be negative.

The last dying patient I'd been to visit in this hospital had been the caretaker of our health centre, in much pain from a carcinoma of the pancreas. Normally the mildest of men, Frank had said, "I'd like some of those bastards who say the NHS is safe in their hands to spend a night in here. Two lasses looking after thirty surgical patients with two admissions on top."

I have very little confidence in the "reforms" being introduced with such a fanfare this month. Rather than eliminating NHS underfunding and the resulting problems, I think they will increase the bureaucracy, without any guarantee of better patient care. And I don't believe it provides a strategy for getting to grips with the underlying causes of ill health.

In London's East End, people, especially the elderly, are often ill-fed, ill-housed and ill-clad as well as being plain ill. These are the people who missed out on the eighties' boom and are now being hit hardest by the recession. How can they hope their asthma will get better in a draughty, poorly insulated flat? What price the "efficiency savings" made by day-surgery and early discharge when the patient leaves hospital with barely controlled pain and becomes infected, or simply can't cope at home and requires readmission? What do I say when I visit an old cockney lady with a fractured leg who has been sent home because the orthopaedic surgeons need her bed for the daily influx of trauma, but who can't stand unaided and who lives alone? Increase her painkillers to a dangerous level, make do with the district nurses and hope she doesn't fall again, which is, in fact, her best chance to get back in hospital.

The ambulance service in London does an outstanding and poorly rewarded job under horrendous pressure. And sometimes it lets you down. A note is pushed under the surgery door: "Mr and Mrs Frederick Saposnik. Cramps top leg. Fainted. Just had heart trouble. Job to breathe. Enard House." I hurry round to Mr Saposnik's dying; Mrs S offers tea. Despite two coronary bypasses, he's now strangled with anoxic pain, face grey, clutching his throat.

We wait for the ambulance, window open so they can identify us, doilies neatly heaped on yellowing copies of the local paper, the cat perturbed by my frantic resuscitation efforts. "Come," she used to say, "as long as you don't think he's wasting your time." That reflex is an old one, prepared to make a tactical retreat but also courtesy. To advance with charm or a curse. He is dead now. The ambulance is late. I try to comfort Mrs S while ringing with the other hand to cancel the 999. Somebody else will need it.

Despite the planners, people are people and fiercely loyal to their hospitals. Mr Morris, an ex-docker with a waggish humour, is one such. "Wotcha got this hammer for then?" he says. "It's not, it's a stethoscope. How's your chest?" "Sounds like someone's playing the flute down there at night. If I go in, I want to go to Bethnal Green Hospital." "Well you can't, you know – it's for older people now." His wife was an orderly there when it was still a general hospital. She knows from inside the sadness of a hospital closure.

Later his wife calls. "Quick. Now put your coat on and come quick. He's faintified and sickified." He's cyanosed, hyperventilating, pneumonia and a possible infarct. "It's a bit dicky, like. Could you give it a once-over? Maybe I'll go in. Just don't make me a geriatric case, Doc."

I spend a long time with the Emergency Bed Service on the neighbour's phone. They can't get hold of the medical referee. "No beds anywhere tonight, sir." The "sir" is supposed to make me feel better. He eventually dies in the ambulance, on the way to a hospital that isn't closed.

And so it goes on. Punks with their dogs piss in the waiting room and ask for money. Saul the furrier is depressed again. When he's depressed he stutters. "I think it's a sin to answer a doctor back," he says, because he's angry and wants to shout at me, at anyone. But can't. I tell him that in a depression, manners are the first casualities. His liver is enormous, and his liver function tests will be sky-high. I go to see his wife the next day. She confides, "He gets a few drinks and wants to wipe everybody out." "Well, how do you feel?" I enquire. "When you feel happy you can share happiness, but we never are. I tell you straight it's useless. Pills – what are they supposed to do?"

The last visit of the day is to Mr Mercer who has myeloma: "It's a disease I can recommend to anyone," he jokes. "He's the kind that won't give in," says his wife. He takes his terminal care in the pub: "Can you make that a large one, Ben, the other one went too quickly." He dies on Christmas Eve, and they don't come for the body till the day after Boxing Day. Some weeks later, I receive a note of thanks along with an engraved beer mug.

Esquire, 1991

ON BLACK CULTURAL POLITICS

A New Way of Seeing

An introduction by Ruth Gregory

I have read most of David Widgery's published essays many times, yet on every occasion they jolt me into a new way of seeing. Even after more than thirty years, they retain the power to illuminate my way, through a confusing present towards a longed-for future. And that, of course, is exactly what David's intentions were.

I first came across him in the 1970s, through his column in *Socialist Worker*, which provided a welcome breeze over sometimes turgid waters. In 1977, I joined him on Rock Against Racism's London committee, and on our militant and creative magazine, *Temporary Hoarding*. David was an eager promoter of the collective spirit of RAR, encouraging both new and seasoned writers to mix a predominately white punk cultural uprising with black reggae resistance in the UK.

Two of the essays in this section were written for *TH*: "What is Racism" and "How Did Biko Die?" Both are delivered with anger and optimism, both are aimed straight at an ill-at-ease and racially divided Britain, and both are battle cries to "get up, stand up for your rights".

There is a hungry optimism in David's work, one which subverts those comforting fairy-tale scenarios we might have been raised to believe and entices us into the culture and politics of his subjects' life stories. He talks of slavery in terms of "specifically sexual terrorism, justified by general myths directed at all blacks", and about Bessie Smith being "a queen on her own terms, black and a woman who made her own sexual life". She and her successor, Billie Holiday, demanded to be heard through their music in a world which "battered and denied their beings".

In the men's liberation magazine *Achilles Heel*, David contrasts a future more sensitive masculinity against the writer James Baldwin's unease with his own sexuality and manhood in the late 1960s, "trapped by the American image of Negro life" and a brutal, homophobic rejection from his peers.

David was a compulsive, but mostly gentle, inquisitor, and would rock up, pen in hand, to gather opinion. Too often history is seemingly constructed to celebrate a white, and male, ruling class and, with the results broadcast at full volume, effectively blocking out those weak, crackly transmissions from the common people. David, meanwhile, did his best to turn up the volume for the masses. His interview with the Trinidadian socialist, activist and writer C.L.R. James is imbued with the admiration, delight, humour and diversity which typifies David's writing.

Music was a shared passion between us, running, river deep, through both our lives. Whilst reading these essays again I found myself rifling my collection, appropriately including some newer material too: Miles Davis, Hortense Ellis, Linton Kwesi Johnson, J.B. Lenoir, Pablo Gad, Misty in Roots, Tappa Zukie, Kate Tempest, Peter Gabriel, The Mighty Sparrow, the Clash, Billie and Bessie; the Wailers, Gil Scott-Heron, Jessie Mae Hemphill...

We should follow the lead of these poets, singers and prophets, and take every disenchanted female, male, black, brown, white, bisexual, straight, gay and transsexual in the village with us. "Stuck on the block," raps Kentish Town's Akala, "read, read! Sittin' in the box, read, read! Don't let them say what you can achieve."[39]

---

39 "Fire in the Booth", *Knowledge Is Power Vol. 1*, Akala, 2012

Baldwin

James Baldwin's literary life overarches the modern Afro-American movement, against it Eldridge Cleaver's career is a brief meteor. He grew up in the Harlem of the second war, the munitions works of New Jersey, the early days of Greenwich Village. He had worked through five years in Paris and the harrowing writing of his first two novels before he began his political writing in the series of essays about the Deep South and the civil rights organisers with the Congress of Racial Equality (CORE) in the early sixties. By the ghetto risings of the mid-sixties he was a veteran, by 1968 and the rise of the Black Panthers judged a has-been. In this decade he lies in retreat in his tent in the south of France, critically and politically defeated. The white critical establishment honoured him with faint praise or mere silence. For the Black Power generation of black intellectuals he became the symbol of the bad old days, the man who never bent his typewriter into a carbine, who was convicted of white envy, assimilationism and cocksucking into the bargain. Rufus, the name of the black anti-hero of *Another Country*, became a term of abuse.[40]

In 1951 Baldwin had begun his startling career as an essayist with an assault on Richard Wright which sought to dispose of the black novelist, who largely defined the upper limits of what was possible in black literature. *Notes of a Native Son* finds itself at length so trapped by the American image of Negro life and by the American necessity to find the ray of hope that "it cannot pursue its own implications".[41] In 1968 Cleaver savaged Baldwin, pinned

---

40 James Baldwin, *Another Country* (Dial Press, 1962)
41 James Baldwin, *Notes of a Native Son* (Beacon Press, 1955)

him mercilessly against the very ghetto doorway he had occupied, robbed him blind of his political possessions. And turning away, sneered in Baldwin's sexual face, that bush-baby face, that he didn't make it because he wasn't enough of a man. Thus, "there is in James Baldwin's work the most gruelling, agonising, total hatred of the blacks, particularly of himself, and the most shameful, fanatical, fawning, syco-phantic love of the whites that one can find in the writings of any black American writer of note." And, "It seems that many Negro homosexuals, acquiescing in this radical death wish, are outraged and frustrated because in their sickness they are unable to bear a baby by a white man." And quite accurately, "Baldwin's essay on Richard Wright reveals that he despised not Richard Wright, but his masculinity. He cannot confront the stud in others – except that he must either submit to it or destroy it."[42]

Ostensibly the clash was political, about whether Baldwin could deal with the civil rights movement when it came north and called itself Black Power. Whether the man who had found his identity in the Paris cafés was any good in the street was between the black city dwellers and the police, the federals and the army. About how a black writer in the sixties should address himself politically, Cleaver found his political footing just as Baldwin lost his; he was the new kid in town, and in quick and brutal fashion he replaced the leader of the pack. On Wright's death, Baldwin had offered a partial retraction and expressed somewhat disingenuous surprise that his essay had been interpreted as an attack. Maybe Cleaver will one day be able to reread his own carve-up, for it catches in the very ferocity of its misunderstanding and the misguidedness of definitions of what is revolutionary, a terrible, self-mutilating weakness

---

42 The three quotations preceding this footnote all come from Eldridge Cleaver's memoir/essay collection, *Soul on Ice* (Ramparts Press, 1968).

in black politics in the late sixties, the sexual dark side of Black Power. Whereas what is so insightful and enduring about Baldwin's writing is that he has always been driven by a need to understand and unravel sexual politics in relation to the black movement. His own blackness and his class-consciousness are utterly wound up with his sexual identity.

As writers they both engineered the devastation of white America's racial and political values, they were both socialists by any reasonable definition of that tradition (whose virtual abolition in post-war America largely explains their appalling isolation). But Cleaver was unable to extend his indictment as far as himself and in the very process of denouncing the system became almost a parody of its persona and values. More self-important, brash and sexually oppressive in his being than the Jericho he sought, for a while, to trumpet down. Baldwin's writing of the fifties and sixties, reread now as it ought to be, possesses on the other hand exceptional decolonising power. Perception not noticed at the time but now stunning in accuracy, intensity and usefulness. Baldwin was never going to be a *Time* magazine revolutionary. He deals in difficulties and therefore often helps us to think rather than act. Yet his perceptions can help us find in ourselves and thereby make our political commitment the more enduring because it is deeply wedded to personal understanding. To find this deeply revolutionary Baldwin is to duck past the unpleasant ring of literary barkers, patronise his anguish and idolise him in impossible abstraction. He must be rescued from the *New York Times*, the not-so-liberal intelligentsia, the black bourgeoisie and probably from himself. Their curious overpraise hung untruthfully in the air; laboured comparisons with Henry James, insincere handshakes of welcome to the Anglo-Saxon literary pantheon, transcripts of trivial interviews with fellow celebrities. One has to trust the tale, not the talk show.

"One writes out of one thing only," Baldwin insists, "one's own experience. Everything depends on how relentlessly one forces from this experience the last drop, sweet or bitter, it can possibly give."[43]

Baldwin's writing *is* extraordinarily dauntingly precise and extensive in its effects. But instead of reaching for references to Dickens and Henry James to explain this fluency, it is more honest to see in its black origins, sources which, since black writing is only yet in its infancy, will be largely outside literature but still in the culture of words and feelings: the tartness and irony of the blues, the extreme mixture of self-assertion and self-expression in jazz, the patois of city talk where whole tales are executed in passing gestures, the sternness and self-summoned gravity of the basement pulpit. For it was this physically barren and emotionally eloquent black city world that shaped his prose. The tendrils of his sensibilities had to find their way, undamaged but not unaltered, through the rust and broken bottles of brutal, enclosed city feelings. His everyday experience was not just about being working class in a family perishing of poverty or the son of a father penetrated by an insane and holy anger which was also an absolute hatred of himself. It was not just being poor in a city where everything, absolutely everything, has its price. It is about his own spiritual and sexual identity – great clichés of sixties comfortable bourgeois self-discovery – but ground together remorselessly in Baldwin's work till they hurt. His religious crisis shaped his subsequent disbelieving. It is to the Church he owes the knowledge that through suffering can come understanding, that it is to be welcomed because of the way it forces a refinement of one's sense of self. He proceeds to apply these maxims, at the time when the movements of sexual liberation were unknown and unanticipated, at a time of

---

43 James Baldwin, *Autobiographical Notes* (A.A. Knopf, 1953); republished in *Notes of a Native Son* (1955)

113

universal and oppressive normality, to his own homosexuality, or, shall we say, lack of heterosexuality. A conscious black writer is drawn to the left, because the constant experience of the disfavour America bestows on their skin must lead to the questioning of that whole society's claim to be civilised. And for a man, to be "on the left" especially in post-war America was to become more of a man, to stand up, to fight and all the rest of the rhetoric of arousal. But to be homosexual is to lack that very ability "to be a man". It is to be put into a white room, a plan where Baldwin, writing of another, says, "He was, briefly and horribly, in a region where there were no definitions of any kind, neither of colour nor of male or female."[44]

In an America in the fifties itself lost in explanations, expectations, advertisements for an impossible self, Baldwin sought, through writing, to discover his real self. Or rather to disentangle it from a series of projections. He was to force this self-discovery at a cruel pitch but then he could never have written about pain without having suffered it, shame without having felt it and self-hatred without being scraped by its sharp edges. Baldwin could be emancipated, he says, from his lack of identity, his hate and self-hatred in two ways: killing it and himself, or exploring it so thoroughly he overcame it. In the nearly untranslatable phrase of Sartre, he "worked himself over". He forced himself through a kind of North American existentialism – a single-handed liberation – insisting, "Though we do not wholly believe it yet, the interior life is a real world, and the intangible dreams of people will have a tangible effect on the world."[45]

What he discovered in that journey about his blackness, although remarkable, is well known. No one, not Frantz Fanon nor poets of Negritude, have written about racialism so delicately. Baldwin's journalism on the then silent zone of

---

44 James Baldwin, *Another Country* (1962)
45 James Baldwin, *Nobody Knows My Name* (Dial Press, 1961)

America below the Mason-Dixon line that opened the tin-can closeness of Mississippi, can still catch breath with its controlled vehemence. But Baldwin's sexual convictions, what he has discovered about love, are more cautiously buried, very far in advance of their time. For when Baldwin wrote, "I think that I know something about the American masculinity which most of my generation do not because they haven't been menaced by it in the way I have,"[46] his vantage point is fundamentally different from that of Cleaver, blundering on about his desire for a "political party that would be the vehicle for galvanising this idea into reality by turning black males into men, by setting the standard of what a black man must be and must be willing to do in our time in order to be a man and in order to say he is fulfilling his duties to secure his tribe". Baldwin has seen that conquering man, and been sexually vulnerable to it, as a woman would be. He understands what a misshapen piece of work such a man would be ... and what a bad lover or leader. In a remarkable essay written for the Paris-based review *Zero* he wrote, in 1949, "In the truly awesome attempt of the American to at once preserve his innocence and arrive at man's estate, that mindless monster, the tough guy, has been created and perfected, whose masculinity is found in the most infantile and elementary externals and whose attitude to women is the wedding of the most abysmal romanticism and the most implacable distrust."[47] He knows too well the "Strong Man" who is quite incompetent with a baby, a sadness, or for that matter a revolution.

Baldwin also insisted, at a time when many radical American novelists were quite literally arguing that the conservatism of America was the fault of women who were

---

46 James Baldwin, "The Black Boy Looks at the White Boy Norman Mailer", *Esquire* (May 1961)
47 James Baldwin, "The Preservation of Innocence", *Zero* 1.2 (1949)

subtly undermining the masculinity of their men, that there was something fundamentally wrong in the relationship between men and women. He saw heterosexual love as bound to be destroyed by the disparity of the power held within the relationship. And he saw the destructiveness of that relationship going both ways, because both sexes were attempting to possess something of the other, while at the same time were obliged to protect themselves with a sliding screen of stereotypes. And there was no way man could so deny the existence of the woman without diminishing themselves utterly. And he catches that strange white North American incompetence at the emotional, that land of being jostled but not touched, rapped with but not talked to and fucked but never loved which has finally given birth to its own psycho-industry selling relaxation, insight and orgasmic potential, all at the appropriate price. Against all that, Baldwin asks for – demands an unoppressive love, which is not about grappling for possession but responsibly entering another person's being. Such a love was not about sexual gadgets of powerful but separated and unknowing sexual release. Love was a journey people had to make together. It could only commence from a measure of self-knowledge; "Everyone wishes to be loved, but in the event, nearly no one can bear it. Everyone desires love but also finds it impossible to believe that he deserves it."[48] Such a lovely concept is very clearly about politics because it is about self-knowledge and change. It makes sense of Baldwin's much misunderstood statement, "If the word integration means anything, this is what it means: that we, with love, shall force our brothers to see themselves as they are, to cease fleeing from reality and begin to change it."[49] As heterosexual men find so hard to accept, the capacity

48 James Baldwin, *Tell Me How Long the Train's Been Gone* (Dial Press, 1968)
49 James Baldwin, *The Fire Next Time* (Dial Press, 1963)

for love is also the capacity for surrender. Read or reread *Giovanni's Room* and *Another Country*.[50] Both novels were critically unpopular because they were novels about sexual liberation before those two words had been placed together. They are now ignored as the bookshops quake with studies of every sort of sexual this, that and the other. Baldwin's publishers rejected the former novel "for his own good" and told him to burn it because portraying a love affair between two men was bad for the career of a promising black writer. Robert Bone's review of *Another Country* is not untypical:

> Five orgasms (two interracial and two homosexual) or approximately one per eighty pages, a significant increase on the Mailer rate. Distracted by this nonsense, how can one attend to the serious business of the novel. To most, homosexuality will seem rather an evasion than an affirmation of human truth. Ostensibly the novel summons us to reality. Actually it substitutes for the illusions of white supremacy those of homosexual love.

Orgasms, Mr Bone, author of *The Negro Novel in America*, feels are not serious. Another critic complains, "Baldwin seems convinced that homosexuality is a liberating force, and he now brings to the subject a certain proselytising zeal."[51] What happens in both books is something quite different: sexual love, orgasms are described with some social meaning, not mysterious skyrockets and grunts, but condensing physically what is happening emotionally between two people. Homosexuals in both novels happen to be the people on best terms with their own sexuality.

It is gently implied that heterosexual relations are more vulnerable to economic and social camouflage which makes

50 James Baldwin, *Giovanni's Room* (Dial Press, 1956)
51 Robert A. Bone, *The Negro Novel in America* (Yale UP, 1958)

the power relations hard to see. That marriages, in contrast to gay relationships, last after they are sexually dead because they are held into shape by society. But homosexuality is never seen, of itself, as a superior form of sexual life: the life of the gay milieu in Paris is quite unsentimentally shown as being dominated by possession and cash values, variants of the very forces that corrupt heterosexual relationships. In fact both novels really advocate bisexuality, that most unpopular but widespread of conditions.

Rufus, the central figure in *Another Country*, is a musician based on a close friend, Eugene Worth, with whom Baldwin joined a socialist organisation and who later, like Rufus, flung himself from a New York bridge. Rufus is invaded by a terrible loneliness, a corroding estrangedness from which he can only escape in violent attacks on his few close friends and in revengeful intercourse, painfully described, with a white southern girl. All his friends let him down, all are haunted by his intensity and shamed by his suicide, all unable to reach across the forces of racism. His catastrophe sends out waves of uncertainty, forces everyone to strip off another layer of illusion. Rufus's sister continues his indicting presence but it is Eric, a gay actor, who can teach, by sexual means, Rufus's mourning friends what love is: to give oneself, to surrender openly. He is capable of acting non-oppressively with men and women against the painful vengeance-ridden sexuality of the first part of the book. It is not like the conventional homosexual novella of the period where gay love is largely conventional in its emotions if different in gender, nor the chirpy but shallow lesbian-picaresque adventure novels of the modern women's movement like *Rubyfruit Jungle* and *Kinflicks*.[52] It is also quite different from the sexual sadism and mysogyny present in Norman Mailer's novels of the period – reread if you can

---

52 Rita Mae Brown, *Rubyfruit Jungle* (Daughters, 1973)
    Lisa Alther, *Kinflicks* (Knopf, 1976)

face it *An American Dream* – whose profanity covers over the Manhattan Jew and the New England Protestant dislike of gays and suspicion/mystification of women.[53] Rather Baldwin is dealing in areas of sexual uncertainty common to both sexes condensed in this passage from *Another Country* into the face of Eric:

> It was the face of a man, of a tormented man. Yet, in precisely the way that great music depends, ultimately on great silence, this masculinity was defined, and made powerful, by something which was not masculine. But it was not feminine, either, and something in Vivaldo resisted the word *androgynous*. It was a quality to which great numbers of people would respond without knowing to what it was they were responding. There was great force in the face, and great gentleness. But, as most women are not gentle, nor are most men strong, it was a face which suggested, resonantly, in the depths, the truth about our natures.

To illustrate quite how advanced was Baldwin's vision, one can contrast the self-abasement of the gay Australian novelist, Colin MacInnes, reviewing *Giovanni's Room* in 1963.[54] MacInnes died tragically of cancer in 1976. His novels of black London are themselves underestimated; they are unique pictures of a certain London at a certain time. After apologising for even mentioning the "tiresome topic of the homosexual dilemma", MacInnes writes with great caution what Baldwin was stating with such force:

---

53 Norman Mailer, *An American Dream* (Dial Press, 1965)
54 The son of singer James Campbell McInnes, Colin MacInnes used both spellings of his last name, though the latter is what he is more commonly known by. MacInnes was actually born in London in 1914, but lived in Australia from 1920 to 1930.

We may see a parallel, which I hope any coloured readers will excuse, between the "homosexual problem" and the "Negro problem". The plain fact about both is that neither is: the Negro is not a problem to himself, but to the racialist; the "problem" of queerdom resides in the heart of the queer-haters and those who, being queers, either glorify the commonplace or deny their own inner natures.

Giovanni's Room was planned quite deliberately to be about the implications of being bisexual, and the first draft was based around the case of Wayne Lonergan, a man rejected twice from the army as a homosexual and then was found involved in a bizarre sexual murder with an heir's wife, which suggested he was no stranger to heterosexual love either. It was to be called *Ignorant Armies*. *Giovanni*, one of Baldwin's favourite books, contains no black characters and is set in Paris. It is about sex and class, about America and Europe, and about the emotional incompetence of white American man once his interpreted ideas of sexual identity with their hygienic compartments are dissolved. David is terrified by the room in which he is physically overwhelmed by the Italian waiter, Giovanni, but what he hates is what is being sexually awakened in him and Giovanni's insistence on feeling. Giovanni simply has an acute sense of what is love and what is not; David's life has been arranged to avoid pain, emotional inconvenience, to reach always for sexual safety.

There is in Baldwin's heterosexual male characters a certain endemic emotional cowardice. They are separated from each other by an inner emptiness to which women are privy but are enjoined to secrecy about. Baldwin shows them vanquished in their attempts to express anything to each other as they meet in public, with too much pride resting on their intactness, unable even in extremity to reveal the feelings that they, in private, thrash against their female companions.

And that, finally, rather than his homosexuality, is why Baldwin is so threatening to Cleaver's politics. For although they share an understanding of how North American capitalism operates, they differ about why and how to fight it. Cleaver is apparently to the left with muscular talk about the struggle, a fast line in sexual insults and quotes from Che Guevara. But although he saw the need for working-class organisation, this sort of tough talking appealed most to the male radical students, the clientele of *Ramparts* magazine. And its politics were intensely individualistic. The revolution became an act of will undertaken as a proof of manhood, and in defence of the helpless, the women and children. When you see Cleaver speaking or on film, he's still operating on the skills of the streets and the prison yard; the parries, the thrusts, the put-downs, the victorious smile as the opponent is lost for a reply. In one particular film interview, a white radical, Bob Scheer, aids and abets this performance with equal egotism but perfectly judged and ingratiating sense of inferiority ... even in Algeria Eldridge is the Black Prince. The hapless pair then stumble round the Algiers streets with that gracelessness peculiar to Americans overseas. But Cleaver's conversational arts are about how black men are absorbed in presenting an exterior. He and Scheer's duet is about the false manhood of men who would do anything to avoid coming to terms with each other. And when that heady individualism falters, as it did for so many of the celebrities of the black revolt, it falls asunder. Because it doesn't understand itself, it can't afford to pause lest it would disintegrate. However much it talks of class-consciousness and collective resistance, the message is plundered of meaning by the isolation of the speaker. In the case of Cleaver, Stokely Carmichael, Huey P. Newton it has resolved in right-wing and nationalistic directions. Baldwin speaks much less explicitly but in a more profoundly political way of a different kind of strength and leadership which has more in common with the initial organising methods of the Student Nonviolent Coordinating Committee (SNCC), the early days of Students for a Democratic Society (SDS) and women's liberation. So to him black groups who were absorbed by hostility to whites, are paying an ironic tribute to their oppressors by remaining defined by them. For Cleaver and Carmichael, for black to be beautiful it had to be feared. Baldwin just remarks, drily, "Black *is* beautiful, and since it's beautiful you haven't got to say so."

Achilles Heel, 1976

What Is Racism?

Racism is as British as Biggles and baked beans. You grow up anti-black, with the golliwogs in the jam, *The Black and White Minstrel Show* on TV and CSE dumbo history at school.[55] Racism is about Jubilee mugs and "Rule, Britannia!" and how we won the War. Gravestones, bayonets, forced starvation and the destruction of the cultures of India and Africa was regrettable, of course. But without our Empire the world's inhabitants would be rolling in the mud still, wouldn't they? However lousy our football team or broken down our Health Service, we've got this private compensation that we're white, British and used to rule the waves. IT WOULD BE PATHETIC, IF IT HAD'NT KILLED AND INJURED AND BRUTALISED SO MANY LIVES. AND IF IT WASN'T STARTING ALL OVER AGAIN.

Most of the time British racialism is veiled behind forced smiles, charming coppers and considerate charities. But when times get hard, the newest arrival is the first to blame. Once they kicked in Protestant French settlers, then tormented the Irish construction workers who built our roads and railways, for the crime of being Micks. From the 1880s until 1939 it was the Jews' turn, refugees from terrible brutality in Eastern Europe who became the victims and the scapegoats again in London and Leeds.

Racism is beaten back by the solidarity of ordinary people. Then eminent people say it will never happen again. Lo and behold, times get bad and jobs get hard to find and wages are washed out and life gets lousy. And then the junk images of racialism, the remains of five hundred years of

---

55 *The Black and White Minstrel Show*, creator George Inns, 1958–1978

"our" Empire surge up again and the Beast begins to stir. They need a racial problem to distract people from the real ones. They need an answer for people who don't want to think. In 1977 the answer is: BLAME THE BLACKS.

Last year in Britain saw racial violence *worse* than the height of Sir Oswald Mosley's anti-Jew campaign in the thirties. Gurdip Singh Chaggar, Dinesh Choudhury and Ribbi Al Hadid were stabbed to death in openly racial murders. Dozens of black people have been injured by the racialists, egged on every morning by the *Mail* and the *Express*'s screaming headlines which make their acts of hatred respectable. Fascists, their spiked Union Jacks and slow military drums under heavy police protection forced their way through Hackney, Bradford, Leicester, despite active and forceful protest. In North London, the police boasted openly that they were using snatch squad techniques to pick out anti-National Front demonstrators "that had been perfected in Ireland". Repatriation, which means forced deportation, which means the rounding up and hunting down of blacks, is informally supported by the Tory Party. And the Labour Party has no answer, except to cringe. It has created the political conditions in which the fascists flourish. From the wire cages in Heathrow Airport's immigrant compounds to the gleaming Alien Registration Computer in Holborn, a new colour bar now stretches. Every retreat by officialdom inflames the appetite of the right. Once again racialism is back. And challenged it must be. For when racialists rule, millions die.

In the 1950s and 1960s, British employers courted black labour, sucking in skills and muscle from the Caribbean and Asia. Black workers filled the jobs that no one else fancied: shift workers in the hospitals, sweeping the airport corridors in the early morning, in the blazing heat of the foundries and the twilight shifts in the mills. They saved for back-to-backs in streets where the refuse somehow never got cleaned up by the council or got pushed into the old council blocks that no one else wanted. Promised the sky, they were slotted in at the bottom. Chapeltown, Manningham, Southall, Brixton; crowded houses, dismal pubs, wet plimsolls, dogs licking dustbins. No fault of the people who had to live there but they got the blame. Black workers were never thanked. They were tolerated, as long as they knew their place and kept to it. And worked their hearts out.

Now the economic furnace which sucked them in is faltering. Prices roar, wages shrink. The economic system is at odds with itself. The more it tries to untie itself, the deeper the knots of inflation and unemployment cut in. To sell your labour now is a privilege; the economy can't use the workers it's got.

Blacks, no matter most are British-born, suddenly become a "problem". Forced into the decaying bits of the big cities, they are accused of causing that decay. Out of work, they are called lazy. Half-educated in overcrowded, bullying schools and they are called educationally subnormal. They are blamed for the conditions they endure and government offices make a living producing books of statistics about how terrible things are. The youth are told on all sides they are worthless. If they fight back, it's proof of their savagery. If they remain passive to the taunts, that testifies to their inferiority. For everyone who feels fear, gloom, guilt, despair, there is a simple answer. If the buses arrive full up, if they don't bother to repair the lifts any more, if Casualty is closed, it's because of the blacks. Racialism is an antidote to thought that offers easy pointless action; a blanket in your head to hide under.

The problem is not just the new fascists from the old slime, a master race whose idea of heroism is ambushing single blacks in darkened streets. These private attacks whose intention, to cow and brutalise, won't work if the community they seek to terrorise instead organises itself. But when the state backs up racialism, it's different.

Outwardly respectable but inside fired with the same mentality and the same fears, the bigger danger is the racist magistrates with their cold sneering authority, the immigration men who mock an Asian mother as she gives birth to a dead child on their office floor, policemen for whom answering back is a crime and every black kid with pride is a challenge.

Because of the change in immigration laws, just to be black is to be half illegal. You become a permanent suspect, always you can be stopped and asked for your passport. The police insist they are impartial but contrast their zeal to force a way through unwelcome streets for the Front and their attempt at Notting Hill Gate last summer to smother a peaceful joyous music festival held by the people in their own neighbourhood with imported riot-trained police. How can we take the police's claim to be impartial seriously when their evidence at the Mangrove, the Metro, the Leeds Bonfire Trials and others is thrown out by the juries, when they accuse an eighteen-year-old girl of assaulting eight policemen or charge the Islington youth with an unnamed crime at an unknown time. How long before they start on white "undesirables", the reds and the queers in the same way?

This new legal viciousness is even more sinister than the hardened fascists' return to the streets. But they can both be resisted. But only when people who realise what's going on come together, black and white, to voice their feelings and show their strength. As a parent of one of the Islington Eighteen said, "We parents should start thinking we've worked too damn hard all these years ... if black parents stand up and say 'We are with our kids', we will win." Another said, "When ordinary black working-class parents start working with white people on a case like this, that's what the police are afraid of. We can go further." Together we can make it.

Temporary Hoarding, 1977

But How Did Biko Die?

On Monday, 17 May 1976, 1600 children at Orlando West Junior School, Soweto, in South Africa, walked out of the gates of their school. They wanted to be taught, as before, in English rather than Afrikaans. They milled around the grounds uncertainly, some dancing and skipping. The teachers waited for them to change their minds. The Inspector of Education asked, "Have you ever heard of thirteen-year-old children striking?"

It spread. One month later fifteen thousand black schoolchildren marched through Soweto carrying exercise book placards saying "Afrikaans is oppressors' language" and "Blacks are not dustbins". The police tried to disperse the march with tear gas. Then a uniformed white policeman shot a thirteen-year-old boy called Hector Pieterson with a revolver: in the back, stone dead.

In the subsequent eighteen months, the black townships rose: barely armed, poorly organised, desperately brave. Teenagers faced armoured cars with sticks, children threw stones back at policemen who were firing submachine guns. On a blackboard in a school in Nyanga, someone drew a crude map and wrote "Cape Town comrades, Mdantsane comrades, Soweto comrades, Maputo comrades ... all these comrades must unite. NO RACIALISM. NO COLONIALISM. EQUALITY." The rising was suppressed with systematic and merciless brutality. In the process South African police have killed 456 people and injured 2160. "Over half of those shot by police around Johannesburg were shot in the back." There are now 662 people held in detention without trial. More than one hundred have been held for over a year. Twenty-three have died in prison.

One of the twenty-three, Steve Biko, a leader of the Black Consciousness grouping, and a believer in non-violent change, was detained in his home town of King William's Town on 18 August 1977. He was alternately interrogated, beaten and then left naked in a police cell. During an all-night interrogation on the night of 6 September, he was attacked by his captors and suffered a brain haemorrhage from which he slowly and excruciatingly died as paralysis spread over his body in the next four days. On the final day of his life, unable to speak, he was driven 750 miles tied up and bouncing in the back of a Land Rover, stark naked.

The Minister of Justice, James Kruger, announced his death at the Transvaal National Party Congress, stating, "It leaves me cold." He stated officially that Biko had died as a result of a hunger strike. When *The World* and *The Rand Daily Mail* published evidence of his post-mortem injuries, the minister attempted to suppress their reports. Fifteen thousand people mourned at Biko's funeral, although buses and trains were halted by police and passengers sjambokked. Fourteen road-blocks were placed on the main road between Johannesburg and the funeral. On 19 October Kruger announced the banning and house arrest of sixty individuals, the two news-papers that had told the truth about Biko and eighteen organisations including the Black People's Convention, the Soweto Students' Representative Council, Black Parents' Association, the Medupi Writers' Association, the Zimele Clinic Trust Fund, the Black Women's Federation and the white-run Christian Institute of Southern Africa.

There is now no one left to arrest or ban. Liberalism is itself outlawed as the search for victims to jail and houses to raid proceeds. The repression feeds on itself. New captives are interrogated to find new victims.

The truth itself is illegal. Mass arrests are an everyday affair. On 18 November during a house-to-house sweep near Pretoria, police arrested 626 blacks. The officer in charge described it as "a perfectly normal raid".

Since the 19 October crackdown, South Africa has made the final turn into a fully fledged fascist state structure. Since 1948, over three hundred pieces of separatist legislation have been passed to create the most repressive system of racial laws in the world. The black population, seventy per cent of the total, are either confined to the black homelands in the thirteen per cent of the most barren of South African territories or live without rights in the cities as migrant labourers. Television and radio are under complete state control. The army has 41,000 regulars with 130,000 reserves ready for call-up at twenty-four hours notice. The National Party itself is controlled by the all-male Afrikaner Broederbond, a secret society with over ten thousand members, including the prime minister.

Now even the facilities for white liberal opinion have been abolished. The Minister of Justice first lied publicly and then openly gloated over the prison cell murder of a non-violent opponent arrested without trial. A judge and ex-member of the National Party, Mr Justice Kowie Marais, has said, after the Biko death, the electors who vote for Vorster in the 30 November elections will be responsible "in the same way the Germans became responsible when they extended a mandate to Hitler". And yet millions of white votes will give that mandate.

The British government voted in the United Nations, yet again, against business sanctions to South Africa, which might do some small good, and for arms sanctions, which are utterly worthless. The South African forces have already stockpiled and anyway are secretly provided for by the Israelis. The reason is twofold. First the Labour Foreign Secretary Dr David Owen relies on Mr Vorster to insist that Ian Smith cooperate in some plan to prevent military victory of the black resistance in Zimbabwe. And second Britain is still South Africa's largest trading partner and investor. Almost a quarter of South Africa's exports go to Britain and four per cent of British exports are destined for South Africa. Major British companies are deeply inter-locked with subsidiaries in a South Africa they profess to disapprove of. Much of the material directly aids the police state. Plessey provides the expertise for electronic weapons guidance systems. Marconi are building an £8 million military communication system. ICI owns forty per cent of the company that manufactured most of the tear gas used in Soweto. British Leyland in South Africa is expanding with British government funds in factories where black unions are illegal, making land rovers for the police. The new head of British Leyland UK won his industrial spurs in Johannesburg.

The state that killed Steve Biko is, despite the diplomatic talk, deeply connected to Britain. To help black Africa to freedom, we will have to free ourselves.

Temporary Hoarding, 1979

C.L.R. James

Optimism is not a proper emotion for a dialectical materialist. But C.L.R. James justified it by his erudition, his political experience and the age he wore so gracefully, and I will always cherish this meeting.

"People are treating me with far greater concern than before," C.L.R. James grimaces. "It's very tiring." James has his feet up in room 384 of the Mayfair Hotel. Beside him lies a John Berger paperback, a brown cardboard folder of manuscript, his wheelchair and a ham sandwich plastered with English mustard. "My feet are tired but my tongue is not. I do not intend to give in." He talks with a rare passion and erudition: of Bolshevism, of Caribbean politics, of calypso, Sartre, cricket and his beloved Uffizi Gallery. His speech is as fresh and pungent as his sandwich.

To the best of my ability, I have attempted not to hero-worship this man who, if Marxists believed in such things, would be the greatest living Marxist. And failed. For my generation, James is the essence of political legend: organising the International African Service Bureau with George Padmore, bearding Trotsky in Coyoacán, organising share-croppers in Missouri, hailing Kwame Nkrumah as the black Lenin in Accra, wandering into a Havana revolutionary congress with a volume of Michelangelo plates. In his wiry, eight-decade-young frame is the historical eloquence of E.P. Thompson, the cricketing connoisseurship of John Arlott, the revolutionary ardour of Tony Cliff and the preciousness of John Berger, all mixed up with a wit and a way with paradox which is entirely West Indian.

The outlaw James had better be resigned to his eminence. The three volumes published this week by Allison & Busby bring together a body of work previously passed from hand to hand as mimeos, photostats and battered American paperbacks. One volume is a collection of "notes" on Hegel, Marx and Lenin; two more bring together stories and essays. (A final selection of essays is promised, and the headstone, a volume of autobiography, is on the way.) But the centrepiece of the present triptych of publications is *The Black Jacobins*, an account of Toussaint L'Ouverture and the San Domingo revolution, which James wrote in Brighton in 1937.[56] The extraordinary narrative power and analytic intensity of this well-known but widely unread book is famous. But James's motive for writing it is not. "I decided," he told me, "that I was going to write the story of some blacks who were not persecuted and sat upon and oppressed, but who did something." The book is not only a pioneering exposition of black pride but is also stamped with James's head-on collision with Marxism.

Cyril Lionel Robert James was born near Port of Spain in 1901. He was the son of a teacher, won a scholarship to Queen's Royal College school (thirty years later, V.S. Naipaul went there, too), and then became a schoolteacher himself. He also began playing club cricket and writing stories. It was Learie Constantine, the Trinidadian cricketer, then playing in the Lancashire League, who suggested James should come over to England.

He arrived from Trinidad in 1932, equipped with an exceptional grounding in the European classics. But at Constantine's home in the small Pennine town of Nelson, he was presented with volume one of Trotsky's *History of the Russian Revolution* and Spengler's *Decline of the West*.[57] "It was then necessary to read the relevant volumes of

---

56 C.L.R. James, *The Black Jacobins* (Dial Press, 1935)
57 Leon Trotsky, *The History of the Russian Revolution Volume 1: The Overthrow of Tzarism* (Granit (Russian), 1931)
  Oswald Spengler, *The Decline of the West, or The Downfall of the Occident*, two volumes (Allen & Unwin, 1918 & 1922)

Stalin. And, of course, I had to read Lenin in order to trace back the quarrel. And thereby I reached volume one of *Das Kapital* and *The 18th Brumaire* of Marx himself."[58]

In a decade in which Stalinist mythology dominated the left, James came to his own conclusion: "I realised the Stalinists were the greatest liars and corrupters of history there ever were. No one convinced me of this. I convinced myself. But having come to this conclusion, I wanted to meet some Trotskyists."

He eventually tracked down this endangered species in Golders Green, noting with some amusement, "I was much more familiar with the political material than the people who ran the group."

As disaster overwhelmed the German left, and Stalin switched to the desperate alliance-mongering of the Popular Front, James – now editor of the Revolutionary Socialist League's paper *Fight* – made regular clandestine visits to the Paris exile grouping of revolutionaries around Trotsky. "They were very serious days," James admonishes, inflecting the adjective "serious" as only an old-time Trotskyist can. "There was a German boy very active in our movement. One day we found him at the bottom of the Seine."

Trotskyism Repressed

James was, with D.D. Harbor, the British delegation to the founding conference of the Trotskyist Fourth International in 1938. This tiny body was established with the hope that, in the holocaust to come, a clear-sighted International might find a way through the chaos. But Trotsky, and effectively Trotskyism, succumbed to the terrible repression.

---

58 Karl Marx, *Capital: Critique of Political Economy*, three volumes (Verlag von Otto Meissner (German), 1867, 1885 & 1894)
Karl Marx, *The Eighteenth Brumaire of Louis Napoleon* (first appeared as an essay in the German magazine *Die Revolution* in 1852, but later published as a book)

In his last years, the Old Man blazed with political imagination, intrigue and epistles, as if beaming out his political SOS. James was duly summoned to Trotsky's fortress in Mexico City. I have read their transcribed discussions and they give a rare glimpse of the Great Exile debating with an intellectual equal. "Although we disagreed, I was tremendously impressed," James recalls. "Trotsky started with the analysis – international, political, philosophical. But the action, the activity, always followed. I got a glimpse of what Bolshevism of the old school meant." James had been lured to North America by the Trotskyist James P. Cannon – some way to remove a "troublesome" element in British Trotskyist politics. And in America, James soon found himself at odds with the orthodoxy, in the same way that Tony Cliff in London and Paul Cardan in Paris were to break with official Trotskyism.

James faced another crossroads. He had friends and, by now, a good job as a cricket correspondent in London. To remain in America and work through his disagreements with Trotskyism was a commitment to ten years of intellectual work. But James accepted the commitment and once again kept his rendezvous with history.

He helped to develop a theory of global state capitalism. He rejected the Bolshevik concept of a vanguard party and emphasised shop floor organisation as the seed of the new society. This meant rediscovering the Young Marx. It is this necessary reshaping of the Marxist ingredients which is presented in *Notes on Dialectics*, one of the reprinted volumes.[59] James reckons, "[It is] one of the most important pieces that I have done. I'm waiting to see what people are going to say about it."

The book was "written in Reno when [James] was seeing about a divorce." It represents the condensation of one of the remarkable political collaborations of modern

---

59 C.L.R. James, *Notes on Dialectics* (Lawrence Hill & Co., 1980)

times: James's political and intellectual prowess, Raya Dunayevskaya's understanding of the Russian material, and Grace Lee Boggs's German studies. It is written with fearsome intensity, calling out names and ferociously bashing down the arguments: it is Marxist philosophy at red heat and ought to be read by those tepid academics who at present monopolise the science in Britain.

The making of C.L.R. James is also presented in the beautifully edited collection of essays which, with E.P. Thompson's recent writings, will do a great deal to revive the fortune of the genre. They demonstrate the sweep, drive and attack of James's Marxism. They move from early fiction, through polemics against racism, to the critical essays he wrote under many Trotskyist pseudonyms on the literature of Shakespeare, Herman Melville and Norman Mailer. (In the early years of *New Society* he wrote on both West Indians and cricket: but those articles are not collected here.)

And James has as good an ear as his eye. He writes beautifully in these essays about the Mighty Sparrow, Trinidad's most famous calypsoan, whom he describes as "the most intelligent and alert person I met in the Caribbean", and with great feeling about the young Paul Robeson, with whose Moscow-line politics he so fundamentally differed (though he and Robeson appeared together in the 1930s at the Westminster Theatre, in a dramatised version of Toussaint's story). We agreed to disagree about reggae, but James pays tribute to the tremendous effectiveness of Rasta music: "The Rastafari are leftists, with no particular programme. But their critique of everything the British left behind, and those blacks who follow it, is very sophisticated."

James came back to England after the Second World War, and remarried. He now divides his time between London and the West Indies, with interludes as, for example, a visiting professor at United States universities or colleges.

When I saw him, he was just back from Kingston, Jamaica, where

> naturally, I had talks with (Jamaican Prime Minister) Manley. But the crisis in the Caribbean is not the problem of the capacity of the individual leaders: it's the tremendous mess the imperialists left them in. What is happening in Kingston today is precisely what happened in Chile under Allende. The same procedures are being carried out: destabilisation, economic manipulation, sabotage, the strategy of tension. And Seaga [the Jamaican opposition leader] promises everything but will bring nothing.

James now plans to return to Trinidad as a guest of the Oilfield Workers' Union. "This organisation is the most powerful political creation of the people of Trinidad and Tobago since the abolition of slavery. It is not that some intellectuals have got hold of it. It has been made by the people themselves." James, the black Cassandra, had sent a public telegram of warning to the young left-winger, Walter Rodney, two months before his assassination in Guyana last month. There is pain, but not disbelief, in his face as he remembers his young friend. One is reminded just how many political deaths James has had to witness, grieve over and endure.

I retain important reservations about James's Leninist libertarianism. He has been insufficiently consistent in applying his own criteria for socialist self-emancipation to Nkrumah, Castro and other revolutionary nationalists. His devastating critique of "vanguard" parties – those toy Bolsheviks who ape and misunderstand Lenin's politics – is in danger of writing off altogether the need for the sinews of socialist organisation. But this is very small beer beside one's respect, admiration and affection for a revolutionary intransigent who inhabits both classical and Marxist culture like a familiar home. He moves from ancient Greece to the Detroit auto plants, and then to Florence, in as many sentences.

Hitler, Stalin, Vietnam

Liberal reviewers of his earlier collection of essays, *The Future in the Present*, found it hard to conceal a certain surprise that such intelligence and such compassion could issue from such a committed Marxist, but this is not remarkable at all.[60] James's excellence is because of his political vantage point, not despite it. "I have seen nothing", James states firmly, "to shift me from the Marxist view of the world I adopted in 1934, have watched nothing but the decline of this capitalist society. I have seen the first war. Hitler, Stalin, the Gulag, Vietnam. And now do I think Jimmy Carter and Ronald Reagan and Mrs Thatcher are going to fix anything?" He waves contempt softly about the bedroom. "And it would seem to me that all this frantic maneuvering in the Labour Party and the trade unions is once again to keep the workers in order."

Then his voice lowers again, and hangs suspended, as if addressing an auditorium: "More and more people, especially black people, are alert. They reject the political choices offered them and are looking for a new way out of the mess. They are the ones who are now turning to Marx and Lenin to see if they have something to say."

They should also be turning to C.L.R. James, who has already answered some of the questions events have yet to pose.

New Society, 1980

---

60 C.L.R. James, *The Future in the Present* (Allison & Busby, 1977)

Billie and Bessie

David Widgery comments: A paid-up blues fanatic, I have never managed to understand the depth of my own obsession. This essay was an attempt to try. I think it was Dennis Potter's brilliant TV series The Singing Detective *which is about, in part, the allure of sentimentality in music, which finally explained it.*[61] *The cynical ballad singer-cum-detective played by Michael Gambon, whose sexual self-repression is a kind of psoriasis, muses at one point, "There are songs to sing. There are feelings to feel. There are thoughts to think. That makes three things. And you can't do three things at the same time. The singing is easy. Syrup in my mouth. The thinking comes with the tune. So that only leaves the feelings. ... But you're not going to catch me feeling the feelings." Which was exactly what Holiday and Smith did. It was also an attempt on my part to write about the rise of black music in this American century and to recall my own shock of seeing segregation in the Deep South in the mid-1960s. And, hopefully, to understand the power of women.*

The blues is a feeling. For most of this century, music has been the only vehicle black America has been permitted to tell its story, to say what it feels and what it wants. From the harshest of slave systems has come the most moving art produced by modern America. And the source of the power of the blues singers has been their ability to empty out their experience of suffering and longing in the most direct and emotionally forceful idiom.

---

61 *The Singing Detective*, dir. Jon Amiel, 1986

For what Bessie Smith and Billie Holiday have in common is not their victimhood – it would be sentimental so to suppose – but their understanding. They knew why America needed victims like themselves. They both could understand not only what it meant to be black when that was a considerable liability, but that it was white society which was deformed and lacking and not themselves.

They knew about capitalism, racism and sexism and sang about them, obliquely, subtly, from within, in words that didn't, mercifully, end with -ism.

The starting point for understanding the blues is the social system of slavery which, first in West Africa and then in the southern United States, created the tonal patterns and the rhythms which remain alive today. The blues have never lost the connection to the condition of being a slave. The chattel slave system began when Europeans used their ships and guns to bring tens of millions of West Africans to work as slaves on the sugar, rice and tobacco plantations of the Deep South of America. But after the discovery of milling methods which could pull the seeds from cotton, it proved possible to extend the types of cotton profitably grown, and the trade spread into the coastal lowlands further across America. The northern states bred slaves to send back to work in the South. Although these northern states were more democratic in flavour, they too depended on the theft of land and slave labour. Slavery was therefore a national system which indirectly benefited the northern merchants and created the capital for America's initial industrial expansion. American slavery was one of the most repressive slave systems ever. The slave was utterly powerless. The only provider the slave knew was the master who was also the source of all punishment, privilege and wealth. Slaves could not assemble unless a white man was present. Blacks were systematically cut off from education; a white woman found guilty of teaching a slave to read in 1855 was sent to prison for five months.

Within slavery had existed a ghastly kind of sexual equality, in that both sexes were equally powerless. Because the white master was the only provider, he became collective father for the whole plantation and the slave father's patriarchal authority as head of his own family was correspondingly weakened. Black women were raised to work outside the family, as field labourers, domestic servants and providers of childcare for the white owners. And their reproductive work providing future workers was only too obvious on plantations whose declared purpose was slave breeding. Under the slave system, the black woman was legally the slave owner's personal property; he had power to do with her sexually as he pleased. Even after the formal abolition of this property relation, the sexual authority persisted. It was usual for the father to relieve himself and for his sons to gain their sexual experience with their black domestic servants, the colour of whose face was considered sufficient invitation to seduction. Black women were painstakingly denied both the big and the little rights and privacies essential to their sexual dignity. There were white ladies and coloured women. On the doors of the toilets it read "Ladies", "Gentlemen" and "Coloured". Laws forbade intermarriage so that no permanent sexual relationship could ever be established with white men. Black women customers were not allowed to try on clothes lest their imagined smell, condensation of their imagined sexuality, might stain clothes whites might have near their white skin. The black woman was not allowed to be modest. Her man was barred from protecting her; she was forced to live without dignity. Then the white man proceeded to announce she was a slut and therefore sexually to assault her because that was only to treat her as she deserved. Having seen to it that neither black man nor woman had social power, they were attributed with an abnormally developed sexuality as a macabre consolation prize.

Specifically sexual sorts of terrorism, justified by general myths directed at all blacks, were used against both men and women. The Ku Klux Klan was formed to organise acts of terror against blacks who attempted to make use of the voting rights won in the Civil War. The midnight raids, murders in broad daylight, pack rapes and the lynchings were justified as protecting the virtue of white women who were said to be under constant threat from black men, roused but not satisfied by their lascivious women and too primitive to control their sexuality.

The right of young, or drunk or niggerhungry whites to rape black women was forcibly reasserted as simply the most extreme symbol of the political defeat of the southern black people after Reconstruction. Not only did it remind the black woman of her state of sexual nothingness on the plantation, it rubbed her man's face in his own powerlessness. To the whites it was morally legitimate to violate a black woman casually because they were all at the moral level of prostitutes. But the black man who defended her or attempted any sexual relation with a white woman was still more severely and publicly humiliated. The white Klansmen who seized blacks from the county jails they had fled to for protection, inefficiently strangled them with a rope over a tree, blew them into lumps with bullets and swigged Jim Crow bourbon from flasks, while white women soaked the dying body with kerosene and set a flame to it all, justified themselves in the name of southern chivalry.

Nor were such rapes and lynchings rarities or isolated excesses. A total of over ten thousand lynchings are said to have occurred by 1920. The first mass black civil rights organisation, the National Association for the Advancement of Coloured People, was formed to combat it. It was black women who led the campaign against lynching, surviving firebombings of their homes and destruction of their printing presses. In doing so, they challenged head-on the myth not only of the rapist black man but of the loose, red-hot, sex-object black woman which buttressed it, answering wild prejudice with dossiers of painstaking evidence and lives of ostentatious propriety. Black life in the South was very far from the high-kicking, high-living, heavy-drinking carnival portrayed by Hollywood dramas of jazz.

The musical traces of this time reflect that inner sadness: the heavy repeated chants of the convict labourers and the melancholy high-pitched near-howl, rasping mouth harp and harsh metallic fingering of country blues singers following work across plains, silent except for a train whistle or the creak of wheels. The racy jolliness was confined to the official popular music of the day, the sheet music for the parlour piano, that symbol of respectability in the big houses, the waltzes, quadrilles, mazurkas, polkas and hymns recorded for the European settlers. For black music, which was to outlast all this jaunty rubbish, was not considered even worth recording until the 1920 Okeh recording of Mamie Smith's "That Thing Called Love" proved money could be made from it. Until then it did not even have the status of novelty value. "Every race has a flag but a coon," said a music publisher; "Negroes just sing about what they eat and who they fuck," thought a Republican senator; and Ralph Peer, business manager of Okeh Records, admitted in 1936, "We had records by all foreign groups: German records, Swedish records, Polish records, but we were afraid to advertise Negro records, so I listed them as 'Race Records' and they are still known as that." The New Orleans instrumental music called jazz, once recognised as commercial, was swiftly imitated for nationwide sales by an all-white band which had the nerve to call itself the Original Dixieland Jazz Band.

The classic blues were the first blues on record. They originated with women singing in the minstrel tradition as one of the acts in a touring variety show which, like the English music hall, might mix serious singing with freaks, jugglers and sword swallowers. But in the 1920s and early 1930s, under the impetus of the record industry, these women singers became performers in their own right, shaping a distinctive body of singing associated with the names of Gertrude "Ma" Rainey, Bessie Smith, Clara Smith, Bertha "Chippie" Hill, Lucille Hegamin and Victoria Spivey. Miss Spivey, the Texas-born pianist and singer, was an especially prolific instrumental blues songwriter. Her "Dope Head Blues" is one of the first songs to deal with cocaine addiction, and "TB Blues", also recorded in 1927, is an open protest against racism. It was she who "discovered" Bob Dylan, strongly influenced his writing and issued his first recording on the Spivey label. She died in October 1976 in Brooklyn.

The classic blues was not and could not be imitated. It caught a unique moment in the history of the American black on the move from rural, southern, mainly peasant and small farmer life into the factories and the big cities of the North. 1914 saw the start of the first mass exodus northwards hankering after factory work (like Mr Ford who could pay you US$5 whatever your colour), in search of jobs, homes and, most important, dignity. It caught the South as it was unsealed but before it dispersed. It captured the blues as they were changing from a folk music directly linked to work to a performed art, but before it was smothered with the showbiz gloss applied for the benefit of a commercial audience. The women singers of the classic era had taken the spirit of the blues but shaped the form into organised performance which had elements of a church but which was quite pagan in its encouragement of sanctified self-expression. Not only did it express black women's social power, it came at the time of the first wave of twentieth-century racial self-assertion, the black risings which followed the First World War, the founding of the National Association for the Advancement of Coloured People and the rise of Marcus Garvey. And, despite the fear of the singers that it would lead to copying and the backstage signs "Recording harms your throat", they are on record, in quantity.

Bessie Smith had begun in poverty as a child singer in dives and tent shows at the edge of a small cotton-gin town for a few pence. She had been taken up and taught by Ma Rainey, the queen of the classical blues, whose records reach back to a more open countrified sound. From that circuit, Bessie worked through minstrel shows, played the black theatres of the Deep South towns, and fronted orchestras in Cleveland and Chicago.

In towns like Memphis, she would give occasional concerts for white people only, complete with pearly smiles and rolling eyes. But singing to black audiences sometimes, as in the Avenue Theatre, Chicago, in May 1924, in the midst of near-uprisings, she could parallel the race pride which in the 1920s took the political form of Marcus Garvey's Back to Africa movement. She sang to the lonesome city migrants the stately blues of their childhood. For though her songs don't mention colour, her performance and repertoire radiated black pride.

As Bessie Smith's records and radio appearances spread her fame, she took on something of the life of a black opera star, dressing at great expense, travelling with a circle of assistants and drinking in quantity and with insistent generosity. She was a queen on her own terms, black and a woman who made her own sexual life. In one of her finest songs, first recorded in 1926 when she was aged twenty-eight, she states her independence in an upright, stately but unanswerable voice:

I'm a young woman and ain't done running round
Some people call me a hobo, some call me a bum
Nobody knows my name, nobody knows what I've done
I'm as good as any in your town
I ain't no high yeller I'm deep yeller brown
I ain't going to marry, ain't gonna settle down
I'm gonna drink good moonshine an' run these browns down.[62]

---

62 "Young Woman's Blues", Bessie Smith, recorded 1926

In the 1937 version, the song is slightly slower with a softer ring and more elegiac tone. But saying as proud as ever: "I am woman." She takes bawdiness from the vaudeville and the old ribald dozens of the medicine show and turns it into something else, a sort of magnificent frankness, insistently physical, proud and defiant, though sung in a slightly funereal and very serious voice.

After a serious but not fatal car accident in 1937, she literally bled to death while segregated hospitals and so-called doctors shunted her from pillar to post in search of a ward lowly enough for the black body of one of the greatest singers of the twentieth century.

The classic blues had died as dramatically as Bessie. The depression had devastated the South; the only way blacks could escape was north aboard the single rail line which ran the one thousand miles from the Delta to Chicago, the home of Sears Roebuck, the *Chicago Defender*, and maybe a job. But women could not easily ride freight or work in the steel mills or car plants, and although they arrived in the North in equal numbers, the move squeezed them out of work. They were forced back into traditional jobs as cooks, nurses and cleaners, or the familiar options as whore or mother of children you couldn't afford to keep. In the same way, women singers seem to retreat into more conventional gospel or pop-romantic styles. Almost none found a footing in the raucous bar blues which developed with such ferocity in Chicago's South Side ghetto or the piano boogie-woogie that thundered out of the rent parties.

In a very short musical period, an almost complete sexual reverse had taken place. Chicago blues is bouncy, raw and male. It held the blues line in the cities and spread by radio to the country blacks. It's an edgy, violent music where the electric guitar is more expressive than the voice, belted out in the cramped, tough bars of the overcrowded, workless slum belt of the South Side where police made captures almost at random and Sunday in the hospital was regularly followed by Monday in the court. All but the most remarkable of women were excluded.

In lots of ways the apparent vitality of rhythm and blues was, like the booze that accompanied it, a prop against the unbearable present, and the sexual blues became a male escape rather than a female celebration.

It was into this world Billie Holiday emerged from nowhere, eight years after Bessie Smith died in 1937. On the radio, the white well-made song and the creamy orchestras of Glenn Miller and Tommy Dorsey were easing the listening public through the Depression. It was a confusing time for a black woman. Bessie Smith could be strong but it was within clear limits, in a musical form which was established and when performance was face-to-face with a black audience. The record industry and music business was at an early and regionally organised stage. Billie Holiday faced the business and sexual pressures with more force and less protection. And while white society was now officially desegregating and would be civil to your face, it was a sham, and the state of being a slave was still a close memory, even if you were wearing a silk gown. When Billie sings about lynching, it's real, not a metaphor, and when she sings about sexual humiliation, it's about her own life and the sexual crossfire she was under every time she went on stage. Because of her autobiography, *Lady Sings the Blues*, much of which was censored at the time of publication, we know at least something about her own attitudes.[63] It's one of the most political books ever written by a musician, which insists on going beyond the clichés of jazz tragedy to the economics of the music business and the pressure of Jim Crow.

Though she came from a show family, her mother was a maid for a white woman. While pregnant, her mother

63 Billie Holiday and William Duffy, *Lady Sings the Blues* (Doubleday, 1956)

scrubbed the floors in the maternity hospital to pay for Billie's hospital delivery. Her grandmother had been a slave and an Irish slave owner's mistress on a big plantation in Virginia, having sixteen children by him. "She used to tell me how it felt to be a slave, to be owned body and soul by a white man who was the father of her children." Billie remembers her first job was as a maid for a woman in Long Beach who would ignore her all day until about fifteen minutes before her husband was due back. She remembers first being called "nigger" with an electric clarity: "Instead of telling me what she wanted me to do, she'd get all excited because her husband was waiting, start hollering at me and calling me 'nigger'. I had never heard that word before. I didn't know what it meant. But I could guess from the sound of her voice." All her life, however successful she was as a singer, racism dogged her, whether it was the drunk at the bar who just had to shout "nigger" at her, the sheriff who came up on the bandstand to drawl "When's darkie going to sing?" or the countless casual taunts and jeers. In 1944, in an integrated club in St Louis, she was refused permission to leave by the front entrance of the building. After a naval officer had called her "nigger" on 52nd Street, she cried for some time, and when soon after a friend asked, "How are you?", she replied, "Well, you know, I'm still a nigger."

Touring with Count Basie's band in Detroit, she had to put on special dark grease because the theatre management thought she looked too white. And in the same city, when having a drink with Chuck Peterson, another drinker came up and said, "What the hell is going on? A man can't bring his wife in a bar any more without you tramp white men bringing a nigger woman in." On tour, eating was difficult, sleeping harder and going to the lavatory impossible. With Artie Shaw's first band, "It got to the point where I hardly ever ate, slept, or went to the bathroom without having a major NAACP-type production." The band supported her and were prepared to go hungry too if Billie was refused service. Being seen with a white man was a special problem; if she'd been a prostitute and he had been paying there would have been no problem. It was because she wasn't a whore that they disapproved of her. Nor were racial attitudes better in the North, just better hidden. At least in the South, Billie noted:

> When they insult you they do it to your face, and you know it. A cracker just wants you to clean up his house or take care of his kids and get the hell out. The big deal hotels, agencies and networks in New York were giving me a fast shove behind my back. This makes life a constant drag. Not only for me but for the people I meet and like. You're always under pressure. You can fight it but you can't lick it. The only time I was free from this kind of pressure was when I was a call girl as a kid and I had white men as my customers. Nobody gave us any trouble. People can forgive any damn thing if they did it for money.

Race was always wound up with money. The New York club scene was still like being on a plantation for all the freedom it offered her. To be recognised as an artist and not just a singer was too much to ask. She was forced into a gruelling touring regime to sing before people she often didn't care for, to raise the money to pay her lawyers and cover expensive addiction cures which didn't work. "If it had been left to the managements and promoters I could have shot myself long ago," she ruefully remarked.

Billie probably got involved with heroin through Joe Guy, and drugs became the third party in all the subsequent sexual encounters. The police used her as a bait, bust her at the end of a residency and got a kick out of her misfortune. There was no remorse. They even made it their business to arrest her on her deathbed.

Nor was her sexual life easy. She had been seduced by her brother and then raped by her uncle when she was twelve. When she and her mother reported the crime and asked the police for help, crying and bleeding, "they treated me as if I had murdered somebody and proceeded to snigger and give dirty looks ... no wonder I was scared to death of sex." She acquired her name Lady because she didn't like showing off her body.

Billie Holiday sang relatively few recognisable blues songs and much of her recordings are of straight pop or the svelte anti-blues crafted by lyricists like Moss Hart, George Gershwin and Cole Porter. Her involvement in cabaret settings is sometimes denounced in the same way as Bessie Smith's vaudeville connection, but for both it was about a way of connecting to a black audience. But she battled not to compromise artistically. "People don't understand," she said, "the kind of fight it takes to record what you want to record the way you want to record it. I've fought for as long as ten years to get to record a song I've loved or wanted to do."

Almost all her songs are about being a woman and being in love. Most are about sexual love, about surrender, loss, need, the moments when feelings make a fool of brains, about coming out with your sexual hands up. She wrote only a few of her own songs but somehow could unwind more personal meaning from other people's lyrics than many modern singers can extract from their own.

It was as if she needed the subjectivity of these songs to regain herself from the constant bruising battles against segregation, the music business and her men. There is almost revenge in the way she creeps up on the words of a song and tips them up. But it is in "Strange Fruit", a classic of political lyricism, that the power of her own experience to rush through her voice is most easy to hear.[64] The song

---

64 "Strange Fruit", *Strange Fruit* (single), Billie Holiday, 1939

was brought to her when she was playing at a club called Café Society, one of the happiest residencies of her career. The club was one of the first in New York to be genuinely racially mixed and the drink was cheap. Its slogan was, "the wrong place for the right people". There were many socialists in the audience and Frankie Newton, the trumpeter, could be found lecturing his band on the economics of Marcus Garvey and the Soviet Five-Year Plan. Billie didn't like the discussions and, since the owner was obliged to run a strict anti-marijuana ruling, used to go out to smoke in the park in intervals. One of the Café Society's regulars, a schoolteacher called Lewis Allan, offered her a lyric about a lynching down south. She was at first suspicious but then took to it with a passion: "I worked like the devil on it because I was never sure I could put it across or I could get across to a plush nightclub audience the things that it meant to me." The song awoke some of the raw political feelings that Billie often hid behind her elegance. It reminded her, she said, of how her father died and she felt it her duty to go on singing the song because of what she knew. "I have to keep on singing it," she wrote, "not only because people ask for it but because twenty years after Pop died the things that killed him are still happening in the South." He had caught pneumonia in Dallas, Texas, on tour with the Don Redman Band and had wandered delirious from hospital to hospital trying to get help from white-only hospitals who wouldn't do as much as take his temperature. He eventually found a veterans' hospital who admitted him to their segregated ward when he proved he had served in the army. Just in time to die.

The song is simple but allowed the full dramatic power of her voice and its richness of texture to blend with the passion she always felt every time she sang the song. It was because it moved her that she could so move an audience, almost flay them with the last eight lines with their mounting of sound, until inside the last elongated, swirling few words you can hear the gallows rope twisting and the wind curling.

Singing live, Billie Holiday exercised a mysterious command over her audience; eyewitness after eyewitness recalls the thickness of the silence, and the live records bear witness to the closeness of their attention, breathing, gasping and laughing to her turns and twists of phrase and weaving of rhythms, then erupting with fierce clapping.

And in the singing of "Strange Fruit", her voice remembers the state of being a slave still, not a chattel slave like her grandmother but a woman who is always owned by another: by men who started as lovers and stayed as businessmen, by managers who cared more for cash registers than music, by the dope that at first had given relief and euphoria but became just a habit. She lived in a formally desegregated but still racist America where black women had in some respects even less social power than they possessed earlier in the century. There was no longer the musical protection which absolute segregation had, ironically, given black music. Her place was in the marketplace. Even as a success, she was always made forcibly aware that celebrity was conditional, provisional, precarious.

She wanted something quite simple: the right to be honest. Her epitaph might be her comment in *Lady Sings the Blues*: "I plain decided one day I wasn't going to do anything unless I meant it. ... You have to be poor and black to know how many times you can get knocked in the head just for trying to do something as simple as that." Male critics have a habit of making remarks about Billie's "difficult" character, her "unreasonable" need for reassurance, "inadequacy" and so on, which, though intended sympathetically, are an insult. Her life as a black woman started and finished in pain; she had to fight constantly for the right to be herself and express her feelings. Her difficulty was that she wasn't dishonest about this; her unreasonableness was that she refused to conform; her inadequacy was simply the erosion of anyone, however gifted, or brave, who takes on the social system alone. And although insecure about her lack of education and suspicious about politics, she felt instinctive solidarity with those who resisted the system. Jimmy Davis, the pianist and composer who wrote "Lover Man" for Billie and served a year in jail for fighting racial segregation in the American army, recalls a performance which in some ways sums up her political feelings: "She came to Paris during the time of the war in Algeria when the Algerians were fighting for their freedom. She went to a clandestine meeting, to sing to encourage the fighters. This is something very strong."[65]

Bessie Smith and Billie Holiday are separated by twenty years, in different parts of America, with the music business in a different phase of its development. But the same collective history and the same personal experience soars behind their singing. Both women sufficiently commanded their art to take charge of the music and transform it. Both were proud to be race women, who did not need to flaunt their blackness but did not deny it either. Both insisted in every note they were women, not men's playthings, committed to passion in their own right. Billie and Bessie were left very hollow and sad at the constant effort of keeping up that exterior alone, drained by constantly giving outwards, haunted by nameless inner insecurities which they unsuccessfully fended off with booze and men. On stage they were acknowledged as outstanding but that was still not enough to entitle them to ordinary rights off it. Just by being black they were non-conformists. By being women and proud of it, they were asking for trouble, and when they got it, deserved it.

---

65 "Lover Man", *Lover Man (Oh, Where Can You Be?)* (single), Billie Holiday, 1945

It was not having been oppressed that made them great. But their greatness lay in their ability to press past a world which battered and denied their beings and turned those bruises and denials inside out – to deny and dwarf the hurts inflicted on them by opening themselves out so completely and profoundly in their singing. Out of that bitter experience came forth something unsurpassingly sweet.

The Wire, 1984 (Shortened)

Culture in Transit

Review of *Ma Rainey's Black Bottom*,
Hackney Empire in January 1990

How do black hip-hoppers end up on *Top of the Pops* and British street fashion find its way on to the Milan catwalks? The transition is one step in the unscrupulous dance made between the creativity of dissident culture, the egos of its performers, politics and profit which is at the tinsel heart of twentiety-century mass culture.

For any artist with an impact on popular politics, from Václav Havel to Vivienne Westwood, this transition involves a calculated set of compromises. (The problem is currently personified in the Clash-worshipping French rebel rockers Mano Negra now in the odd position of being the French Minister of Culture's favourite band.) But the deal and its consequences are most intense, most persistent and most imbalanced within twentieth-century black culture. This is the subject of the black American playwright August Wilson's *Ma Rainey's Black Bottom* which examines, in the course of a Chicago recording session in the late 1920s, the way the classic blues forms, forged in the relative isolation of the Deep South, were adapted by whites and in the process weakened, to sell on record to a mixed audience. The play's tremendous success at the Cottesloe Theatre probably depended on its brilliant ensemble acting. But its (unresolved) argument is what makes it so relevant today. It could just as easily be about Public Enemy, Soul II Soul or Neneh Cherry.

So it's significant that it's this play, rather than *Salome* or *The Shaughraun*, that David Aukin, executive director of the National Threatre, has selected as the first-ever production to tour to an "alternative" inner-city venue.[66] And doubly interesting that it's going to London's East End, stronghold of reggae, hip hop, and to the reborn Hackney Empire, home of uncompromisingly radical new variety stand-up comedy, which makes Hackney to Margaret Thatcher what East Berlin's Prenzlauer Berg was to Erich Honecker.

Perhaps the transfer to Hackney, four miles by map but very much further in social geography, marks a new direction for the NT. And, just possibly, the very public traumas of the post-Peter Hall Royal Shakespeare Company, now inextricably embedded in their Barbican bunker, have been a factor. Despite the savagely anti-Murdoch *Pravda*, the current *Good Person of Szechwan* and Adrian Mitchell's *Pied Piper*, the NT audience remains pretty solidly bourgeois, pricey seats occupied by tourists and advance-booked suburbanites.[67] Aukin's may be a very shrewd move. "We see this as the first of many," he predicts, "and we may have to make the case to our sponsors that taking an NT production to Hackney is as culturally important as touring the provinces."

Interestingly too, the move makes artistic sense in Hackney. It was clear last summer at the Edinburgh Festival that stand-up comedians were moving towards longer, more structured theatrical pieces (Arthur Smith's *Bed Play* was the classic example).[68] It was the energy and audience for new variety that reopened the Hackney Empire, but they are keen to get more theatre on stage and are currently

---

66 *Salome*, Oscar Wilde, 1893 in French (1894 in English)
   The Shaughraun, Dion Boucicault, 1874
67 *Pravda*, David Hare and Howard Brenton, 1985
   The Good Person of Szechwan, Bertolt Brecht, 1943
   The Pied Piper, Adrian Mitchell, 1987
68 *Live Bed Show*, Arthur Smith, 1989

in negotiations with Unity about possibilities. Roland Muldoon of the Empire, a once renowned denouncer of elitist theatre, is now more emollient: "We have to recognise that the NT is one of the last great sources of theatrical energy in this country."

Finally there is the sheer beauty of the theatre, preserved by bingo from post-war demolition and the last of what was once a ring of suburban variety theatres. Theatre historian, Andrew Patenall, believes it may be the finest left in southern England and "the absolute zenith" of Frank Matcham's work, architecturally more imaginative than his later Coliseum or Victoria Palace. The National Theatre are not exactly going to your average community hall.

The Empire has also proved, in three years of independent and largely unsubsidised operation, that it can attract varied audiences: Jewish OAPs for Frankie Vaughan, the clubbers who filled Billy Bragg and Hank Wangford's ambulance strike buckets during packed new year shows, world music fans, ethnic audiences and gay cult hits.

But in some ways the theatre's most remarkable success was the boisterous black audiences who cheered on the semi-pro black history show *Black Heroes in the Hall of Fame* or became a noisy jury for the trial play *Ragamuffin* which juxtaposed Broadwater Farm with the Haiti slave uprising.[69] Using intensive fly-posting, leafleting and a specially recorded commercial by the show's star Carol Woods pumping out on E8 pirate radio shows like *Supreme*, *Eurojam* and *City*, The Empire is hoping the same audience might warm to *Ma Rainey*.[70] Kenneth Tynan must be applauding, off, in his grave.

Black Theatre, 1990

---

69 *Black Heroes in the Hall of Fame*, Sandy Flip Fraser, 1987
   Ragamuffin, Amani Naphtali, 1988
70 *Ma Rainey's Black Bottom*, August Wilson, 1982

Above: David Widgery sitting in a doorway in Soho in 1973 – perhaps dreaming of the revolution? (image: Michael Gray). Left: The politically active ex-OZ contributor and trainee doctor in May 1976 (image: Michael Kidron).

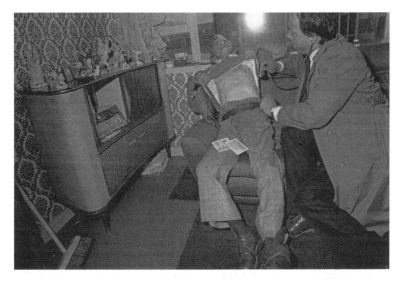

Doctor on call, September 1983: Sixty-one-year-old George McDowell, suffering from pneumonia, receives a visit from his National Health GP – David Widgery – in his council flat overlooking the Roman Road Market in London's East End. This photo first appeared in *A Day in the Life of London* (Jonathan Cape, 1984) (image: Syd Shelton).

Doctor on call in a council estate in Limehouse after being mugged in 1989 (image: Syd Shelton).

David Widgery in 1990 showing a victory sign over the number of doctors balloted by the British Medical Association who were against the formation of Foundation Trust Hospitals as the first step in their privatisation. The struggle had a catchy slogan: "Don›t Trust the Trust? Ditch the Trust!" (image: Vanda Playford).

Memorial card designed by Ruth Gregory for David Widgery's funeral in 1992, music chosen by Juliet, Jesse and Anny, and distributed to those who attended his funeral.

ARTS

An introduction by Tony Gould

In 1990, when I gave up books-editing at *New Society* (or what had become the *New Statesman & Society*), David wrote me a lovely letter in which he said: "My only real regret is that I have at last become word-processed and was looking forward to presenting you with reviews which lacked the usual Widgery misspellings and barely comprehensible afterthoughts which you have had to remedy over the years ..." Spelling was never David's strong point but compared with some other valued contributors – Richard Cobb and Raphael Samuel, to name but two – editing David was a doddle. At least he wrote to the commissioned length.

He was a contributor who became a friend. We met infrequently, but there was a warmth in our relationship that may have stemmed from the fact that we were both polio survivors. His early death was a personal, as well as a public loss. In a review I wrote for the *TLS* of Patrick Hutt's book about him, *Confronting an Ill Society*, I described David as "avid for life", and on rereading the arts-related articles selected here that phrase seems apt.[71] These essays are characterised by enthusiasm and generosity of spirit; his eagerness to share his discoveries with others is infectious.

His piece on William Carlos Williams, a writer I am equally keen on, is a good example of one of his strengths as

---

71 Patrick Hutt et al., *Confronting an Ill Society: David Widgery, General Practice, Idealism and the Chase for Change* (Radcliffe, 2005)

a reviewer: he does not hide behind the mask of impersonality. There is no mystery about WCW's appeal for David: both were doctors, as well as writers. David provides a list of other medical practitioners who were also writers and points out that with "almost all of them ... if they are any good as writers, the stethoscope takes second place". But not with WCW, who succeeded at both in a way that David can only envy. While Chekhov likened medicine to a wife and writing to a mistress, Williams saw no such dichotomy. He wrote simply, "I have never felt that medicine interfered with me but rather that it was my very food and drink, the very thing which made it possible for me to write."

WCW, whose poetic credo was "No ideas but in things", is an unlikely Widgery hero. "Politically polemical" poets like Blake, the young Auden, Mayakovsky and Ginsberg are more predictable choices. But David was nothing if not a maverick, and his ability to surprise was a large part of his appeal to me.

It is a challenge for any literary editor to find the perfect match of book and reviewer, the obvious choice not always being the right one. If I sent David books about the politics of medicine I would have had a pretty shrewd idea of what he'd make of them, but in sending him a book like Reggie Kray's memoir, the last one I ever asked him to review, I had no idea what he would come up with. He liked the challenge and I trusted him to come up with the goods which – in my experience – he always did.

The Kerouac Connection

David Widgery comments: *The Beats are at present doing well in the laundromat of style, and a complicated and scholarly circle of enthusiasts meet and correspond, in part through Dave Moore's excellent little mag* The Kerouac Connection. *Whether this leads to people actually reading Kerouac rather than attempting to dress like him, I don't know. But he was a prodigiously gifted writer quite apart from the myth. And his premature death was a much deeper shock than the regrettably predictable death of the various rock stars our generation is supposed to have spent the 1970s mourning.*

Ti Jean, Jack Duluoz, Sal Paradise, you're gone now. You died age forty-six in your house in Lowell, Massachusetts, where you lived with your crippled mother and suspicious wife of one year, Stella, and they decided to do to you the American death thing and have you mummified, thread your veins with formaldehyde, tie a bow tie in position and clad your face in certain deathly cosmetics. And though Allen Ginsberg, Peter Orlovsky and John Clellon Holmes stayed by you gently all night, dawn was soon and a Massachusetts funeral.

Marmite and Bop

To read Kerouac when you were fifteen, scrabbling through the Ks of Slough Public Library, was a coded message of discontent: the sudden realisation of an utter subversiveness and licence. He legitimised all the papery efforts of a child writer, dream books, pretend novellas, invented games, planned and described walkouts. He expressed a solution to the pent-upness, exitlessness of youth, that feeling of wanking off inside all the time. Everyone I know remembers where they were when they read *On the Road*, whether newly expelled from school, public librarians (trainee) in Hammersmith, car park attendants in Dorking, knowledgeable Eisenhower drunks or hospital porters, because of the sudden sense of infinite possibility.[72] You could, just like that, get off out of it into infinite hitch-hiking futures. Armed only with a duffle coat, you could be listening to wild jazz on the banks of the Tyne or travelling east-west, across the Pennines. Mostly we never actually went, or the beer wore off by Baldock High Street and you were sober and so cold. But we were able to recognise each other by that fine, wild, windy prose and the running-away motif that made so much sense. I, like ten thousand other fifth-formers, wrote a series of letters in imitation of Kerouac, spiralling indiscriminate word patterns and being able, in his shadow, to write thewordstogether if I so wanted to. A Canadian friend who thought he was Dean Moriarty sent me a notebook bound in smelly red cellophane about his runaway with an autocycle and packet of Marmite sandwiches which he was forced to abandon in a snowdrift after two miles. The notebook was about eighty pages yet seemed proper and as it ought to happen and all accountable within the terms of spontaneous bop prosody. Jazz was the other part of our underground because it meant beer and beards and arguing about the fourth trumpet in Stan Kenton's reconstructed front line like stamp collectors.

We would get three-quarters drunk and listen to Charlie Parker who seemed to be trying to sound like Kerouac too if you listened to the breath sounds and the oral punctuation:

> Yes, jazz and bop, in the sense of a, say, a tenor man drawing a breath and blowing a phrase on his saxophone, till he runs out of breath, and when he does,

---

72 Jack Kerouac, *On the Road* (Viking Press, 1957)

his sentence, his statement's been made ... That's how I therefore separate my sentences, as breath separations of the mind ... [...] Then there's the raciness and freedom and humour of jazz instead of all that dreary analysis and things like «James entered the room, and lit a cigarette. He thought Jane might have thought this too vague a gesture ...»[73]

When Hoagy Carmichael heard Bix Beiderbecke, he fell off his chair. When Tom Paine was in hiding, he found shelter at the home of William Blake. Now I'd been getting bored with the stereotyped changes that were being used all the time and I kept thinking there's bound to be something else. I could hear it sometimes but I couldn't play it. I was doing all right until I tried double tempo on "Body and Soul".[74] Everyone fell out laughing. I went home and cried and didn't play again for three months.

Red Shift, Big Bang

Kerouac's writing started with home-drawn comic strips, home-made comics, whole childhood exercise book novels, long systems for horse racing and basketball games in the comfort of your front room, played with symbols and pieces of paper money:

At eighteen I read Hemingway and Saroyan and began writing terse little stories in that general style. Then I read Tom Wolfe and began to

73 Kerouac interviewed by Ted Berrigan in *the Paris Review* (Issue 43, Summer 1968), in answer to the question "What about jazz and bop as influences rather than ... Hemingway, and Wolfe?"

74 "Body and Soul" is a jazz standard written in 1930 for British performer Gertrude Lawrence, but performed by countless others, including tenor saxophonist Coleman Hawkins, whose 1939 recording of the song is one of the most famous versions.

write in the rolling style. Then I read Joyce and wrote a juvenile novel like *Ulysses* called *Vanity of Duluoz*. Then came Dostoevsky. Finally, I entered a romantic phase with Rimbaud and Blake which I called my "self-ultimacy period", burning what I wrote in order to be self-ultimate. At the age of twenty-four, I was groomed for the Western idea-listic concept of letters from reading Goethe's *Dichtung und Wahrheit*. The discovery of a style of my own based on a spontaneous get-with-it, came after reading the marvellous free narrative letters of Neal Cassady, a great writer who happens to be the Dean Moriarty of *On the Road*.[75]

Cassady might, reluctantly, be compared to Trotsky in his historical span. Just as Trotsky is the sole link between Bolshevism and the post-war revolutionary movement, so it was Cassady who was the only human link between the West Coast Beats and the post-Timothy Leary hippies, acting as the driver of Ken Kesey's acidic bus Further. He stayed magnificently the same. In Kerouac he's this incre-dible talker, lost into a blue streak that's going to last all his life, pulsating even when silent:

> …Where once Dean would have talked his way out, he now feels silent himself, but standing in front of everyone, ragged and broken and idiotic, right in front of the light bulbs, his mad face covered with sweat and throbbing veins, saying «Yes, yes, yes» as though tremendous revelations were pouring into him the whole time now, and I am convinced they were, and the others suspected as much and were

75 Kerouac in a letter to his friend Donald Allen; can be found in *Selected Letters: 1957–69*, ed. Ann Charters (Penguin Books, 1995)

frightened. He was BEAT-the-root, the soul of Beatific.[76]

And ten years later, when drug-casseroled ex-novelist Kesey makes his American migration, there Cassady sat driving the bus:

> Cassady had been a rock on this trip, the totally dependable person. When everyone else was stroked out with fatigue or the various pressures, Cassady could be still counted on the move. It was as if he never slept and didn't need to. For all his wild driving, he always made it through the last oiled gap in the maze, like he knew it would be there all the time, which it always was. When the bus broke down, Cassady drove into its innards and fixed it. He changed tyres, lugging and heaving and jolting and bolting with his fantastic muscles popping out striation by striation and his basilic veins gorged with blood and speed.[77]

Now Cassady's dead too. His body was found beside a railroad track outside the town of San Miguel de Allende in Mexico. It was said that he had been despondent and felt that he was growing old and had been on a long downer and had made the mistake of drinking alcohol on top of barbiturates. His body was cremated.

Bullet Beat

Cassady's writing had started, like Kerouac's, in the slow, painstaking, creative-writing-course-by-post way. Then he wrote *The First Third*, a novel about his childhood with

---

76 From *On the Road*
77 Tom Wolfe, *The Electric Kool-aid Acid Test* (Farrar, Straus and Giroux, 1968)

his alcoholic father in the Denver alley wine shops and Greyhound station Johns and the way they talked to each other (like Kesey's acid-soaked Pranksters) with "minds weakened by liquor and an obsequious manner of existence, seeming continually preoccupied with bringing up short observations of obvious trash, said in such a way as to be instantly recognisable by the listener, who has heard it all before and whose own prime concern was to nod at everything said, then continue the conversation with a remark of his own, equally transparent and loaded with generalities".[78] Cassady sent Kerouac a forty-thousand-word letter (now called *The Joan Anderson Letter*) which Kerouac describes as "the greatest piece of writing I ever saw, better'n anyone in America, or at least enough to make Melville, Twain, Dreiser, Wolfe, I dunno who, spin in their graves", and which disappeared overboard into the sea.[79] Kerouac and Cassady could talk each other into a state of semi-trance where their unrepressed word-slinging hotted up into a big shoot-out, bullet words whizzing backwards and forwards with words that were slippery without being gelatinous and made you tremble when you read them. "We did much fast talking, on tape recorders, way back in 1952 and listened to them so much we both got the secret of LINGO in telling a tale and figured that was the only way to express the speed and tension and the ecstatic tomfoolery of the age."[80] Kerouac/Cassady learned from this to curve and move their acoustic prose in

---

78 Neal Cassady, *The First Third & Other Writings* (San Francisco City Lights Books, 1971)

79 Written in December 1950, the letter was believed to be lost at sea until 2012, when it was found amongst the boxes of unopened letters and poems sent to Golden Goose press (now defunct) in Oakland. The Kerouac quote on the letter is from his aforementioned 1968 interview with Ted Berrigan in the *Paris Review*.

80 From Kerouac's aforementioned 1968 *Paris Review* interview

the air, sustaining the long line by breath, rubbish image, riff, dazzling phrasing making an awkward tightrope walk like Chaplin about to fall but never quite doing so since able to "add alluvials to the end of your line when all is exhausted but something has to be said for some specified irrational reason".[81] It's Kerouac's sound, not the coterie poetics of Robert Creeley/Charles Olson, that is behind Ginsberg's rush on language. And from all three Americans the florid young British poets of the 1950s fed, snatching bootlegged copies from Lawrence Ferlinghetti's City Lights Books and the other artistic contraband which made possible the dense undergrowth of the British small poetry magazines (especially *Poetmeat*, early *Underdog*, and the short-breathed and "substantial" *New Departure*). Mike Horovitz, whose mattress prose, too, is interior sprung, describes the impact of the American orals on off-the-page British poetry wonderfully well in his afterword to Penguin's *Children of Albion: Poetry of the Underground in Britain*.[82]

Ferlinghetti had always been social and political – "All this droopy corn about the Beat generation and its being 'existentialist' is as phoney as a four-dollar piece of lettuce ... only the dead are disengaged. And the wiggy nihilism of the Beat hipster, if carried to its logical consequences, actually means the death of the creative artist himself."[83]

Ginsberg increasingly became political after his decision to "expose self and accuse America". But sez Kerouac, "I

---

81 Jack Kerouac, "Statement on Poetics", *The New American Poetry: 1945–1960*, ed. Donald Allen (Grove Press, 1960)

82 Michael Horovitz, *Children of Albion: Poetry of the Underground in Britain* (Penguin, 1969)

83 Widgery is quoting Ferlinghetti's response to Beats insulted by the criticism in his poem titled "Tentative Description of a Dinner to Promote the Impeachment of President Eisenhower" (published in *Liberation* 3 (August 1958)), that "some men ... sat down in Bohemia and were too busy to come".

agree with Joyce, as Joyce said to Ezra Pound in the 1920s, 'Don't bother me with politics, the only thing that interests me is style.'" Nowadays he seems to dismiss the holy goofing groin cats and wine lips of the San Francisco poetry gang: "Ferlinghetti and Ginsberg, they are very socialistically minded and wanted everyone to live in some sort of frantic kibbutz, solidarity and all that. I'm a loner." [84] Kerouac was the lonesome traveller jumping out of cars, into fruit wagons, merchant holds, going and going as if by his movement alone he could become a molecule in a marvellous unity. He deeply wanted to believe in a total unification of the Golden Buddhist eternity; his religion was his ultimate resource and he saw it mostly in nature – the misty swelling and blooming of the seasons, sea and redwood trees he watched over for a spell. This was the wonderful still centre within all his energy; the baby Ti Jean with kitten and candy bar on a pillow while the absolutely evil Dr Sax caused the swollen oily river to rise sucking and slapping in the streets of Lowell.

It is said that as a child Kerouac was discovered trying to fuck the world; found with his prick buried in soil.

What Happened

This handsome travelling man who sings and writes across the hugeness of the States is a great figure of the real migrant American. In the false America of the 1950s of Ike and Perry Mason's fight against freedom, in the symbol-worshipping, silent, bad sociology writing, thick 1950s, his very existence was a protest. Against that world's addiction to the inanimate, Kerouac's response was not political or critical – he just damned them with his energy. Against the moral ruin of the world, he replied in every second of his hour with the creative act. He insulted them, almost without knowing it himself, with his exuberance, his wonder, his emotions, almost crazed by the

---

84 Both of the preceding quotations are from Kerouac's aforementioned 1968 *Paris Review* interview.

torrent of experience and finally devoured by its own appetite. Compared with him, the alleged novelists of dissent on this side of the Atlantic look and were mean, conservative and trivial.

But he seemed imprisoned within his wonder and his age, the 1950s. He doesn't so much develop as a writer as accumulate, reworking the themes of his witness of the Beats, of his brother Gerard and family, of Mexico City and Paris with a steadily growing intensity. The compulsive nature of his writing could turn pathological; drugs and writing were the organising principles of his life, and death. "Notoriety and public confession in literary form is a frazzler of the heart you were born with, believe me."[85] He was unable to alter the pace set by his mind, which was as out of breath at forty-five as it was at his hallucinated fifteen. He wrote, like Victor Serge, single spacing on a continuous typewriter roll at a punishing rate (in Tangier he typed *Naked Lunch* for William Burroughs).[86] *The Subterraneans* was written in three days, a physical feat much harder than the athletic struggles of the windy field, leaving him as white as a sheet and having lost fifteen pounds and looking strange in the mirror.[87] His babble-brook book *Satori in Paris* was written on cognac and malt whisky.[88] *Tristessa*, the fine mystic novel about a Mexican girl faint for morphine, and the remarkable Mexico City poems, were direct from his life in Mexico where his life and writing intersected dangerously.[89] The vain records of the pageantry of the West Coast Beats, *Desolation Angels*, *Big Sur* and *The Subterraneans*, indicate the pace at which he lived, the tension level at which the books are charged.[90]

---

85 From Kerouac's aforementioned 1968 *Paris Review* interview
86 William S. Burroughs, *Naked Lunch* (Olympia Press, 1959)
87 Jack Kerouac, *The Subterraneans* (Grove Press, 1958)
88 Jack Kerouac, *Satori in Paris* (Grove Press, 1966)
89 Jack Kerouac, *Tristessa* (Avon, 1960)
90 Jack Kerouac, *Desolation Angels* (Coward-McCann, 1965)
　　Jack Kerouac, *Big Sur* (Farrar, Straus and Cudahy, 1962)

Book of Dreams used even his sleeping life for material "in a style of a person half awake from sleep and ripping it out in pencil by the bed ... yes, pencil ... what a job, bleary eyes, insaned mind bemused and mystified by sleep, details that pop out even as you write them, you don't know what they mean till you wake up, have coffee, look at it and see the logic of the dream from the language itself."[91] He was the last American to write quite like this: the great Romantic, a naked sheet wound round experience and registering it in wonder – "the true story of what I saw and how I saw it."

As he grew unrelentingly older, he grew, logically, patriotic and sentimental. A rare public meeting he spoke to in southern Italy was broken up by dumbfounded Italian kids when he defended the American war in Vietnam. His drunkenness, male adventuring, lumberjack clothes (now looking uncannily like the handsome Ronald Reagan) were of a different world now. He must have sensed it was impossible to keep hold of his old human universe when he retreated to his bungalow in Lowell. Like Dylan, his quietism is only objectionable if you interpret it politically; which of course you have to. When people started fighting back against the monster America, the nutcase radicals, Trotskyists, Black Panthers, they do so in a way that excludes him ... even disgusts him. For now protest is nowhere near enough. It's too conventional and we need to fight America with all the science it is using to destroy us. And we must win.

We have to blaspheme against Kerouac's religiosity and be wary of his colossal nervous system. His is a precious voice but from the past. When we win we can name streets and stars after him.

OZ, 1969

---

91 Jack Kerouac, *Book of Dreams* (City Lights Books, 1961)

The Streets Are Our Palettes

A tribute to Vladimir Mayakovsky[92]

David Widgery comments: One of the delights of growing up politically lies in discovering one's own traditions. In art they were nearly obliterated by Stalinism, declared redundant by the long post-war boom and generally buried in a "modernism" which was often apolitical and trite. It was exhilarating to unearth in Soviet Russia the most genuinely modern of modern art movements and Mayakovsky, the original "hooligan communist".

Vladimir Mayakovsky, the poetic loudspeaker of the Russian Revolution, came to socialist ideas with the enthusiasm of youth. He began to read Engels and illegal pamphlets under his desk-lid when he was twelve. When later the same year his school was closed by military edict because of the 1905 uprising, he became chief school leaflet distributor. When he made his first contact with the illegal Bolshevik Party, he immediately presented them with his forester father's shotgun. Aged fifteen, he was arrested in Moscow for helping to organise the escape of political prisoners from jail and was himself held in Novinsky Prison where he began to write poems. For the following twenty years he served the revolution as a poet-agitator with the same audacity and passion. And when he shot himself in Moscow in 1930, he died a Bolshevik, brandishing his poems:[93]

---

92 Originally published in *International Socialism* (July–September 1972) as "Mayakovsky and Revolutionary Art".

93 Most of the poems quoted in this article are from the following

When I appear
at the CCC
of coming bright decades
above the band of poetic grafters and crooks
I'll lift up high,
like a Bolshevik party-card
All the hundred volumes of my
ComParty books![94]

Mayakovsky's communism was, like him, broad-shouldered
and larger than life, impatient, rude and necessary:

Proletarians come to Communism from the depths
beneath
the depths of the mines
sickles
and factories.
I plunge into Communism from the heights of poetry
above,
because for me
without it
there is no love![95]

But his passion was neither sentimental nor cosy, like the
clichés of modern Soviet art: those cheery collective far-
mers, the harmonious choristers and the agile folk dancers.
In his complex love poems like "A Cloud in Trousers" and
"About This", he explores the nature of revolutionary love,
trying to untangle his private passions from his larger love

two books: Herbert Marshall, *Mayakovsky and his Poetry* (Pilot
Press, 1942); *Mayakovsky*, ed. & trans. Herbert Marshall
(Dobson Books, 1965)
94 Vladimir Mayakovsky, "At the Top of My Voice: First Prelude to
a Poem on the Five Year Plan" (1930)
95 Vladimir Mayakovsky, "Home!" (1925)

of the revolution as the expression of human solidarity and vitality. Through his poems, we can gain a glimpse of the boisterous spirit and feverish energy of the real Russian communism so deeply buried under the false images of Stalinism. As his last poem insisted:

> I abhor
> every kind of deathliness
> I adore
> every kind of life.[96]

Mayakovsky also abhored literary pretentiousness and adored being rude and down to earth:

> I know –
> a nail in my boot that's hurting
> is more nightmarish than all the fantasies of Goethe.[97]

"I've become a terribly proletarian poet," he wrote to Lilya Brik, the woman he loved, in a letter covered with cartoons of himself as a bear. "I've got no money and write no poems."[98]

The Russia Mayakovsky grew up in was still paralysed by its own political and economic backwardness, its industrial potential locked up in its underdevelopment, its possibilities imprisoned by the absolute power of the tsar and the vast empty plains of the east with their huddled villages of thatched wooden houses. But by 1900, Russia's very backwardness had acted to suck in new manufacturing techniques from the advanced capitalist nations of the West. Cheap mass production began in a few large

---

96 Vladimir Mayakovsky, "At the Top of My Voice: First Prelude to a Poem on the Five Year Plan" (1930)
97 Vladimir Mayakovsky, "A Cloud in Trousers" (1915)
98 Letter from Mayakovsky to Lilya Brik, 1926

factories, and Moscow and Petersburg became familiar with telephones, bicycles, irons and wirelesses, the new products of the machine age. To Mayakovsky, perhaps over-optimistically, the new forces of steam and electricity represented a promise of a new future and required a new form of art. Previously the Russian left had admired the realist novelists of the nineteenth century; Lenin's favourites and inspiration were Pushkin and Tolstoy. Systematic Marxist writers on art like Georgi Plekhanov and György Lukács were aesthetic conservatives. But Mayakovsky wanted to alter the form of his painting and writing to suit an age of advertising and electricity and the altered perceptions of citizens of the twentieth century.

The Russian tradition of the realist novel sat in his way, "like enormous bronze backsides".[99] So in the first manifesto of the Futurist Group, characteristically entitled "A Slap in the Face of Public Taste" and issued in 1912, it was denounced: "Let us throw Pushkin, Tolstoy, Dostoevsky from the steamship of modernity." In the name of Futurism, he and fellow poets and sculptors travelled Russia, reading poems, denouncing the tsar and unfurling their manifesto. In many towns they were banned on sight and they remained unpublished. "Publishers do not touch us. Their capitalistic noses sensed the dynamiters in us."

And in Italy too, which had also experienced violent and abrupt industrialisation in a backward, mainly peasant

---

99 Source unclear, but possibly from the following edition: Vladimir Mayakovsky, "Kak delat' stikhi" ("How Are Verses Made?"), *PSS* (aka *Polnoe sobranie sochinenii*) (1928). One translator describes Mayakovsky as complaining, with reference to the classics, "Learn them, love them in the time in which they were working. But don't let their big bronze backsides block the road to young poets who are on the road today." (Source: James Rann's dissertation titled *A Stowaway on the Steamship of Modernity: Pushkin and the Futurists* (UCL, accessed 1 June 2017)).

country, Futurism emerged with its explosive language and fierce hostility to old forms. But while Mayakovsky's hatred for poetic marzipan and literary dust was linked to a movement to socialise art, the Italian Futurist poet Marinetti wrote with jagged, bombastic phrases, and his destructive spirit led him to press towards war as a means of artistic gratification. Italian Futurism became openly fascist. As the German critic Walter Benjamin put it, "Its own self-alienation has reached such a degree that it can experience its own destruction as an aesthetic pleasure of the first order."[100] Marinetti and Mayakovsky met only once and hated each other's guts.

But in Russia, the Futurists were the first organised grouping of artists to clearly devote themselves to the October Revolution and to express the ambition of those years. Mayakovsky became involved in a series of magazines – *Art of the Commune, Lef* which he edited and its successor *New Lef* – which championed the most avant-garde of the Russian art movements, Constructivism, which aimed at an artistic counterpart of the social revolution. The Constructivists differed sharply from the traditional defenders of realism who were grouped round the magazine *Krasnaya Nov*, edited by a supporter of the left Opposition, Voronsky, and the proletkult magazine *On Guard* which had grown out of pre-revolutionary working-class cultural institutions and stressed a fairly crude and agitational art (these tendencies had permanent bombastic quarrels and repeatedly demanded the censorship of their rivals). The Constructivists wanted an end to old elitist forms of art: the novel in its morocco binding and the oil painting with its bulbous gilt frame. They demanded instead a motivated art in new forms which related to industrial techniques in a workers' state. As John Berger says, "Their works were like

---

100 Walter Benjamin, "The Work of Art in the Age of Mechanical Reproduction" (German essay, 1935)

hinged doors, connecting activity with activity. Art with engineering; music with painting; poetry with design; fine art with propaganda; photography with typography; diagrams with action; the studio with the street."[101]

They wanted to be master-executors of social command, not priest-creators awaiting inspiration. At its most extreme, it was an attempt to bulldoze down the wall between art and life, subordinating aesthetics to the actual needs of the workers' state. As the sculptor Gabo announced in his Realist Manifesto of 1920:

> In the squares and on the streets we are placing our work convinced that art must not remain a sanctuary for the idle, a consolation for the weary, and a justification for the lazy. Art should attend us everywhere that life flows and acts, at the bench, at the table, at work, at rest, at play; on working days and holidays; at home and on the road; – in order that the flame to live should not extinguish in mankind.

It represented the release of artistic energy from the cages which boxed it up under capitalism, the energy in Mayakovsky's triumphant poem "The 150,000,000":[102]

> We will smash the old world
> wildly
> we will thunder
> a new myth over the world.
> We will trample the fence
> of time beneath our feet.
> We will make a musical scale
> of the rainbow.

---

101 John Berger, *About Looking* (Pantheon, 1980)
102 Vladimir Mayakovsky, "The 150,000,000" (1921)

Roses and dreams
Debased by poets
will unfold
in a new light
for the delight of our eyes
the eyes of big children.
We will invent new roses
roses of capitals with petals of squares.

The movement tended towards an oversimple anti-art feeling similar to Dadaism which had exploded in the West as a response to the First World War. And it was also magnificently unrealistic. As the Constructivist architect Lavinsky wrote: "We are condemned to aestheticism until a bridge towards production can be found. But how can this bridge be built in a country where production itself is scarcely alive?"[103]

But amazingly, the Constructivists managed to alter the artistic means of production in fundamental ways which the capitalist "avant-garde" has yet to come to terms with. In Russia of the revolution amazing things were possible. Mayakovsky meant it when he pronounced, "The streets shall be our brushes, the squares our palettes."[104] Tatlin was quite serious when he demanded the movement "into real space and real materials".

Tsarist cinema, for example, had been dominated by foreign production companies who took themselves and most of their equipment home on hearing of the revolution. Censorship had been comprehensive, even scenes of hard work and mention of the French Revolution were banned. But after the revolution what cinema industry that remained

103 Boris Arvatov, "Materialised Utopia", *Lef* 1 (1923)
104 Vladimir Mayakovsky, "An Order to the Art Army" (1918); can be found on *Socialist Worker* website, article titled "Vladimir Mayakovsky: the Poet of the Revolution" (23 October 2004)

was nationalised and new equipment procured with which to make feature and news films. The way the films were made was revolutionised. The camera was emancipated from being merely a version of the human eye, and film-makers explored the possibilities of editing and reorganising the rhythms and images on celluloid. Vertov produced revolutionary news reels: "a swift review of VISUAL events deciphered by the film camera, pieces of REAL energy brought together at intervals to form an accumulatory whole by means of highly skilled montage."[105] Eisenstein began his series of epic feature films, and Mayakovsky wrote amazing movie scripts featuring, as usual, himself as the hero. He worked alternatively on plans to reorganise the nationalised film industry (Sovkino) and on denouncing it for underestimating the masses.

Russian architecture had previously been oblivious to working-class housing and produced only rhetorical and overdecorated impersonations of Western styles. Constructivist architects, organised around the magazine *Sovremennaya arkhitektura* or *SA*, stripped away the larded decoration and disguises and used glass, aluminium, steel and asbestos frankly and elegantly. They invented the ideas of integrated design, as used on the new *Pravda* offices, flexible homes with interchangable units to alter homes as families grew and shrunk, and "new towns" like the one planned at Magnitogorsk. They stressed communal designs which aimed at maximum pooling and collectivisation of domestic duties and the socialisation of housework. As the Constructivist architect Moisei Ginzburg stressed, "The Constructivists' approach to the problem with maximum considerations for those shifts and changes in our way of life that are preparing the way for a completely new type of housing ... that is to say for us the goal is not the execution

---

105 Dziga Vertov, "Film Directors: A Revolution" (Russian essay, 1923)

of a commission as such, but collaboration with the proletariat in its task of building a new life, a new way of living."[106]

The Soviet Pavilion at the Paris International Exposition in 1925, on whose design committee Mayakovsky had sat, staggered the bourgeois world by the use of Constructivist principles. In the theatre, Constructivists produced mobile stage settings, hung the auditorium with placards and bombarded the audience with leaflets during the interval. Vsevolod Meyerhold produced Mayakovsky's play *Mystery Bouffe*, a *Pilgrim's Progress*-like account of the revolution for the international delegates to the Third International.[107] The storming of the Winter Palace was re-enacted and the streets, squares and monuments were dyed and redecorated to celebrate revolutionary anniversaries. Printing presses were hugely expanded and poetry jostled with posters and edicts to be printed in cheap editions with experimental typography and photo-montaged covers. Art academies were turned into polytechnics and student numbers increased. "We have taken by storm the Bastille of the Academy," the students claimed. But, as if to strike a note of realistic warning Vladimir Tatlin announced in 1925, "We must look neither to what is old nor what is new but only to what is needed." He was to follow his desire for the fusion of art and industry into the design of "maximum heat, minimum fuel" stoves, collapsible furniture and utensils, reflecting the needs of a virtually nomadic proletariat.

Of course Mayakovsky was in his element: "The work of the revolutionary poet does not stop at the book; meetings, speeches, front-line limericks, one-day agitprop playlets,

---

106 Quotation can be found in Arts Council of Great Britain, *Art in Revolution: Soviet Art and Design Since 1917* (Arts Council of Great Britain, 1971)

107 *Mystery-Bouffe*, Vladimir Mayakovsky, 1918
John Bunyan, *The Pilgrim's Progress from this World, to that Which Is to Come* (Two parts published in 1678 & 1684)

the living radio voice and the slogan flashing by on trams."
He travelled and declaimed on the agitprop trains and boats
which linked Moscow and Petrograd with the war fronts. He
wrote slangy poems abusing the Whites and rhymed advice
against drinking unboiled water and kissing ikons. He drew
and wrote simple and direct story-poems (which echoed the
old Russian "lubok" picture and text street literature) to
be displayed in post office windows. These ROSTA posters
were printed daily in thirty-four towns by poster collectives
and became immensely popular. He wrote advertisements
for state-produced matches and sweets, held auctions of his
manuscripts to raise money for the Volga famine, planned
a book to answer the twenty thousand questions he had
been asked when reading, wrote nineteen children's books,
conducted incendiary debates with rivals and fell in love
several times.

Highly popular among workers and the young, he gained
enemies elsewhere. Lenin disliked Futurism and did his
best to halt publication of "The 150,000,000". Since the
Commissar for Culture Anatoly Lunacharsky protected the
Futurists (he had called them "the virtuoso drummers of
our red culture"), Lenin sent a memo direct to the head of
the State Publishing House: "Isn't it possible to find some
dependable anti-Futurists?"

But Lenin seemed to warm to Mayakovsky, who he had
called on first meeting "a hooligan communist". In a 1922
speech to the communist faction of the Metal Workers'
Union, he mentioned the Mayakovsky poem "In Re
Conferences" which satirised the Bolshevik obsession with
meetings. Lenin said, "I don't know about the poetry, but as
for the politics, I can vouch for it that he is absolutely right."
In some of Lenin's more lyrical phrases – "Socialism equals
Soviets plus electrification", and "Revolution is the festival of the oppressed" – one can almost sense Mayakovsky's
presence.

But as the heady days of war communism were followed by

the compromises of the New Economic Policy, Mayakovsky became bitter against "the academics, singly and in bunches beginning to knock at the door", and suspicious of "the old familiar face of the aesthete peering out from under the mask of the engineer". His plays, *The Bedbug* and *The Bathhouse*, satirised the arse-licking and pomposity of the New Economic Policy's NEP men and red bureaucrats.[108] "From the philistinism of living comes the philistinism of politics," he wrote. He hated the dishonest obituaries, writing after the death of a friend, "Stop once and for all these reverential centenary jubilees, the worship by posthumous publication. Let's have articles for the living! Bread for the living! Paper for the living!" In his extended political poem "Lenin", he warns that if Lenin is turned into a God figure:

I'd have found enough curse words for blasting ears
and before they could smother my cry and drown me
I'd have hurled to heaven blasphemies,
and battered the Kremlin with bombs.
Down with![109]

And in 1923, a poetic leading article in *Lef* speaks concretely against what was to be called "the cult of the personality":

We insist
Don't stereotype Lenin
Don't print his portrait on placards, stickybacks,
plates, mugs and cigarette cases.
Don't bronze-over Lenin
Don't take from him the living gait and countenance.

---

108 *The Bedbug*, Vladimir Mayakovsky, 1928-9 in Russian
    The Bathhouse, Vladimir Mayakovsky, 1929 in Russian
109 Vladimir Mayakovsky, "Lenin" (1924)

And in a 1929 poem Mayakovsky characteristically ima-
gines himself delivering a poetic report to the jovial ghost
of Lenin:

> Many
> without you
> got right out of hand
> So many
> different
> rascals and blackguards
> Prowl
> round and about
> our Soviet land
> There's no end
> to their numbers
> and aliases
> A whole assembly belt
> of types
> are unloaded
> Kulaks
> bureaucrats
> and red tapists
> Sectarians
> drunkards
> and toadies.
> Chest sticking out
> they arrogantly strut;
> pocketfuls of pens
> breastfuls of Orders.[110]

The Bathhouse was attacked and boycotted. *New Lef* came
under fiercer criticism, most sadly from the poets of RAPP,
the newly formed writers' union which Mayakovsky eventually agreed to join. His photograph was cut out of the

---

110 Vladimir Mayakovsky, "A Talk with Comrade Lenin" (1929)

printed copies of *The Press and Revolution* for April 1930.[111]
He was prevented from visiting his new love Tatiana in Paris
and could not persuade her to come to Moscow. He told an
audience at a Mayakovsky exhibition, "I demand help, not
the glorification of non-existent virtues." He wrote:

> I'm fed
> to the teeth
> with agit-prop, too
> I'd like
> to scribble love-ballads
> for you
> they're profitable
> charming and halcyon
> But I
> mastered myself
> and crushed under foot
> The throat
> of my very own songs.[112]

It was as if he realised what the future held, that the
Constructivists' enthusiastic application to "social command" and the principle of utility would be used by Stalin
and Andrei Zhdanov to trim all which was revolutionary
and truly modern down to tidy slabs of a "socialist realism"
which was in fact a nineteenth-century naturalism. For
by 1930 the Constructivist impetus was faltering, a safer
art which was prepared to lend dignity to socialism in one

---

111 *The Press and Revolution* was a Lenin-approved journal founded
   in 1921 that mainly covered literary criticism, literature and
   art (according to the *Cambridge Companion to Twentieth-
   Century Russian Literature*, ed. Evgeny Dobrenko & Marina
   Balina (2011)).
112 Vladimir Mayakovsky, "At the Top of My Voice: First Prelude
   to a Poem on the Five Year Plan" (1930)

country was better received by the artistic authorities. While Constructivists' designs were halted on the drawing board, their new towns remained unbuilt and their journals were closed down, an ornate and pompous "Palace of the Soviets" was constructed to house a "Soviet" which no longer met. Dignitaries were now taken to the Bolshoi Ballet and the Grand Opera instead of Vsevolod Meyerhold's theatre and the street exhibitions. Oil paints, smocks, easels and professors of fine art found their way back to the studios. Stalin ruled. On 14 April 1930, Mayakovsky shot himself with a revolver. In his suicide poem he said simply enough: "... the love-boat of life has crashed upon philistine reefs ..."[113]

International Socialism, July 1972

---

113 Vladimir Mayakovsky, "At the Top of My Voice: Unfinished Prelude to the Second Part of a Poem on the Five Year Plan" (1930); can also be found under the title "Past One O'Clock"

William Blake

The London of two hundred years ago seems a strangely familiar world. The regime is in constant fear of its own downfall by popular agitation and private plotting, by working-class violence and middle-class dissent.

Radical workers, weavers, cutlers and potters are reading the *Rights of Man*, a banned book whose author is outlawed. A demo of 200,000 obstructs George III's attempt to open Parliament with missiles and chants of "No king" and "Give us bread and peace".

The successful revolt of black slaves is encouraged and supported by white revolutionaries in London and Paris. In Ireland, British troops and secret police brutally suppress a rising aimed at setting up a revolutionary democracy in the whole of Ireland.

In this riotous world the poet and painter William Blake wrote, etched and saw visions. His work is one of the first yet one of the bitterest protests against life in industrial capitalism.

His longing for social upheaval and an end to individual alienation was a call for revolution of the deepest kind. A socialist before the word was known, Blake grew up in a London which was beginning to assume its current layout, character and importance.

New trading and manufacturing centres were growing up in the east of the city, where the livery men and free-men who made up the "monied interest" had once ruled alone. A new labouring class was being born, not into factories yet, but in the tanneries of Bermondsey, the silk looms of Bethnal Green, the docks of Wapping and Limehouse, the print shops of St Giles and the hatteries of Charing Cross.

It was a class born into pain; it died young and unattended from convulsions, consumption and the pox, and commonly worked twelve hours a day simply to purchase bread and lodging. Adults dissolved their pain in gin, the babies were comforted with opium.

Pleasure itself was brutal; huge crowds watched female prizefighters mutilate each other with knuckledusters, bears devouring each other alive, and turned hanging into holidays. Yet the ordinary people, thrown into new kinds of work, new social relationships, the systems of capitalist trade and labour, were quite capable of scaring the wits out of their "masters" in the court and city.

What the coffee house wits and the Whig historians called "the Mob" in fact consisted mainly of wage earners and was bent not on riot but defiant demonstration of working-class anger, especially militant at times of shortage and price rises.

In London the periodic demonstrations were often aimed directly at the homes and property of the responsible politicians, and the last great outbreak of the century was directed against the "crimping houses", as the army recruiting centres were known.

As a child, Blake would have seen the street fighting by the blue-cockade-wearing supporters of "Wilkes and Liberty". He would have heard the voice of London dissent demanding freedom of the press, a larger loaf and support for the Freedom Boys of Boston and Philadelphia.

He had been near the front of the crowd when Newgate Prison was forced and the gates and hinges dissolved in flames during the Gordon riots of 1780. Blake's first major political awakening must have been the American War of Independence which he saw as a "mighty and awful change".[114]

---

114 William Blake, "Letter to Mr John Flaxman, Buckingham Street, Fitzroy Square", 12 September 1800

Popular Revolt

This overthrow of tyranny set him on the path of political poetry. In his allegory *America, a Prophecy*, he asserts that if George III is to re-enact the oppressions of biblical times, then he will take up his bardic duty and prostrate the tyrant with his art.[115]

In the French Revolution, which sent the wave of popular revolt against kingly authority around the world, Blake saw not only the disintegration of despotism but the spirits of Voltaire and Rousseau arising to drive out the priesthood and reassert civic patriotism. 1789 was a year of international revolution no less than 1848, 1917 or 1968.

An American wrote home from Paris, "Republicanism is absolutely a moral influenza from which neither titles, places or even the diadem can guard their possessor; the Lord preserve us from a hot summer."[116]

But by the turn of the century the Tory hue and cry against radical societies in Britain, and the downhill course of the French and American revolutions had saddened and silenced Blake. His poem on the French Revolution went unpublished. And he increasingly criticised the limitations of the bourgeois revolutions of the 1780s.

He saw that the American Revolution was not solely an act of liberation but the establishment of an independent right to buy and sell. The Declaration of Independence had nothing new to say to women and black slaves.

This was not Blake's idea of a revolution where "everything is holy and without price and every line and lineament is itself and not intermeasurable with or by anything else."[117] But Blake's attitude towards those

---

115 William Blake, *America, a Prophecy* (1793)

116 Written by American politician (and one of the Founding Fathers) Gouverneur Morris during a business trip to Paris in 1789.

117 Widgery appears to be quoting from David V. Erdman's analysis

who had still failed to free themselves was no longer a religious pity.

Rather his compassion for their plight had moved politically towards an understanding of their struggles and an interest in the means of their insurrection. In the remarkable poem "What Is the Price of Experience?" he argued against poetic liberalism:

> It is an easy thing to talk of patience
> to the afflicted
> To speak of the laws of prudence to the
> houseless wanderer,
> It is an easy thing to rejoice in the tents
> of prosperity
> Thus could I sing and thus rejoice; but it
> is not so with me.[118]

Blake was deeply interested in the slave revolt in Santo Dominigo, which ranked with the Roman Spartacus rising in its power and organisation. It came at a time when revolts had broken out in Peru and Mexico, when the Sultan of Mysore had taken to calling himself "Citizen" and the *Times* was talking of "the instability of rule in India". The black revolt was supported by the revolutionary armies of France (the story is wonderfully retold in C.L.R. James's book *The Black Jacobins*).

---

of a letter Blake wrote to George Cumberland on 12 April 1927, which can be found in Erdman's book, *Blake: Prophet Against Empire* (Princeton UP, 1954)

118 Here Widgery is quoting part ("Night the Second") of an epic poem titled "Vala, or The Four Zoas", which Blake began in 1797 and wrote over the course of ten years. Blake died without publishing it, but in 1893 it was found and published in *The Writings of William Blake*, III, ed. Edwin J. Ellis & William Butler Yeats (source: British Library).

Blake was at this time hired to make illustrations for the journal of a liberal English mercenary, Stedman, who had been employed to crush the slave revolts. Blake seems fascinated by the docility of the slaves, their obedience as slaves and their good behaviour as cargoes. In Blake's allegorical poem "Visions of the Daughters of Albion", Bromion talks of "the swarthy children of the sun who are so obedient that they resist not, they obey the scourge".[119]

Blake knew what underlay the fears of men like Lord Abingdon, an eighteenth-century Powellite, who had said that the slave revolts had "dried up the rivers of commerce and replaced them with fountains of blood where, all being equal, blacks and whites, English and French, wolves and lambs, all shall be merry, companions everyone, promiscuously pigs together; engendering a new species of man as a product of this new philosophy".[120] Abingdon's fear of French commercial competition, his hatred of revolutionary doctrines of democracy, lay at the roots of his sexual and racial fears and insults.

Racialism was not challenged in the arguments of the "moral politicians" like William Wilberforce, who, with the backing of Adam Smith, opposed slavery because it was no longer economically necessary. But Blake's hatred for the slavery of anyone and his joy in revolt went much deeper.

Crippling Code

He saw how slavery, soldiery and tyranny were equally the products of private property and wealth. And he saw how the owners of property preserved their power by a crippling

---

119 William Blake, "Visions of the Daughters of Albion" (1793)

120 From a transcript of the Earl of Abingdon's speech during the debate in the Lords on the abolition of the slave trade on 11 April 1793 (Possible source: *The Parliamentary History of England, from the Earliest Period to the Year 1803*, Vol. 3: 1792–1794 (T.C. Hansard, 1817))

moral code based on religious self-denial: the priest who "with branches and briars, bind my desires".[121] He hated the cruel and inflexible school system which defeated the "happy ones" by compelling them to " spend the day | In sighing and dismay".[122] Even more he hated those who cynically "protect" the innocence of children. He, who evaded formal education, woke each morning to the sound of the regimented London charity children. He once wrote, as an introduction, "Those who are offended with anything in this book would be offended by the innocence of a child and for the same reason – for it reproaches them with the errors of acquired folly."[123]

He saw bourgeois morality, the "Thou shalt not" written over the door, as hypocrisy to cover the realities of colonial plunder, soldiery, harlotry and apprentice slavery. And Blake constantly stressed experience and instinct against the thwarting of both under capitalist rationality and legalism (which he portrayed in poem and picture as the tyrannical and blind figures of Urizen and Los).

Perhaps this more than anything else has made his poems into slogans once again: Notting Hill Gate and London School of Economics walls carry such Blakean commands as "The tigers of wrath are wiser than the horses of instruction," and "The road to excess leads to the Palace of Wisdom."[124]

Before Marx and long before Wilhelm Reich, Blake was the first and finest guide to the alienation imposed by urban

---

121 William Blake, "The Garden of Love", *Songs of Innocence and of Experience* (1794)

122 William Blake, "The School Boy", *Songs of Innocence and of Experience* (1794)

123 William Blake, "Annotations to Lavater's *Aphorisms on Man*", London 1788

124 "Proverbs of Hell" from William Blake's *The Marriage of Heaven and Hell* (1793)

capitalism. His London was still a garden city whose pillars stood at its boundaries of Islington, Kentish Town, Primrose Hill and St John's Wood.

But in one of his best known and finest poems, he shows how capitalism corrupts his idyll. The streets are now given over to trading and charters; everything in life is reduced to buying and selling, not just of goods but of childhood (the chimney sweep), life itself (the soldier) and love, the source of life itself (the syphilitic whore):

> I wander thro' each charter'd street
> Near where the charter'd Thames does flow,
> And mark in every face I meet
> Marks of weakness, marks of woe.
>
> In every cry of every Man
> In every Infant's cry of fear
> In every voice, in every ban,
> The mind-forg'd manacles I hear
>
> How the Chimney-sweepers cry
> Every blackning Church appalls;
> And the hapless soldiers sigh
> Runs in blood down Palace walls.
>
> But most thro' midnight streets I hear
> How the youthful Harlots curse
> Blasts the new born Infants tear,
> and blights with plagues the Marriage Hearse.[125]

Socialist Worker, 1971

---

125 William Blake, "London", *Songs of Innocence and of Experience* (1794)

Enter Stage Left

Much of the theatrical radicalism of the 1960s and 1970s has compromised or just vanished. But some hasn't and theatre remains a vital source of political insight and inspiration. Indeed I think one should support live entertainment in itself against the deluge of video pap, style mags and bland pop. I'm afraid I prefer Ken Dodd on stage to Sammy and Rosie in the front room.[126]

It started with the domes, the bulbous, terracotta knobs with which the architect Frank Matcham crowned his thousand-seat, three-tier, cantilever-balconied Hackney Empire whose construction was one of the last great architectural acts of nineteenth-century London. The Empire, which opened on 9 December 1901, is a place which sets theatre historians atremble. A "Number One" Stoll theatre, it put on everyone, from Lily Langtry, Stan Laurel and Little Tich through Max Miller and the Fields (W.C. and Gracie) to Tony Hancock and Gerry and the Pacemakers.[127] But it was theatre history. In the somnambulant TV-sated 1950s when *Sunday Night at the London Palladium* killed live entertainment, Mecca bought the carcass, hung a huge housey-housey board over the stage and sealed the proscenium. Until in 1979 when, almost by magic, terracotta tiles started to fly loose, the domes looked dangerous and Mecca, injudiciously but Mecca-like, removed them.

Hackney Council, whose own mausoleum-like town hall is fifty feet up Mare Street, managed to notice. And so did English

---

126 *Sammy and Rosie Get Laid*, dir. Stephen Frears, 1987
127 Stoll theatres (Newcastle, London) were named after Oswald Stoll, who took control over certain theatres in the early twentieth century, including a popular one in Lond's West End.

Heritage who confirmed, to everyone's amazement, that in the heart of Hackney, wedged between the doner-kebab takeaway and the plastic training-shoe retailers of the borough's main shopping street, was a building of international significance. Listed, inside and out, Grade Two. Even Pevsner had missed it (while he noted a "not bad" 1930s Odeon up the road). Repair of the domes alone (they are being recast in specialist kilns in Lancashire) would have set back Mecca £250,000. The other potential fines and penalties for neglect or destruction, which can be exerted retrospectively, gave Mecca's accountant paroxysmal nocturnal dyspnoea. So, "Theatre for Sale: Excellent Location, Period Features, Needs Some Work".

Enter stage extreme left, Roland Muldoon, accompanied by Claire Muldoon ("my partner in life, in theatre, in everything"), in search of ... a theatre. For twenty years, first with CAST (the Cartoon Archetypical Slogan Theatre), then with New Variety. They had been performing, producing and promoting radical live entertainment in the upstairs rooms of pubs, trade union halls and, once in a blue moon, on a stage: the Ziegfelds of alternative cabaret. Muldoon's ginger-nut beard, demented beanie and demotic -psychedelic-cockney diction are not unknown on the theatrical left (an Arts Council official has called him "a combative, dogged, awkward cuss"). Brought up on an overspill council estate in Weybridge, he did the theatre management course in the Bristol Old Vic and gravitated to the old Unity Theatre in King's Cross from where he and Claire were said to have been expelled in 1965 by Stalinists on the bar committee for "Freudian-Trotskyism".

In revenge they set up CAST, the independent theatre group famous for its acrobatic style, fast pace and roll-neck black sweaters. They started in folk-club intervals with cartoon Marxism: hitting the audience before it could get to the bar, scaring them, making them laugh, pointing out the contradictions and pissing off before anyone could think up the answers.

After the ferment of 1968 and the proliferation of agitational theatre, CAST eventually entered the era of subsidised theatre. Mercedes vans and Equity rates – not without a good deal of vituperative debate in the style of the Soviet artists of the twenties; that is, ferociously extolling their own virtues and denouncing everyone else in sight. But Arts Council money was, in the Thatcher era, bound to come to an end. And CAST was never a very grateful recipient. "The grants were bound to stop," remembers Muldoon. "So we did everything possible to insult them and be as horrible as possible. We thought it was our duty." In *Sedition 81* they handed out large joints to the audience, telling them it was a government rebate; they also cut the Queen's head off, shot Prince Charles, threw the chairman of Turner & Newalls into a vat of boiling asbestos, and sent all the left-wing playwrights to the House of Lords. Their grant was not renewed.[128]

The Greater London Council came to the rescue. "We were looking for new angles," says Muldoon, "and this man called Tony Banks came along with some bumptious plan to bring culture to London. So we said we had some experience in this field." Instead of compulsory Acker Bilk and Arnold Wesker in draughty town halls, New Variety set up pub and community centre venues across London, putting on not just the stand-up comedians the Comedy Store were breaking in Soho but live acts: socialist magicians, radical ventriloquists, interminable mime duos with funny names and general mayhem. New Variety was the new line and launched the Joeys, Benjamin Zephaniah, Happy End and, literally, hundreds of others. In the process, the Muldoons became, themselves, a mini-Arts Council. It was classic cheer-ups for the New Depression but bubbling with angry, extreme talent and, for once, paying the union rate. And it

---

128 *Sedition 81* was a variety show put on by CAST which opened on 10 February 1981.

was still political, if less explicit: in the year of the miners' strike the groups performed non-stop and, against the stereotype of the north-south divide, were part of the great fundraising movement by London workers which did so much to feed the strikers and their families.

But the GLC was also doomed. And most of the money was ending up in the brewers' pockets anyway (bar takings are a key element in the finances of live shows). And when the acts got big, the venues were far too small and they had to crawl back to the West End managements. The GLC was interested in the purchase of a large theatre and so the Muldoons found themselves auditioning auditoriums in Kilburn, Tottenham and, eventually, trying to sneak a look past Harry the Doorman of the Hackney Empire. It was love at first sight or perhaps *folie à deux* between the raga-muffin hustlers of New Variety and Matcham's glorious, imperial theatre.

The Lyceum is majestic but seldom a theatre nowadays; in Wyndham's you need oxygen to get to the upper circle, the view is lousy and the gin and tonics expensive. The Theatre Royal at Stratford is exquisite but quite small. The Empire is as beautiful architecturally, and underneath Mecca's decorative efforts has a real proletarian grandeur. Empty it is formidable; with a full house it exudes warmth, majesty and sheer size.

Matcham (creator of the Coliseum and son-in-law of the then Lord Chamberlain, which helped with planning per-mission) managed to arrange the pillarless balconies, circles and nook-like boxes so that every seat has a good sight line.

The New Variety coup was executed with precision. A provisional deal was hammered out with Mecca with the incumbents taking responsibility for renovation of the domes and, in October 1986, the new management were let in the back door by Harry Godding, newly employed as live theatre custodian. They raced past the bewildered bingo persons to start dismantling the stage to see if the fire curtain was intact. The following weeks became an E8 version of 42nd Street with frenetic preparation to reopen on the theatre's eighty-sixth birthday, 9 December 1986. It was a dream come true: the old theatre alive again with a capacity crowd, the best of the alternative performers queuing up to give their all.

"It was like a wedding day," remembers the greasepaint gamin side of Muldoon. "Everyone was special that night. The acts went down a storm. The audience just wouldn't stop clapping."

But as even the surly estate agents' weekly, the *Hackney Gazette,* was moved to remark, "It was an occasion as joyous and historic as any gala West End premiere ... this is one show that must go on."

What happened was rather more complex. The Hackney Empire Preservation Trust (chairman Benjamin Zephaniah) is the charitable (and therefore "non-political") body which will own the theatre. New Variety (Hackney), which is funded, although not by Hackney Council, arranges the day-to-day running of the venue which is leased to independent producers as well as putting on its own shows and running the bar. So in the first months when the theatre was inundated by acts who thought bonanza time was here, the Empire's first advice was, get yourself a producer. It's not like putting on mates in a pub room; it's the biggest light entertainment venue this side of Wimbledon.

This also explains the use of the theatre by the local police for a pensioners' benefit, and the appearance of Frankie Vaughan, Ken Dodd and David Essex over the last year, which has raised some eyebrows on the purist left. It was, in fact, the phone call from Dodd's agent in April 1987 which proved that the Empire was in the big league. (Backstage Dodd to Muldoon, impressed: "This is all paid for by the loony left?" Muldoon, justifiably sore about lack of support from Hackney Council: "I wish it was.") And Vaughan, who works the stage superbly, was in fact an early showbiz sponsor of the Anti-Nazi League, even if he does play "God Save the Queen" at the end of his act (to the bafflement of most of the staff). Essex is said to have insisted to his promoter, Mel Bush, that he played the Empire, being something of a sentimentalist about old theatres.

But the first lesson of the first year is that the Empire is not some sort of theatrical Red Base. What it is, is the biggest theatre in London controlled by a non-commercial management with sympathies to the left. And that management takes the view that if Dodd and Essex hiring the theatre can enable them to put on things like the South African workers' play *The Long March* then so be it.[129]

The Empire would obviously not stage, or allow back, anything offensive to a modern Hackney audience, which would certainly rule out the acts the Empire used to house like *The Chocolate Coloured Coon*.[130] But someone like Alf Garnett is more problematical. Muldoon, but not all the theatre's board, was for staging Garnett: "I think he is passing comment on something that exists and which white liberals find very hard to admit exists." But Warren Mitchell won't be asked back. The act was repetitive and fairly unfunny.

Harry Enfield's character Stavros the Greek has also troubled the dinner parties of Mr and Ms Hackney-Fluorescent-Bicycle-Clips who see it as "offensive for Greek men". In fact, Enfield's creation, based on a kebab-house philosopher in a local takeaway, is one of the best things the theatre has put on, selling out by word of mouth and much applauded by the chef on whom it is modelled. The act is classic Chaplin.

---

129 *The Long March*, creator Sarmcol Workers Cooperative (SAWCO), 1986

130 British music hall performer G.H. Elliott (1882–1962) was known as the Chocolate Coloured Coon; he performed in black face, contrasted with all-white attire.

In fact it was a considerable achievement to keep the theatre open, let alone to stage such a wide variety of acts.

The audiences have been equally varied: white East End Cortina-boys worship Lenny Henry; Hackney Muslims use the Empire as their most important auditorium west of Frankfurt; there is a strong lesbian following for women comedians and musicians, notably Sweet Honey on the Rock, the acappella virtuosi. Vaughan brings in the older, often Jewish, Hackney residents who remember the Empire in the old days; the *Rocky Horror Show* still has a big troupe of transvestites in its entourage.[131] In audience terms the most remarkable was *Black Heroes in the Hall of Fame*, a virtually amateur show which puts Huey Newton alongside Toussaint L'Ouverture, and Sojourner Truth which had a word-of-mouth sell-out to a ninety per cent black working-class audience packing Hackney with Brixton BMWs.[132]

It's too early yet for the audiences to cross over and the old ladies to enjoy the Joan Collins Fan Club (another darling of the Empire) and for the Turks to get into the Wolfe Tones, but the presence of the building and the management's enlightened booking policy is doing more against racism and for working-class unity than mounds of windy declaration. Roland's old sparring partners are certainly impressed. Pam Brighton, ex-CAST and the co-founder of the Half Moon Theatre in neighbouring Tower Hamlets, now retired wounded from live theatre and qualified as a solicitor, simply says: "He's done it at last. What we all dreamed of." And Chris Rawlence of Red Ladder, CAST's

---

131 Musical: *The Rocky Horror Show* (dir. Jim Sharman, 1973 (in London)); Film: *The Rocky Horror Picture Show* (dir. Jim Sharman, 1975)

132 Sojourner Truth (née Isabella Baumfree, 1797–1883) was an African-American abolitionist and women's rights activist. Born into slavery, she escaped with her infant daughter in 1827; she changed her name to Sojourner Truth in 1843.

old adversaries, and now a TV producer and writer, thinks simply: "It's marvellous."

Hackney itself is the same inner-urban mess of desolation, poverty, rowdiness and HGVs, and the Empire won't change that. But it has given a new pride, elan and a sense of possibility to the borough. At the first annual general meeting last month there was much anguishing about the mistakes and the scale of the fundraising challenge (the first £50,000 is now needed in four months). But a commercial management would have been patting itself on the back if it had achieved a tenth of what the Empire's team have done in just a year. Harry the Doorman seemed to think it was all very simple. A great theatre is lit again. And the volunteer who operates the follow-spot thought the same sort of thing: "All I know is that I see a lot of heads. There's grey and bald and dreadlocks. But they all love being here."

New Society, 1987

William Carlos Williams

The first thing any practising doctor who also writes gets asked is, "How do you find the time?" A combined career ought, in theory, to be perfectly possible: writers and doctors are both only trained observers. And there is a distinguished medico-literary roster: Abse, Brecht, Bridges, Büchner, Bulgakov, Coleridge, Conan Doyle, Cronin, Chekhov, Döblin, Goldsmith ... and that's only seven letters into the alphabet. Even Roget, the writer's friend, was medically qualified. But almost all end up doing one or the other. And if they are any good as writers, the stethoscope takes second place. There never seems to be time to do both properly.

But William Carlos Williams, the great Modernist poet, succeeded. Williams, who was born in 1883 and died in 1963 after a series of strokes, was not only a prolific poet, critic, novelist and dramatist, but also a lifelong full-time general practitioner in Rutherford, New Jersey. Although he could have easily set up in private practice in Manhattan, he chose instead to work in a working-class industrial township with many recent immigrants from Italy and Eastern Europe who spoke little English.

His *Doctor Stories*, some written fifty years ago, deal with crises understood by any contemporary inner-city GP: stillbirth, autopsy, patients who refuse examination or cannot understand reassurance, never-ending evening surgeries ("that hellish drag"), extended family consultations in broken English, the particular test of night-visiting.[133] My visits are made to the concrete tower blocks of Tower

---

133 William Carlos Williams, *The Doctor Stories*, compiled by Robert Coles, MD (New Directions, 1984)

Hamlets, and the new immigrants are from North Vietnam and Bangladesh. But the emotions Williams records are heart-achingly familiar. There is no other writer who deals so well with how to listen, how to care, how to be there at *the* moment of physical need. He must have jotted these feelings down on prescription pad or notebook, then transcribed them on his laboratory typewriter, whose hammering often awoke his children. "By the time we assembled for breakfast, he had probably already done an hour's stint," recalls his physician son William.

As much as his industry, I like his laconic tone. His tenderness is hard-edged, his humanism slightly cynical; best of all, he is never sentimental about the oppressed. This quality he shares with that great revolutionary Luis Buñuel, and the older Jewish doctors I first worked for in the East End. And there is the sheer quality of his literary work.

When Williams was very unfashionable in Britain, Allen Ginsberg first introduced his originality to me. Ginsberg, who had just been expelled from both Havana and Prague, was in London for the 1965 Albert Hall reading. He was staying in a Soho garret transcribing a poem by Williams about Piccadilly Circus. It was Williams, he explained, who turned him away from pseudo-Elizabethan symbolic abstractions towards the minute, everyday particulars of his long poem "Howl". Somehow springing from his lotus position, horn-rims akimbo, Ginsberg declaimed Williams's poetic credo, "No ideas but in things," over the sleeping rooftops of London.

Williams, whose mother was Puerto Rican, was only a second-generation English speaker, so he struggled to develop a truly American voice, partly by the study of Native American history he undertook in *In the American Grain*.[134] His innovations were a simile-free, metaphor-stripped

---

134 William Carlos Williams, *In the American Grain* (New Directions, 1925)

diction arranged with a syntax and prosody based on lung breaths. It produced a wonderful, still woefully underrated body of work ranging from the long love poem Auden so admired, "Asphodel", to the haiku-like lilts in "Pictures from Brueghel".[135] For often this "difficult Modernist" was an old-fashioned pastoral poet. He is certainly the literary link between Whitman's Leaves of Grass and the post-war Beats.[136]

Williams was never polemically political like my other favourite modern poets, the young Auden, Mayakovsky, and Ginsberg himself. Since I come from an intellectual background shaped by the twin rigours of Trotskyism and R 'n' B, it's a little embarrassing to have chosen a poet as my hero, rather than a writer-activist like Victor Serge, Antonio Gramsci or C.L.R. James. But I think, perhaps idiosyncratically, that the point of modern Marxism is not to build power stations or palaces but to put the imagination in power (and then see what gets built). And thus poets are the unacknowledged legislators of the societies we must create in the twenty-first century.

Williams is heroic because he was a prophet in his own land, because he reclaimed poetry from European-imitating academics and because he stayed a working doctor – and enjoyed it. So whenever I become disgruntled about the workload, or Tory politicians' attempts to turn me into an accountant, I mutter a phrase of Williams's about one of his patients which sums up my own mixed feelings about practising in the East End: "Her smile, with a shrug, always won me."

Underneath the apparently laconic prose of Williams's Doctor Stories seethes the clinical passion and human

135 William Carlos Williams, "Asphodel, That Greeny Flower", Journey to Love (Random House, 1965)

William Carlos Williams, Pictures from Brueghel and Other Poems: Collected Poems, 1950–1962 (J. Laughlin, 1962)

136 Walt Whitman, Leaves of Grass (Walt Whitman, 1855)

desperation of life "in the ischiorectal recess". The most powerful story, "Old Doc Rivers", a portrait of an addicted doctor who is also an effective healer, indeed concludes: "It is a little inherent in medicine itself – mystery, necromancy, cures – charms of all sorts."

Surely much which is theorised about Williams's poetry is to be explained here in the circumstances of its making, in his finding, as GPs must, of explanatory colloquialisms; in his untangling of the broken American of his Jewish and Italian patients, himself, as Pound used to jeer, only a second-generation American. And in his doctor's delight in the concrete, the local and the particular, and in the way that part of making a diagnosis lies in registering the turns you make in your own mind. There is, too, in a brilliant story about a company nurse's hypocrisy, a reference to his constant but unobtrusive radicalism.

Above all, there is the genuine humility of a great writer who has also spent a lifetime of careful listening, unsentimental caring and just being there. Williams writes, "I have never felt that medicine interfered with me but rather that it was my very food and drink, the very thing which made it possible for me to write. For it provided not just the subject matter but a presence at the moment of articulating, the opportunity to actually witness words being born."

This wonderful book will reinfect us all with Williams's hard-eyed humanity and should forcibly remind medical readers what a privilege it is to be called Doc.

The Independent Magazine, 1990

Simon Guttmann: Agent in Shot

Simon Guttmann, the pioneer photo editor who has died at the age of ninety-seven, was a committed revolutionary socialist and principled anti-racist. Guttmann, who boasted in his guttural German accent that he had never taken a photograph in his life, was an important influence on modern photojournalism. With Alfred Marks, he founded the most eminent of the interwar photogroups, Deutsche Photodienst, and in 1954 set up the Oxford street photo agency called Report, which trained many now-eminent photojournalists, provided the socialist and labour press with its first professional picture agency, and built up a unique archive of documentary pictures of working-class conditions and activity. "When they want to know what it was like during those terrible years in Britain and who fought and why, our photographs will tell the story," he used to say with a sardonic sadness.

The only son in an upper-middle-class Budapest Jewish family, he liked to claim a father who had manned the 1848 revolutionary barricades and was also awarded the Order of Isabella by the Spanish Ambassador for services rendered in the supply of horses to the Spanish cavalry. His family fled Hungarian anti-Semitism for Berlin where Simon became a socialist in his teens, first in response to economic inequality and secondly "because of the daily experience of the superficiality of the teaching at school". First taught orthodox (Bernstein Second International) socialism "by the proprietor of a very shabby department store", Guttmann became an anarchic poet declaiming at the celebrated Cabaret Voltaire in Zurich.

After the Russian Revolution, he followed Lenin to the Soviet Union, stayed with Mayakovsky in Moscow, drank with Brecht and collaborated with Willi Münzenberg. After open and clandestine anti-fascist action in Germany he retreated to London, but never faltered in his commitment to the left.

Hunched in his Oxford Street office no bigger than a bedsit, dwarfed by heaps of mouldering newspapers and wrapped in bandages, he would take lemon tea and sweet biscuits and interrogate, cajole and charm political visitors. Woe betide any editor who incorrectly cropped his pictures or a photographer who missed a deadline. More than anyone he changed the visual appearance of the post-sixties socialist press (from awful to merely bad), and he leaves behind an important catalogue of new photographs which will be long cherished as a record of oppression and resistance.

The Guardian, 22 January 1990

Twice Met: Sedgwick and Serge

The contemporary admirers of Victor Serge owe much to another revolutionary socialist, polemicist and self-taught historian, Peter Sedgwick, who died in a still unexplained drowning incident in Yorkshire in 1983.

Peter, whose edition of *Memoirs of a Revolutionary* was published by OUP in 1963, was not merely a translator but himself a partisan of Serge's undogmatic Marxism and a writer of great wit, compassion and political precision.[137]

The 1963 publication of the *Memoirs* (now in their fourth paperback edition) was to have a definite political impact on the reemerging British revolutionary left, one of the many impetuses to the eruptions of '68. This was principally because of the inspiring and intransigent example of Serge's remarkable life at a time when, despite '56, the orthodoxies of Stalinist ideas were still widely accepted on the left. But it was also because of the special enthusiasm which Peter contributed to recovering the story of Serge, and thus a whole generation which had been written out of socialist history.

Peter was a classicist by training but, having been introduced by the French surrealist Pierre Marteau to the 1951 Éditions du Seuil edition in Oxford in 1958, he devoted himself to the preparation of an English edition, teaching himself French to do so.

He pursued the work, including the remarkably erudite footnotes, while working as a psychology demonstrator at Liverpool University, and probably completed it after he was sacked from the university for his political activity.

---

137 Victor Serge, *Memoirs of a Revolutionary, 1901–1941*, trans. Peter Sedgwick (Oxford UP, 1963)

As is well known, Serge was keen to have an English edition and had sent George Orwell a manuscript. And it was Isaac Deutscher (whose biography of Trotsky was the only easily accessible account of the Soviet Union from an anti-Stalinist perspective) who supported Sedgwick's proposal to OUP – of all people – to make his translation.

Early extracts from the work were published in the journal *International Socialism* in 1963, and Peter went on to translate and edit the magisterial *Year One of the Russian Revolution* for Allen Lane in 1972.[138] Serge never completely went out of intellectual circulation (the Shachtman translation of *Destiny of a Revolution* was published in London in 1937, and Serge contributed to the famous New International Symposium on Kronstadt alongside Rudolf Rocker, Emma Goldman and Leon Trotsky).[139] But the British anti-Stalinist left was much less familiar with him than the French.

Indeed, it is reasonable to speculate that when Sartre saluted Serge's intransigence in the famous passage of the 1956 declaration *The Hungarian Tragedy*, a good many British readers would have scratched their heads.[140]

It was certainly due to Peter's enthusiasm that the early seventies saw a small renaissance of Serge publication in Britain, including the Penguin editions of Richard Greeman's translations of the novels. But more importantly the books fed into the political mood of the time. Serge's and Sedgwick's politics were of Bolshevism at its most libertarian, and Marxism at its most warm-hearted and witty. Peter, whose most important book was the 1982 *Psycho Politics* – a study of theories of mental health – was a self-taught historian but had tremendous feeling for the

---

138 Victor Serge, *Year One of the Russian Revolution*, trans. Peter Sedgwick (Allen Lane, 1972)

139 Victor Serge, *Destiny of a Revolution*, trans. Max Shachtman (Jarrolds, 1937)

140 Peter Fryer, *Hungarian Tragedy* (Dobson Books, 1956)

material and made an early friendship with Serge's son Vlady.[141]

When Peter died he was working on the Serge-Trotsky correspondence. He dressed like a Basque beatnik, wrote footnotes to his own footnotes, typed (like Serge) in single, uncorrected spacing on flimsy paper, collected tins of mulligatawny soup and was the founding editor of *Red Wank: Journal of Rank and File Masturbation*, whose second (and unpublished) issue was to feature "Great Autoerotic Revolutionary Acts" and "Coming Out as a Worker: Problems in a TU Branch".

Sedgwick was one of the few "new left" who stayed moving leftwards in the sixties, serving as an active and valued member of the International Socialists from 1963 until his resignation in 1977.

Characteristically, he regarded the organisation as the one doing the resigning by renaming itself the SWP, and he half-seriously proposed to continue under the old nomenclature. It is sad that Peter has not lived to witness the first steps in the rehabilitation and rediscovery in Eastern Europe of a fellow writer and revolutionary of world-stature Serge clearly merits.

The words of André Giacometti, in his review of the 1963 edition of the *Memoirs* in the journal *International Socialism*, could apply to both translator and subject: "He had qualities of which there is a great dearth on the radical left of today; compassion, sanity, a sense of humour, optimism. He did not move like an enemy agent in the midst of ordinary humanity: to him to be a revolutionary meant to participate in every aspect of the life of ordinary people, and he never allowed himself to forget this is where socialism must come from if it is to come at all."

Serge Centenary Group Newsletter, January 1991

---

141 Peter Sedgwick, *Psycho Politics* (Harper & Row, 1982)

PERSONAL POLITICS

Spanning Contradictions

An introduction by Sheila Rowbotham

The affirmation of sexual love was integral to David Widgery's revolutionary socialism. In "Why Do Lovers Break Each Others' Hearts?" he sees love in utopian terms as transformative in a double sense. Through intimate union we are all potentially capable of glimpsing ourselves through union with the other. At the same time he wants to change how sexuality might be experienced, criticising the manner in which capitalist power relations and values impinge upon our innermost consciousness. Impatient with external convention and constraint he asserts love as unbounded and free, while being aware that in existing society male sexual needs and interests tend to be culturally dominant.

David collected inspiration from many sources: from the Surrealists, especially André Breton, from William Blake, from Karl Marx, from the sex psychologist Wilhelm Reich, the communist Christopher Caudwell and from the American thinker Norman O. Brown. He was also a supporter of the women's liberation and gay liberation movements from the late 1960s and early 1970s, assimilating ideas from them.

The idea of learning from social movements that focused on sexual politics may not seem particularly iconoclastic nowadays. But, unlike now, when he was writing, these were marginal indeed, and socialism was actually closer to British mainstream culture than either women's liberation or gay liberation. In "The Other Love" in *Gay Left* magazine in 1974, David challenged fellow revolutionary socialists, loyally but defiantly.

He recognised the power of culture and the need to situate opposing ideas within traditions of dissent. His essay on Sylvia Pankhurst expresses his enthusiasm for a woman who linked nineteenth-century rebels to the twentieth century and was committed to extending democracy through revolution and the emancipation of all women. Louise Michel, Eleanor Marx and Dora Russell, the socialist feminist campaigner for birth control and sexual happiness, were also among his favourites.

Spanning contradictions was part of his make-up. The same young man who wrote on unrestrained "cominglings" was also imbued with a sense of moral service to society. One major empathetic influence was his mother, Margaret Widgery, a Christian socialist active in the Campaign for Nuclear Disarmament whose own mother had been a supporter of women's suffrage. David, the only boy, suffered from polio and tuberculosis in childhood and grumbled bitterly against his father Jack Widgery's anxious attempts to teach him manly craft skills. He emerged with an edgy relationship with 1950s codes of masculinity.

In "Women Are Goddesses or Sloppy Beasts", David mounts an incisive assault on Norman Mailer's overweening male chauvinist posturings, hitting deftly below the belt. This early critique of Mailer's display of man-power reveals how David exulted in words as weapons. David angry, like David on love moreover tends to reject the external trappings of form. Sentences are stretched into seemingly impossible shapes, like those long-nosed animals made from balloons.

David's writing retains its relevance. The persecution of gays and lesbians noted in "Gay Was Good" persists along with the hateful class and gender contempt he excoriated in terms like "scrubber" – which still feature in such august publications as the *Guardian*.

Women Are Goddesses or Sloppy Beasts

A comment on *The Prisoner of Sex*, by Norman Mailer[142]

> We've had a load of scrubbers answering our ads for dishy nude model dollies. Surely there are some really pretty girls with nice faces as well as figures who will bare their boobs for £20 a day? Please don't ring if you're horrible.

> – A small ad from *Time Out*'s "Special Women's Liberation" issue[143]

We left Mailer driving his land rover through the mud and tide of Provincetown Bay, mourning his marriage and the moon, now both gone. Prose exhausted, weary in every comma and colon with inventing metaphysics for the sex-stripped mysteries of the moonmen and their machines. Well known for his well-knowness, celebrated for his fame, Aquarius was running out of eponyms. The Mailer who had uncannily foreseen the black uprising, guided us through the livid heat of Beat, comprehended and fought the advancing order of brutality of Vietnam, seemed emptied. In *Cannibals and Christians* he had promised, "This country is entering the most desperate nightmarish time of its history. Unless everyone in America gets a good deal braver, everything is going to get a lot worse."[144] And in *The Armies of the Night*, he recognised the future as a twenty-year battle for the soul

---

142 Norman Mailer, *The Prisoner of Sex* (Little, Brown, 1971)
143 Likely published in or around 1971
144 Norman Mailer, *Cannibals and Christians* (Dial Press, 1966)

of America.[145] But now he seems to have caught weightlessness; the ideas he had been juggling for fifteen years were floating out of his reach; his moralism had turned sanctimonious, his paradoxes anaesthetic, his toying with a pop-Marxism and a mock-existentialism simply a whim. His break with James Baldwin was the first clear sign. Mailer was prepared to offer the blacks an abstract right to liberate themselves. Baldwin understood that one of the first things it was necessary to be liberated from was people like Mailer projecting their own unrealised desire for animality on to them. Mailer loved the revolution as long as it remained an enigma; Baldwin could no longer afford to make a mystery of politics: "If they take you in the morning, they will be coming for us that night," he wrote to Angela Davis.[146] Now Mailer, who has always led with his prick, was finding women, too, less grateful for being sexually exploited to fit his fantasies.

The publication of *The Prisoner of Sex*, his frontal attack on women's lib (as they cosily and diminutively call it, those admen and novelists who thought it would all be over in a year), marks the end of any kind of sympathy for the revolutionary movement in America. His picture of women is not flattering, so clearly designed to shock, so sad. He says women are goddesses or sloppy beasts, they should live in temples or in cages, and he is showing off, desperately. It's a classic "masculine" double bind, common both in the saloon bars and around the hookah, a "real man" hates piety and so denies himself the possibility of many of his feelings. Mailer likes to prime his thoughts with viciousness, but

---

145 Norman Mailer, *The Armies of the Night: History as a Novel, the Novel as History* (New American Library, 1968)
146 James Baldwin, "An Open Letter to My Sister, Miss Angela Davis", 19 November 1970 (appeared in the 7 January 1971 issue of the *New York Review of Books* (Volume 15, Number 12))

the pain explodes in his own face. Or conversely he lays a mawkish mysticism on to women in a way that obliges them to become tangled in false versions of themselves, if only in escaping his. He glories in a picture of woman stripped of cities and corruption where she can do little else but act out the Christian symbolism of flesh, animality and fertility.

It's nothing new. Olive Schreiner, the nineteenth-century feminist, knew such "lofty theorist[s who stood] before the drawing room fire in spotless shirt front and perfectly fitting clothes" who talked so passionately of the wonders of childbirth. Does, she asks, the same man say "to the elderly house drudge who rises at dawn while he sleeps to make him tea and clean his boots, 'Divine childbearer! Potential Mother of the Race! Why should you clean my boots or bring up my tea?'"[147] No, no Norman: "He would love a woman and she might sprain her back before one hundred sinks of dishes in a month, yet he would not be happy to help her if his own work would suffer, no, not unless her work was as valuable as his own"... and you can guess who decides that.[148] Woman's work becomes miraculously no work at all; Mailer leans across a nation of invisible women on all fours to treasure "femininity" and "love", so obviously the projections of his own distorted masculinity. For from the women's liberation view, the traits of women rolled out by Mailer – the passivity, the inner-directedness, the proximity to eternity – are not timeless mysteries but historically determined, no more mysterious than the grinning nigger. Stepin Fetchit became Stokely Carmichael, so die "woman" die.

His old megalomania is now reinforced by a new condescension toward women: "Obviously no journalist could have done the job – it was work which called for a novelist."[149] The job is selecting a kind of Debrett's of women's writing

---

147 Olive Schreiner, *Woman and Labour* (T.F. Unwin, 1911)
148 Here Widgery is quoting from *The Prisoner of Sex*.
149 Here Widgery is quoting from *The Prisoner of Sex*.

which he congratulates on being penned "in no way women had ever written before" (has he read Mary Wollstonecraft, Flora Tristan, Emma Goldman, Eleanor Marx, Sylvia Pankhurst ... a whole submerged and passionate feminist literature?). He builds up a parody picture of the woman's movement, all bras, Valerie Solanas and scissor-women, designed to be easy to beat. Germaine Greer's "liberal heart" and Ti-Grace Atkinson's extrauterine plans are neither central to women's liberation (except in the media's eyes) or dangerous to Mailer's right conservatism.

He grudgingly quotes a pamphlet which argues that "women will not respond to an appeal to live the kind of lives they see men living and if they tried to do so in large numbers, they would cause a crisis in society." Mailer is stunned by this "echo of Bolshevism" (the Bolsheviks apparently being an all-male organisation) and concludes that it is probably true that men and women will not get anything fundamental without changing the economic system. He immediately drops the point. He's bored with statistics anyhow.

Never serious about Marxism, Mailer did have a period of thinking of himself as a "Marxist existentialist". Now his existentialism is just a poetic conceit, everything has consciousness, even his snot, and the Marxism is just a belief that technology, not the men that control it, is anti-human. The ideas he borrows, unacknowledged, from Wilhelm Reich, are those of cancer being caused by a failure of the psyche, the obsession with molecular forms of energy, the fear of homosexuality, and the insulting tones of his last persecuted days. What gets left out, as so often, is Reich's personal and practical commitment to working-class struggle and socialism as the only route out of the Weimar sexual hypocrisy. Reich's intransigent advocacy of Marxism in the Freudian front parlours, the work of SexPol, and his scientific use of the psychoanalytic method began the study of how it is that the values of capitalism and imperialism take route inside people's heads.[150] Marxist thinkers like him and Frantz Fanon, Sartre, De Beauvoir and R.D. Laing may be inaccessible and except ions to the general conversion of Marxism into the doctrine of the Russian ruling class, but their work has been crucial to the black and women's movements. All that lies behind Mailer's heaps of adjectives is theology: underneath the talk of "science", a dreary catalogue of the biology of illiteracy from thoughts on the emotional life of the sperm to Hans Eysenck on psychoanalysis.

Kate Millett has clearly wounded the old prizefighter: he can't stand a serious woman and so he sneers at her precision and brandishes his hornyness. He has not the beginning of an understanding of how great is the effort of breaking through the silence, to what extent the ideas which make up the intellectual world are all seen through men's eyes ("We must learn to see them through the eyes of women," wrote Trotsky).[151] Millett's book is an attempt to reinterpret sociology, anthropology and literary criticism's inadequacies from a feminist viewpoint.[152] For in every bourgeois science and a good deal of Marxism, women are made into invisible objects. We are only beginning to understand the process of the social education into femininity, the learning of how to "please" men. It is beginning to be possible to see how men's notion of their own masculinity (derived, in my case, not from D.H. Lawrence and Henry Miller but *Blonde on Blonde* and Jean-Paul Belmondo) acts to sexually divide women, to prevent their solidarity, to force them to police themselves

---

150 SexPol was an organisation founded in Berlin in 1931 by Wilhelm Reich as an official subsection of the Communist Party of Germany. (Not to be confused with Wilhelm Reich's book of essays, titled *Sex-pol*.)

151 Leon Trotsky, "Against Bureaucracy, Progressive and Unprogressive", *Problems of Life* (Methuen, 1924)

152 Kate Millett, *Sexual Politics* (Doubleday, 1968)

in our interest.[153] Even in orgasm, Mailer is reasserting the domination of women which exists in the outside world: "A man can become more male and a woman more female in the full rigours of the fuck."[154] It's a soap opera, even in the come. Perhaps we should assert the reverse, that women's liberation allows the possibility of man discovering his own femininity, anality and the memories of sex before puberty, almost before birth.

As David Cooper puts it, and it's an acid discovery, "Orgasm is the total experience of the trans sexuality."[155] The fucker is fucked in the course of his or her fucking. One becomes not only both genders and all generations, but for Mailer sex stays defined as the anatomy of the genitals: a woman's passivity from her "damned sponge" of a womb and her narcissism from her ova, man's ambition from his penis and his wealth from his semen. Whereas the kind of sexuality which might be hoped for once man and woman have finally laid down their last false demand on each other would be truly as William Blake and our Norman O. Brown, longed for:

> Embraces are cominglings
> from the head
> even to the feet.
> And not a pompous High Priest
> entering by
> a secret place[156]

It has been argued, more cynically by Peter Sedgwick, that "the vista of communist society in which genital sexuality

---

153 *Blonde on Blonde*, Bob Dylan, 1966
154 Norman Mailer, *The Prisoner of Sex* (Little, Brown, 1971)
155 David Cooper, *The Death of the Family* (Vintage, 1971)
156 William Blake, *Jerusalem, the Emanation of the Giant Albion* (William Blake, 1877)

is dethroned and diffused into body tone, work and the outdoor life is not too far from the ideology of sublimation festered by some public schools (and is liable to be no less unrealistic in practice)."[157] But it is clear that the lineaments of gratified desire are quite contradictory to Mailer's rigid semen economy which sees disaster in every wasted sperm, whether it be in a gay rectum, a schoolboy's hanky or a woman wearing a diaphragm. Mailer refuses to see that contraceptives increase woman's control over her own body. Like Orwell he hates rubberwear (Orwell ends a poem by accusing the cash nexus of being responsible for "the sleek estranging shield | Between a lover and his bride"; in that fantasia of studhood *An American Dream*, Mailer-Rojack brings the nightclub hostess Cherry to her first orgasm ever only after removing his Durex).[158] The definition of a successful fuck is that it produces offspring. He hates the fact that abortion is at last being made available early enough to make it an operation no more serious than a big dental job. He actually hankers after the era when puerperal fever made childbirth always pass close to fatal risk: "Sometimes the Prisoner thought it likely that women had begun to withdraw respect from men about the time pregnancy lost its dangers," a remark of such offhand sadism that there is little indignation left to recall that Semmelweis's discovery of the cause of puerperal fever was prevented from saving women's lives for years because of all-male doctors' refusal to introduce elementary hygiene.[159] The extreme violence of man on woman could not be put more beautifully; Mailer still wants his sperm to have the possibility of causing the death of its recipient, it will have "respect" that way. And if his victim dies, the streptococcus will kill

---

157 Peter Sedgwick, "Natural Science and Human Theory: A Critique of Herbert Marcuse", *The Socialist Register* (1966)
158 George Orwell, "St Andrew's Day" (1935)
159 Norman Mailer, *The Prisoner of Sex* (Little, Brown, 1971)

other women simply because doctors are too proud to wash their hands. Just as syphilis of the prostitute was the reality of the Victorian saloon's waistcoats and crinolines, so what underlies Mailer's sexual delicacies is the power to kill, the mentality of My Lai. The religious respect for mystic womanhood becomes the reality of the sexual punishment of the actual woman who must fall short of male fantasy: the anal rapes of Mailer's novels, the phallic murders of Eldridge Cleaver's writing, the use of female genitals as ashtrays, urinals and punchbags in Henry Miller, Mailer's "Old Master". The hatred and the hyprocrisy for women who won't accept their own subordination. When the Paris Commune was finally destroyed one hundred years ago, the women, accused by the victorious aristocracy of free love, were treated with especial sadism. As middle-aged women were marching to prison a young aristocratic hussar, how Mailer would have admired him, bent over from his horse and shouted at one, "When we get you to prison, you red bitch, we will fuck you with a hot iron."

But in a way the extremism of Mailer and, it must be added, his epigones in England – Christopher Ricks and Clive James, who crawled out of the senior common room woodwork to waggle their manhood once Mailer gave the go-ahead – makes it too easy on the rest of us. Most men on the left and the underground are more like the male communards who visited the women's clubs of the Paris Commune and whose rowdy interventions caused their closure. We oscillate between smugness and fear. It is to men much like us that a female communard said, with dignity and perhaps more patience than we deserve, "We don't want to act as playthings or entertainment for anyone ... behind your catcalls despotism is strengthened. You know very well that we don't want to lower you in any way but you are afraid to see us rise." Men in movements against capitalism often find their own definition at the expense of women. At one level the underground's sexual fantasy is a threat to the kind of pornography which actually caters for self-hatred. And it's clear that Lord Longford's minature McCarthyism will do nothing about the "pornography" in existence precisely because of the sexual hypocrites so well represented on his panel. Instead he will attack the subversive use of sexuality. But the underground just can't go on seeing every nipple and grunt as an attack on capitalism. *Ink* newspaper shows how little is really left when *OZ* is shorn of the porn. It's simply not enough to publish a perfunctory "Women's Issue" and still be saying like the proprietor of *Time Out* Tony Elliot, "an extra five thousand copies if we put boobs on the cover". The underground can no longer go on evading the issue, with the aid of token women and the whole reactionary supergroupy sludge, any more than the left can think the promise of a socialist revolution then is a reason to stop women's liberation now.

OZ 36, 1971

Why Do Lovers Break Each Other's Hearts?

David Widgery comments: *This is rather an impudent attempt to fit sexual love into a Marxist schema.*

Sexual love is the moment that breaks the rules; an uprising of the senses that abolishes propriety. Time alters. A gasp lasts an hour, a night separates into a heap of minutes, a conversation journeys from bar to bed to bus stop, and has it been a fortnight or a day? Objects flood with sudden meanings; a weed becomes a flower beside a canal that is an ocean. A shell swells with feelings. Touches echo, nerves misbehave, hands ricochet. Eyes kindle and melt in a world of constantly altering surfaces. Love offers a glimpse of the most intense communication that we have experienced. Everything that's said about love is true, except the happy ending.

To love in capitalism has an especially bitter intensity. It is to repossess feelings to which we have become foreign. Emotions without rules or price or power attached to them. In love's bed, mutual subjectivity allows absolute altruism. The precious is given without price, the delight lies in delighting another. We recover that which we have been taught to withhold or avoid or simply have shaken out of us by parents and teachers and each other. It is a state of revolution against the discoloured flatness which is "normal", sleep-work-play life. Lovers win a short parole permission to trail after the ditch-flowers, to stare through the swirls of harbour water to the stone and become entranced by the dart and hover and spill of storm clouds. Sexual love cannot be hoarded, accumulated or displayed. Neither moth nor rust can corrupt it.

In general, the individualism so avidly developed in us by the capitalist system is for external application. We are persuaded to distrust our emotions when they conflict, as they usually do, with competitive success. If we are going to "get somewhere" and "make something of ourselves", education not experience should be our guide. The adverts school us, the slogans batter down. Get without giving. Take what you can. Look after No. 1. "The less you are, the less you express your life; the more you *have*, the greater is your *alienated* life and the greater is the saving of your alienated being," wrote Marx.[160] But even the bourgeoisie flounders on love which it is obliged to honour however much it loathes its expression. For love is a zone of subjectivity which also has official approval – a precarious holiday where feelings, not finance, are supposed to rule. Love allows you, briefly, to return to what was once yourself.

Such a chaotic state, so randomly entered, would be a madness if it were not mutual. Courtly, romantic and platonic loves are myths designed to console or to gain power, a species of religion undertaken when the beloved is an object, never an agent, a screen against which the devotee projects desires. "If you are not able, by the *manifestation* of yourself as a loving person, to make yourself a beloved person, then your love is impotent and a misfortune," Marx reflects.[161] But love is not an unfortunate emotion, all poetic gestures and unwanted flowers, when its subjectivity and intensity are mutual. Then it is

---

160 Karl Marx, "Human Requirements and Division of Labour Under the Rule of Private Property", *Economic and Philosophic Manuscripts of 1844* (aka *The Paris Manuscripts*); This was unpublished during Marx's lifetime, but released in the Soviet Union (in original Russian) in 1932 and published in English in 1959.

161 Karl Marx, "The Power of Money", *Economic and Philosophic Manuscripts of 1844* (1932)

neither smothering nor bossy. For lovers can teach each other to find and trust their feelings and their bodies. It is a moment of shared aloneness, of laying down masks and disregarding appearances. Lovemaking is for delight and pleasure and surprise. The whys and wherefores are not determined.

It is not hard to see why such an unruly state of mind has to be strictly rationed and kept controlled with greeting cards, marriage licences and marzipan cakes. It is unpredictable, disorderly and bad for industrial relations. It's too simple and too difficult and doesn't consume enough. For the effective growth of commerce, it should occur only once in life; its emotions must be surrounded with regulations, icing sugar and lace, made as well behaved as possible. It would be easier if it didn't exist, this love, and for many it never does. But it has proved quite impossible to remove the gnaw or eradicate the itch. So it has been turned into something different – a mouldy, consoling sort of emotion which, for men, is made palatable by bouts of "sexy" sexuality which must be purchased or forced rather than discovered. Sex itself must be turned into work, with its own rules and games. It is forced back into the black sack of marriage, a contract to feel in a matter whose very essence lies in its voluntary nature.

It's not just a case of love "withering under constraint", as Blake, one of the first of the rebels against the laws of trade, marriage and scholarship, put it. Love is buried by love's forms, and sexual love or eroticism becomes an acted insincerity. Love does not wither, it sprouts unreal blooms, a tired romanticism which is a self-defeating fuss. Attempting to nurture a private exotic zone which escapes from the general pressure of society, it collapses into its own overweight luxuriance. As Christopher Caudwell wrote in 1938 in his essay on love in *Studies in a Dying Culture*, "It is as if love and economic relations have gathered at two opposite poles. All the unused tenderness of man's instincts gather at one pole and at the other are economic relations, reduced to bare coercive rights, to commodities."[162] By the forced separation of sensual emotion from the world of property relations, both love and life are twisted out of shape.

The echoing senses and unbraked subjectivity are made silly and impossible to sustain, for such love needs leisure and more space than five football fields. That kind of love becomes, in practice, a privilege for the rich. The rest of us are left to read about the affaires of ballet dancers and the loves of princesses. Ordinary love is locked up in its own company, given guards called Jealousy and Fidelity, taken out in public once a month, and stifles to death between the TV and the nappies. The underside of love surfaces and passion now wants its penalties. A once equal love capsizes and itself becomes the subject of the division of labour. The man is the human being who has to be kept fuelled and sustained, fit to do *his* stuff in the outside world. As time passes, it is mysteriously the man who comes to determine the terms of the emotional bargain. It's the woman who fits it, placates, anticipates, mollifies, sacrifices and then becomes bitter and made lonely by what love has become. The labour of love becomes just another labour.

Love can quickly become a species of tyranny, a word offered and withheld like a dog's biscuit. A word that turns suddenly into a slap, a trap, a threat. "Do you love your mummy?" means "Reward me for your dependence." "Mother knifed baby to prove she loved it," says the local paper. Love becomes involuntary, a system of emotional Green Stamps, promised, stored and exchanged.[163] The platitude that love is close to pain

---

162 Christopher Caudwell, "Love: a Study in Changing Values", *Studies in a Dying Culture* (Lane, 1938)

163 Green Shield Stamps was a popular scheme introduced in the

comes cruelly true, the intensity of violence replaces the gentleness of love. Not just broken alcoholic men but the smart young executives find violence sexy when the fun has gone out of love.

Violence is the occupational disease of a wife. Men beat their spouses regularly who would never harm their dog. But the slow death of love is a different sort of pain, full of guilt and dread and exhaustion. Love becomes an oath or a pang or a regret: the grease on the spoon, the hook in the tune. Women are less keen to forget, that is why they are called sentimental. But mulling over memories while contriving to be lovely-to-come-home-to is apt to produce a mawkish and sickly romanticism, no use to anyone. The evidence of loveless marriage lies concealed and unrecorded in doorstep grumbles and corner shop intimacies and smoothed-over rows in public bars, to be kept from the outside world if it can be. The consequences of such undeclared unhappiness crowd the doctor's surgery, fuel the terrible scorn in the popular Sunday press for the "abnormal", produce the bitter titters for those tributes to British sexual repression, the *Carry On* films.[164]

How the economic set-up of the family mutilates the emotions of love and how the unequal relations of the sexes turn a particular pair of lovers into sparring partners are not the most important crimes of a system which can starve whole continents and destroy and make ugly

---

UK in 1958 with the goal of promoting consumerism. The scheme lost popularity in the 1980s and ceased altogether in 1991.

164 Produced and directed by Peter Rogers and Gerald Thomas, respectively, the *Carry On* films comprise thirty-one low-budget British comedies released between 1958 and 1992. The franchise also includes Christmas specials, a TV series and stage plays. At the time of writing (May 2017), a new *Carry On* film is reportedly in development.

entire cities. But they are amongst the saddest. Feelings which have regulated life itself are relegated to a mere memory. A glimpse of something which has become a taunt. Once mixed up with marriage and corrupted with cash, love is bent into certain shapes which no longer fit feelings. People are sorted out into twos and marched up to the wedding cake while relatives make bitter jokes behind their backs and hire-purchase agents lick their pencils. The family is a convenient self-financing unit of competitive consumption and indoctrination, the original sweatshop where production and repair and reproduction are carried out by an unsafe, unpaid and underappreciated female workforce. For the state it is cheap at the price. How much easier than spending on good public transport or comprehensive group care for young children, or community centres and restaurants which provide much better and cheaper food and entertainment than the commercial outfits, if everyone does it at home one by one? Exhaustingly, inefficiently, expensively. And then sits in front of the nuclear TV to watch still more invented happy families serving out their Shreddies. The family provides certain certainties and keeps us all well wadded with stupidities. If it is breaking down, that is an occasion for rejoicing, not dismay. We need to start finding alternatives and demanding the facilities to make them work, not trying to force the broken pieces back together again. "The new society," wrote Dora Russell, "demands that women should give up rearing their families in small exclusive homes, treating their children as possessions and as pawns in the game of social rivalry with the neighbours. Women should give up catching a husband and assuming the right thereafter to dispose as they please of everything within the home that he provides. Men have to give up the idea that all within this home is their personal property, bought and paid for by them, theirs to fling into want or theirs to wrap up in the cotton wool of luxury, whichever their personal ambition dictates. These little fireside kings and queens must abdicate."[165]

Written 1972[166]

165 Most probably from Dora Russell's *Tamarisk Tree* (Elek/ Pemberton, 1975) or *The Right to be Happy* (Harper & Brothers, 1927), but at time of publication, unsourced.

166 Published in *Red Pepper* magazine's Valentine's Day issue on 14 February 2017, but otherwise not lawfully published previously.

Sylvia Pankhurst

David Widgery comments: *Sylvia Pankhurst is one of the few British revolutionaries to have publicly debated with Lenin. Indeed, she is largely known for having come off the worse for it. But she was a link between the British revolutionary movement of the nineteenth century, the world of Engels, Eleanor Marx, Kropotkin, Louise Michel and William Morris, and the era of briefly triumphant Bolshevism and the Third International of Lenin, Antonio Gramsci and Amadeo Bordiga. In her journey between the two, she collaborated politically with the outstanding revolutionaries and labour leaders of the time: Ben Tillett, Will Thorne, Tom Mann, Harry Pollitt, Jim Larkin and Victor Grayson. And in East London she sought to build a "strong self-reliant movement among working women" and succeeded in editing a genuine worker's paper, the Dreadnought, perhaps the first British socialist paper to use the phrase "rank-and-file movement". So if I am allowed one hero, it is her. There is still no biography which does her political justice, but I was given invaluable help in writing this tribute by the historians Lucia Jones and Sheila Rowbotham.*

Three women of the Pankhurst family dominated the struggle for women's suffrage in Britain. Mrs Emmeline Pankhurst married into a family with a history of radical and suffrage agitation, and moved towards the socialism of the Independent Labour Party in the 1890s. The Women's Social and Political Union (WSPU) was founded in her front room in 1903 with the slogan "Votes for Women". Christabel, born 1880, her favoured elder daughter, was her fiery lieutenant in the suffragettes' war of broken windows, slashed paintings and burnt-out churches as the Votes for Women agitation reached its crescendo. Sylvia, born 1882, middle, less glamorous and less well-known daughter, broke, painfully, from her mother and sister. Between 1912 and 1922, she attempted to remake the once intimate connections between socialism and feminism, not in the industrial north where the women's suffrage began, but in proletarian London.

My interest, affection, it's hard not to call it love, for Sylvia Pankhurst has grown over the last five years spent practising as a doctor not half a mile from her old home in the Old Ford Road. East London is different now, studded with tower blocks and fenced with corrugated iron. But curiously the same. Still solidly proletarian, still the sweatshops and street fights and rent strikes and plenty of old lady patients who remember "our Sylvia" with a twinkle. Still the migrants, speaking Bangladeshi rather than Yiddish, still the dole queues, longer now than ever. And still a revolutionary socialist minority, of which I'm part, spouting at street corners, dishing out leaflets, spreading union membership, occupying hospitals due for closure. Sometimes I feel Sylvia's presence so sharply, it's like a political ghost leaning over my shoulder to look with anger and compassion at the wheezy infants and cooped-up young mothers and panicky grannies who live in the council blocks the council has had the nerve to name after Percy Bysshe Shelley, William Morris and Israel Zangwill.

From 1910 onwards there was growing unease within the Pankhurst family and the WSPU. After 1912, on Christabel's instructions, the organisation concentrated on direct attacks on the property and person of the male members of the ruling class, carried out with much melodrama. Yet only two years later the same women became the most fervent opponents of Germany and Mrs Pankhurst transferred her vitriol to new targets – "conscientious objectors, passive resisters and shirkers". Workingmen did have a role after all, to bayonet each other in the trenches of the Somme. Christabel had been early to complain at Sylvia's speaking at mixed meetings; by the end of the First World War, she had bundled Bolshevism, sexual intercourse, strikes and venereal disease into a unified masculine conspiracy. As the WSPU became more despotic, it relied more and more on rich women who appear to have combined a radical break with sexual orthodoxy with a fairly conventional upper-class mixture of patronage and loathing for the lower orders.

In 1914 the long-awaited breach between Emmeline Pankhurst and her socialist daughter was made public with Sylvia's expulsion from the WSPU. Sylvia reported that the split came because "we had more faith in what could be done by stirring up working women than was felt at headquarters, where they had more faith in what could be done for the vote by people of means and influence. In other words, they said they were working from the top down, we from the bottom up."[167]

She had moved in 1909 to live at Bow at the house of the Paynes, who were both shoemakers, and began to build suffragette branches with the help of a handful of middle-class friends who shared her politics. She first approached known radicals, but soon attracted a group of working-class women leaders who were born agitators. Women like Charlotte Drake, ex-barmaid, labourer's wife and mother of five; Melvina Walker, a one-time ladies' maid and, like many of Sylvia's supporters, a docker's wife

---

167 Noted in the ELF (East London Federation of Suffragettes) meeting minutes from 27 January 1914, in which Sylvia said that while in Paris Christabel had asked – in front of their mother – her to change the federation's name and leave the WSPU (source: Elizabeth Crawford, *The Women's Suffrage Movement: A Reference Guide 1866–1928* (UCL Press, 1999)).

whose scandalous tales of high society made her a favourite speaker; and Nellie Cressall, a mother of six and married to a paint factory worker, who eventually became mayor of Poplar, one of the most radical of the dock area boroughs of London. At first the message spread among the tailoresses, serving women, factory girls and wives of Stepney, Limehouse, Poplar and Bermondsey, by word of mouth. The East London Federation's minutes record: "Membership is growing through afternoon tea parties. The outdoor meetings were not successful; too cold." But the colours of the East London Federation, the old suffragette purple and green with red added, were soon seen at early morning dock-gate meetings, Mothering Sunday marches, the traditional speaking sites at Victoria Park and Gardiner's Corner – where the male listeners raised the traditional cry, "Wot about the old man's kippers!" – and on street pitches and outside picture places.

Sylvia's constant and hectic political activity in those early days taught her details of the life of East London people. She got to know her way round the blank walls of the docks with their fortified entrances where the wealth of the empire passed through the hands of the very poorest. She sold papers outside gates which became an early morning parading ground of the workless desperate for casual labour. She was at home down the mean backstreets with their barrack dwellings, hard to keep clean, dangerous for play, costly to heat in winter and airless and dark in summer. She knew how hard it was to keep up the rent when work was uncertain. She sheltered in the blackness of the Blackwall Tunnel at night, the only underground shelter during the war's bombing raids where mothers and babies huddled next to munitions wagons awaiting shipment to the front, with the horses shivering and rearing with terror at the noise. Describing a 22 bus ride through London ending in the Isle of Dogs, she wrote:

Leaving the broad river in its quiet. Leave the wide sky, mount again to the narrow streets, to the mean streets, to the tumbledown hovels among the massive factories, to the lovers with nowhere to go, who clasp each other in gloomy doorways. Great chimneys, gaunt; great chimneys, fantastic shapes of elevators, and Venus that shines up there in the quiet sky. Majestic sadness. Stores of wealth kept here in bond amid the poverty.[168]

East London, then as now, presents particular problems for political organisation. Its long history as a national port and merchant capital defined the geography of the city before industry grew up. Londoners remained divided according to trade and transport, with most manufacturers small, and many service industries. Paper flower-making, hat finishing or driving a cart was more likely than factory work. There are no mines and little shipbuilding in London. There were pockets of high capital investment where working conditions and union politics were more like Glasgow or Yorkshire (the Beckton Gas Works was the world's largest and employed twenty thousand), but light engineering, woodworking and clothing manufacture in small workplaces were much more general. One in three working women were in service, mainly as cleaners. London trade unionism had been weakened by the "commuting artisan", by the conservative outlook of the skilled craftsman, the isolation and powerlessness of the unskilled casual worker, by the relatively large proportion and poor organisation of the migrant and women workers. Nonetheless, in the national patchwork of pre-war militancy, London workers of both sexes were as active as those in the provinces. There were long strikes

168 Sylvia Pankhurst, *The Suffragette Movement: An Intimate Account of Persons and Ideals* (Longmans, Green & Co, 1931)

of women cleaners, biscuit makers and jam packers in 1909 and 1910.

With Sylvia's leadership, these problems were addressed by the *Woman's Dreadnought*, newspaper of the East London Federation, established in 1913. It exposed the conditions of women homeworkers, campaigned on behalf of single mothers and the victims of hatpin abortions, published articles on the schooling of the future and international affairs. It sold about 8000 copies, with the Bow branch holding the record with a regular 800 a week and a claimed 1600 in one week. Some sellers complained of the police, the difficulty of selling to immigrants who could not speak English and of male hecklers who "crowded but did not buy ... giving us a very rough time". But these problems were countered by determined and imaginative publicity campaigns with late-night *Dreadnought* "chalking parties", "red sticky-backs" and the hiring of a pleasure boat in Victoria Park from which were unfurled parasols spelling out *DREADNOUGHT*.

Sylvia found her first real happiness among the cockneys, who despite her middle-class background took her to their hearts, calling her "Our Sylvia" and providing her with a bodyguard called Kosher Hunt, a local prizefighter. From 1912, Mrs Pankhurst and Christabel, while stepping up the apparent militancy of their campaign for the vote, were moving to the right. After years of public organising and exhausting constitutionalism, the WSPU was transformed into an upper-middle-class urban guerilla army, commanded from a secret HQ in Paris.

By contrast, Sylvia's efforts to build an independent working women's movement in East London brought her in contact and cooperation with the revolutionary left. In 1914 she intended the *Dreadnought* to widen the East London Federation's political interests. But by 1917 the paper was more concerned with the unity of the left and full of optimism for the Russian Revolution. In October 1917, it was renamed the *Workers' Dreadnought*. But the insistence on women's issues continued, both on local matters and in republishing articles by Alexandra Kollontai, Clara Zetkin and Grigory Zinoviev on the necessity for women's councils and a Women's International Congress. The extent and the sophistication of socialist feminist agitation carried out by the women's organisations of the Third International in the early 1920s remains curiously neglected even by feminist historians.

The war had effectively put a pistol to the head of every political organisation and interrupted the steady growth of the causes of women and labour. It enabled state-organised official obedience to push back the initiatives being taken by the women, the workers and the Irish. The overwhelming majority of the socialist organisations, with various complicated rationales, ended up backing the most pointless and brutal military slaughter in history, even those who had pledged, at conference after conference, their utter opposition.

The suffrage movement also fell first obediently, then enthusiastically, behind the war effort. Just as Sylvia moved away from the women's vote issue towards general political agitation, so in 1915 her mother, financed by leading industrialists, went on a speaking tour of industrial and mining areas of Britain appealing to wives to resist Bolshevism and stop supporting the shop stewards. The polarisation was to gather speed; just before Sylvia arrived in Moscow eager to debate with Lenin, her mother had been in the same city trying to rally support for the dying Kerensky regime. But even by 1914 the ways were parting. The prospect of martyrdom and glory did not appeal to the working women who had until then supported the suffrage campaign. The ladies broke the windows but the working women hung back.

Sylvia's sustained community organising in East London tried instead to get to grips with their more immediate problems – food, rent and working conditions. The East London Federation campaigned against government calls for food rationing. When bread prices went up, they suggested: "Someone should go into the shop and ask for it at normal prices and if it were refused, go and get a number to back her up and then take it." They tried to start a "No Vote, No Rent" strike but the idea was rejected by the WSPU because "it was impossible to work it through their organisations as their people were widely scattered and it is only in working-class homes that women pay the rent."[169] They also suggested to the Poplar trades council that "the Russian example can be followed and the empty houses in any part be commandeered for people now in the workhouse."[170] The federation was accustomed to working with local men trade unionists. They joined the general campaign against the "sweated trades" and particularly took up the cause of women finishers who sewed buttons and seams on soldiers' trousers and demanded that "if a woman does a man's work she shall have a man's pay." Equal pay was of particular importance because women were sucked into traditionally male jobs when those men were sent to war. Union branches of the Stratford and Bromley railmen heard women speakers on adult suffrage, and the trades councils turned their members out on suffrage demonstrations.

The federation was also adept at disguise and decoy so that Sylvia and others could defy the 1913 Prisoner's (Temporary Discharge for Ill Health) Act, the "Cat and Mouse" Act aimed to neutralise the tactic of hunger strike

---

169 Attributed to the WPSU Pankhursts, according to Sylvia Pankhurst in the 27 January 1914 ELF meeting minutes (source: Sheila Rowbotham, *Hidden from History: 300 Years of Women's Oppression and the Fight Against It* (Pluto Press, 1973))
170 Proposed by Norah Smythe of the WSF in June 1918 (source: Rowbotham)

by allowing for temporary release and return to prison once health improved. Once out, Sylvia resisted rearrest and made a defiant speech to the faces of the police in Trafalgar Square. The federation also took up a campaign about the conditions in Holloway jail where the women succeeded in getting the garters and proper teaspoons they had pleaded for, tiny victories that meant so much to women crushed by well-regimented pain. The scale of this East London agitation challenged the government. In 1920, during the intervention into Russia, the British Socialist Party, the Workers' Suffrage Federation and the shop stewards' movement led a united campaign for "Hands Off Russia". Dockers refused to load munitions for the Polish army of invasion and the heavers refused to coal the ship. The Workers' Suffrage Federation called on dockers' wives to support not only their husbands' campaigns but also to agitate at their own workplaces and on the public housing estates. This activity, which at one point had public speakers operative at over thirty open-air speaking sites in East London, did much for the Hands Off Russia campaign. British support for the Poles was stopped in its tracks.

Sylvia spread her ideas to other industrial towns in Britain and lectured in Denmark, Norway, Budapest and Vienna on socialism, suffrage, education and childcare. In America she spoke on "the garment workers" strike, drug fiends and juvenile delinquents, the "Negro question". She had particularly close links with the male engineering workers in Glasgow. But the activities in East London were in continual danger of caving in under the sheer weight of misery. The federation had to create places where working-class housewives could meet and support each other practically before it led them on to the streets and into the grim cells of Holloway jail. A toy factory was started in Bethnal Green for workless women and run under a kind of workers' control with equal pay. From it sprang a crèche where "working mothers can leave their babies for the day at a charge of threepence a head. For this the children receive three meals, the loan of suitable clothes and are cared for in every way."[171] A pub, the Gunmakers Arms, was converted to a maternity centre, the Mothers Arms, with a resident nurse, cheap maternity foods and hygiene and health talks. By 1915 mother and baby clinics had been set up in Bow, Bromley, Poplar and West Ham, connected to *Dreadnought* readers' groups. Cost-price restaurants linked to the paper served stew and rice and meat pie and potatoes in Bow and Poplar. In Walthamstow a League of Rights was set up by the wives of soldiers and sailors to campaign for better treatment for servicemen.

It is true that by 1917 the East London Federation had not produced great results. The distress relief always tended to become a disguised form of charity instead of the working women's self-activity that was intended. What with people running off with the cash, the cooperative factory being bankrupted by commercial firms and the maternity nurse watering down the milk, only bits of the federation's private welfare schemes remained to be taken up by Poplar Council. The federation was aware of the danger of merely providing services as a form of political charity, but certain that without collective provision for some of the working woman's burdens, it was fanciful to demand she step forward and emancipate herself. And the crèches, kitchens, choirs and clinics were themselves organised in a radical fashion. Socialist doctors and psychologists gave talks on sexual matters, the nursery nurses practised Montessori methods, advice

---

171 This is how Sylvia Pankhurst explained it whilst seeking funding. The quotation is taken from Sylvia's "Letter to the *Times*, 11 December 1914", which can be found in the Sylvia Pankhurst Collection ELFS, available from the Institute of Social History Amsterdam (source: Rowbotham).

on contraception was almost certainly given informally. During the war the federation spread itself from its East London heartland to form branches in Birmingham, Nottingham, Glasgow and Wales. By 1918 it had small groupings in twelve of the major towns which emphasised day-to-day women's issues within a wider framework of socialist demands.

Sylvia's fierce and consistent opposition to the war, although applauded by the Scots engineers and Welsh colliers, in fact cut her off from her old friends in East London. Hope came only from afar, from the Bolsheviks and the Soviets in Russia. It was to them and the communist parties being organised throughout the world in the glow of the Russian Revolution that Sylvia and her supporters turned. Like most British socialists, she was probably unsure what exactly Bolshevism was and certainly unclear about its relationship to her feminism, but she was to adopt wholly for the next few years its aim, the revolutionary overthrow of capitalism. As she told the judge who tried her in 1919 for agitating among the forces:

> I started four clinics and have sat up night after night with the little ones. I also set up a day nursery but all my experience shows me it was useless to try to palliate an impossible system. It is the wrong system and has got to be smashed. I would give my life to smash it.

When Sylvia drew up the agenda for the rank-and-file convention which met in 1919 to discuss the theories of soviet power, and to which she proposed her idea of the "social soviet" which would organise workers where they lived, far from abandoning her feminism, she was attempting to relate it to a new political era. For example, in an article on the shop steward movement published in Gramsci's *L'Ordine Nuovo*, she explained to Italian readers the meaning of the foreign phrase "rank-and-file movement".[172] Her perception of the potential of the rank-and-file movement and the need to link the factory council with the social soviet, the need to "translate" the soviet experience into Western European conditions, are a contribution which make her a founding mother of today's revolutionary movement, even if she was fated to make connections in her theory which she couldn't forge in practice.

Radical America, 1974

---

172 Gramsci met Sylvia Pankhurst in October 1919, and afterwards published a series of her "Letters from England" (translated into Italian by Togliatti as "Lettere dall'Inghilterra") in *L'Ordine Nuovo*, a weekly newspaper established in May 1919.

The Other Love

David Widgery comments: *Don Milligan's self-produced pamphlet* The Politics of Homosexuality *was one of the first British attempts to define gay liberation from a socialist point of view.*[173] *After the initial horror, the idea made a lot of sense politically, although not at this time to the editors of* Socialist Worker, *which explains why this review was published in the independent journal* Gay Left. *Still,* Gay Left, *like so many sexual politics publications, is long gone now, while* Socialist Worker, *if a little slow off the mark, is nowadays a resolute and reliable defender of the threats against gay rights which have materialised in the 1990s.*

Homosexuality has been a taboo subject on the left for one hundred years. It's always been somebody else's problem; something to do with bourgeois degenerates or Stalinist spies. Socialists who wanted to go to bed with lovers of their own sex have done so in great secrecy or simply become celibate and submerged their sexual longings in political activity. Although homosexual writers like Edward Carpenter, active in the Sheffield labour movement early this century, were very widely read in the movement (*Love's Coming of Age* went through twelve editions), their analysis could never advance beyond a desperate pleading for their form of love to be tolerated.[174]

Radical homosexual writers who were drawn towards socialist ideas because of their own experience of the

---

173 Don Milligan, *The Politics of Homosexuality* (Pluto Press, 1973)
174 Edward Carpenter, *Love's Coming of Age: A Series of Papers on the Relations of the Sexes* (Labour Press, 1896)

hypocrisy of capitalism were seldom welcomed. Oscar Wilde, openly prosecuted in an atmosphere of pre-Boer War patriotic hysteria, was unmentioned by the socialist press of the day. Walt Whitman, the American poet, whose proletarian following in northern England corresponded and sent money to their hero, was never able to openly link his homosexuality to his political feelings, although privately they were inseparable.

Of female homosexuals we know only sneers and silence. The left has occasionally included homosexuals somewhere in its list of oppressed minorities but the perspective has been reformist and legislative. For example, a warm-hearted article in *Socialist Review*, commenting on the Wolfenden Report which made homosexuality legal between consenting adults, still saw homosexuality as an evil and perverted form of love, a product of capitalist society which would be cleansed after the revolution. In the meantime, queers are supposed to keep their heads well down and wait for more tolerant laws to be passed from above. And although the Bolsheviks acted to legalise homosexuality, since 1934 in Russia and in most of the state-capitalist regimes, especially Cuba, homosexuals have been singled out for the most vigorous persecution.

The emergence, out of the political Pandora's box of 1968, of the gay liberation movement has altered the whole terms of the discussion. A movement of homosexuals of an entirely new kind was born in collective struggle (literally in a fist fight with New York cops attempting to make arrests in a New York homosexual bar). They asked not for integration and tolerance but shouted defiance and challenged heterosexual society to examine the seamy side of its own "normality". A sexual minority, apparently contained in their own guilt-ridden ghettoised sub-society, suddenly in the late 1960s began to organise politically and look for radical explanations of their own situation. Seldom has Engels's remark that "in the fore of every great revolution the question of free love is bound to arise" proved truer.[175]

The reaction of socialists has been embarrassed and uncertain. At one extreme the freak left, by giving uncritical support to every whim of gay liberation (and there have been many), in fact took a liberal and also a rather patronising attitude. At the other extreme, those socialists who denied that homosexuals were a "genuine" minority, and suspect it's all a middle-class problem anyhow, ended up utilising revolutionary phrases to cloak straightforward prejudice (at the World Youth Festival 1973, for example, socialist homosexuals were beaten up when they attempted to raise a Gay Liberation Front banner).

Milligan's pamphlet documents quite clearly how homosexuals are oppressed by law prejudice, the specific attacks made by psychiatrists and queer-bashers and, most importantly, the personal self-denial of a life of furtiveness and enforced secrecy. In reply to those who argue that this oppression has no relation to the class struggle, he quotes the words of the Bolshevik central committee member Alexandra Kollontai who wrote in 1919, "The problems of sex concern the largest section of society – they concern the working class in its daily life."[176]

It is hard to understand why this vital and urgent subject is treated with such indifference. The indifference is unforgivable. Milligan argues that homosexuals are an affront to capitalism because they challenge the system's division of people into small competitive family units of obedient producers and consumers house-trained in obedience and rigid

175 Friedrich Engels, "The Book of Revelation" (1883); can be found in *Marx and Engels on Religion*, trans. Andy Blunden (Progress Publishers, 1957)

176 Alexandra Kollontai, "Sexual Relations and the Class Struggle" (1921); can be found in *Alexandra Kollontai, Selected Writings*, trans. Alix Holt (Allison & Busby, 1977)

sex roles. For, like the Women's Question, any adequate Marxist analysis of homosexuality is bound to deal with sexuality, child-rearing and psychology, topics not raised within the Marxist movement since the late 1920s. These questions are not being raised again in the working-class movement by accident; it is inevitable they will be asked once again in new guises as we transform our revolutionary socialism from the dogma of the few into the faith of the multitude. Indeed, a modern revolutionary party unable to come to terms with feminism and the gay movement is storing up trouble for itself.

The struggle for a Marxist theory of homosexuality will continue and will only finally be made by working-class homosexuals themselves. As Connolly says, "It is those who wear the chains who are most qualified to begin throwing them off."[177] In the meantime, socialist homosexuals are entitled to expect the active support of their heterosexual comrades. Socialists who are weak on this question will undoubtedly show themselves weak on other perhaps more important questions of principle. For it is not a question of moralism but one of class solidarity. For a male worker who sneers at queers, just like one who talks of niggers and slags, is finally only sneering at himself and his class.

Gay Left, Edition 1, 1975

---

177 James Connolly, *The Re-Conquest of Ireland* (1915)

Gay Was Good

David Widgery comments: Gay News, *the national newspaper of the gay movement in Britain, collapsed in 1983. Its demise, partly self-inflicted, was another indication of the sexual-political left's difficulties adapting to a new and harsher era. Had it survived, it could have been an invaluable defender of gay rights in the age of AIDS and Section 28.*

After *Gay News*'s unexpected demise last month, I traipsed out to the periodicals section of the British Library at Colindale to inspect the corpse. "Oh, no, you won't find that here," said the lady at the issue desk. "It's a cupboard number, you see." So back to the special section of the North Library in the British Museum, where readers of material deemed obscene have to sit under direct and constant observation – presumably to prevent them playing with themselves. Homosexuality out of the closet? After fourteen brave years of gay liberation, it hasn't even got out of the British Library's dirty books cupboard.

When Heaven is awash with amyl, leather and sweat, gay men can be glad to be gay. But as the Blunt-hunt and the vile hounding of Peter Tatchell have shown with a chilling clarity, while attitudes and amenities have improved no end, to be homosexual is still to be at constant risk. And there are a lot of people more powerful than the trustees of the BM, or even the judge who in 1977 sentenced *Gay News*'s editor to a (suspended) six-month jail sentence for blasphemy, who want it to stay that way.

Take just a handful of the letters *Gay News* staff received in the week of the closure. A young lesbian writes, "I am a homosexual and have not been able to face up to this fact at all. I find the worry, secrecy and self-hate extremely crushing and destroying." A married milkman writes of his persecution and probable sack when he was discovered to have a male lover. There is a letter of thanks from Wilfred Blunt over-underlined in crabbed courteous longhand: "By far the best account of my brother I have read in any paper .... I don't know if I can re-Xerox it?"

Indeed, given the obvious practical importance of *Gay News* (not to mention its political import and literary merit, which are both considerable), it is quite extraordinary that its liquidation has hardly been mentioned, let alone analysed, in the media which are otherwise obsessed with matters homosexual.

It is hard not to detect, in the deafening silence of the liberal establishment, a private relief that yet another of those damned hornets that escaped the Pandora's box of 1968 has been eradicated. For the permanent loss of *Gay News* will be a grave loss not only to 200,000 regular readers for whom it was a unique source of information, communication and solidarity, but to everyone who wishes to resist the rolling back of the gains – and they were genuine, if often double-edged – of sexual-political movements of the 1970s.

The blow is all the more cruel in that it is, to some extent, self-inflicted. Denis Lemon, who emerged as the editor and then the owner of *Gay News* in the 1970s, is universally respected for his consistency, capabilities and energy. But it is hard not to see his secret sale, at a ridiculous sum, of the paper's assets to a not very gifted businessman, as smacking of avarice. And the Greater London Council's much vaunted Enterprise Board appears to have given false hopes of a major loan to the staff, which deprived them of time which might otherwise have been used to muster funds to purchase the title and maintain the all-important continuity of publication.

Andrew Lumsden, who succeeded Lemon as editor and

is otherwise surprisingly un-bitter about the situation, permits himself the single sardonic observation that "a newspaper for men who like to make men, and women who like to make women, was destroyed by men who like to make money."

A Trifle Sandy-and-Julian

The first issue, published in June 1972, had a front cover of Jimmy Savile – for some reason – in a bilious green. It was printed on the International Marxist Group's press, priced at 10p and boasted a simple editorial line: that gay was good. The initial tone is a trifle Sandy-and-Julian (the Biograph Cinema is "that little haven by Victoria Station" and there are pieces on trolling in Capri) considering the gender-bending flamboyance of the Gay Liberation Front who at the time seemed to have discovered the epicentre of the world revolution wearing a frock outside the Coleherne pub in Earls Court.

But backstage things were more raunchy. "If I buy one, can I have you?" one street seller was asked. "The answer was yes but the guy didn't wait!" And a later reminiscence describes the magazine "germinating in a soil of male love, acid, red wine and poverty". Yet the newspaper survived, consolidated and overcame the trials, the traumas and the people, like James Pope-Hennessy, who "did not see why homosexuals should have their own newspaper any more than people who like aubergines". By its hundredth issue in 1976 it had fourteen staff and thirty contributors – an extraordinary achievement for a paper which had originated in the margins of a counterculture which was pretty marginal itself.

It was not just journalistic survival. *Gay News* contributed practically to many of the institutions and groups that make up the modern gay community. The Gay Switchboard, the pioneering twenty-four-hours-a-day information exchange, much imitated but without peer, was initially founded to hive off the shoals of telephone inquiries the *Gay News* staff had to answer while trying to get their paper out. (It is said of the switchboard that gays in Dallas ring to find out what's on ... in Dallas.) From Gay Sweatshop to Parents Enquiry, there is hardly a gay grouping that *Gay News* hasn't at some time helped with national publicity, energy, resources and sometimes personnel.

If the endless editorials about the state of the newspaper's finances, or Peter Katin's benefit being banned in Harrogate, or whether Richmond Library will or will not stock *Gay News*, get a bit obsessional sometimes, well, being a bit obsessional is a necessary quality when trying to dent the sexual conservatism of the British establishment.

Above all, it existed. As the pop star Tom Robinson wrote, "The great thing about your newspaper is the dignity it lends the whole gay movement by remaining just that – a newspaper, not a wank-rag." And in the late 1970s, though there is clear evidence of growing strain between the post-blasphemy-trial Lemon and his staff, and a sometimes infuriatingly wilful and unwise apoliticism, there is also, in the writing of Keith Howes, Alison Hennegan and Jack Babuscio, journalism of the highest calibre.

The tenth anniversary issue (No. 243 in June 1982) adopted a well-justified tone of celebration: "Only ten, we should be one hundred or one thousand. But as it is, it's a fantastic achievement. Some credit to us, but much more to the tens of thousands who in ten years have rejected all the misnomers that society has given gays and have accordingly bought us."

Andrew Lumsden seemed to be bringing a new editorial impetus to the paper, widening its concerns and making a long overdue commitment to gay women readers in the autonomous "Visible Lesbian" supplement. This was all the more important after the closure of *Sappho* in 1981, and the section earned the support of initially highly sceptical women. He may be a little large in his claim that "*Gay News* is the bravest publishing venture of the twentieth century," but it was certainly a paper of integrity, intelligence and not a little experience.

If the abruptness of the liquidation was a universal surprise, there are differing views on its impact on gay morale. There are those who are critical of *Gay News*'s involvement with the commercial scene which, among other things, gets expensive for UB40s. And some gay veterans argue that for isolated homosexuals and organisations, the loss of the paper for any length of time would be a devastating blow. Others see the movement getting going again and are less worried about Ferdinand Mount's ability to organise the sexual counter-revolution.

The new GLC-aided London Gay Centre, for example, though a quite common municipal venture in North America, would have been unthinkable only a few years ago. And there is no question of the generation of gay men and women who grew up post-GLF being made to take the shit and the shame again. Denis Lemon has announced the launch of a new fornightly, *Gay Reporter,* and the majority of *Gay News* staff and contributors are also committed to a relaunch of a paper. So, whatever the opinion of the trustees of the British Museum, gays are not about to be consigned to the closet once again.

New Society, 1983

MISCELLANY

An introduction by Michael Rosen

David Widgery loved to get things right, and he loved the struggle in doing so. Part of this process was for him (and many others before him and since) to look closely at what others in his line of work were saying and distinguish himself from them. He did this with wit and passion in everyday chats, in meetings and on paper.

The first time I ever saw him was at a rally at the time of the student occupations at the London School of Economics in 1968. When it was his turn to speak, he moved swiftly to the front of the stage, spoke louder than anyone else and, though I don't remember the specifics of the moment, he ended by urging us all to be positive: we could win.

The point was – and still is – there are things worth fighting for, and if you get your tactics right, you get the support and you can win. In my many chats with him later, something else emerged: that doing these things is what makes life possible. As the old song says it, "The world is ill-divided."[178] From that simple but grim truth, a lot of things flow: if we want to have the right to a peaceful, secure and flourishing life for all, we have to fight for things like the NHS. Yet, winning it is not even half the battle, or a third of it: we have to struggle to defend it, keep it and make it better. David knew this better than anyone, and the articles

---

178 "The Jute Mill Song" is a union song written by Scottish jute worker Mary Brooksbank some time around 1920.

he wrote in this struggle – along with his book, *Some Lives!: A GP's East End* – sustained many of us at the time and still do.

The book was also part of urbanism, the attempt to figure out how cities grow and change, how we live in them and why we end up where we do. His engagement with Paul Harrison reminds me of the way in which he would sometimes turn up on my doorstep and begin a conversation in what was in reality the middle. He had read something, seen someone on TV and was engaging with it in his head. By the time he reached me – I'm sure it could have been anyone else – he was bursting with indignation and would open with "What do you think of...?" In fact, I can remember him asking me that very question about Paul Harrison's book. What really irked him was its pessimism. This is not simply a matter of style. The problem with pessimism is that it raises the question, Why are you telling me this stuff, then?

Satire cheered us up. When we put together *The Chatto Book of Dissent*, we found ourselves looking into the precise details of how parody, sarcasm and irony can expose the ways of the powerful.[179] Were we, "anything goes" people, or were there some things that were off limits, and if so, why? *Private Eye*, we accepted, was often acute and dangerous, but why was it sometimes not much better than snobbish? Snobbery never made the world a better place.

None of these thoughts came to an end when David died, but of course his voice disappeared. For that I'm sorry in more ways than I can express here.

---

179 *The Chatto Book of Dissent*, ed. David Widgery & Michael Rosen (Chatto & Windus, 1991)

The Eye's Privates

There was a time when it seemed magazines might change the world instead of merely entertaining it. At the height of the epidemic of radical publishing in the early seventies, an offset litho equivalent of the unstamped press almost unsettled our political establishment. In 1972, OZ celebrated its fifth birthday and IT and Time Out both clocked up their one hundredth issues. In those days, Time Out still advertised "Revolution" as one of its consumer services, sited somewhere between "Restaurants" and "Rock and Roll", and although Frendz was still "dedicated to the spirit of Woodstock" and the politics of well-meaning chaos, Ink and Seven Days were using the underground press's breakthroughs in design and production to push hard-headed and well-argued left politics. Spare Rib and Gay News were busy being born, and the socialist press, notably Socialist Worker under Roger Protz, was undergoing a renaissance in quality and circulation.

There was a good deal of rancour and rivalry between the papers, and much fostering of the eccentric display, competitive chemical research and aggressive sarcasm characteristic of male literary bohemias: Ink wouldn't talk to Seven Days, IT hated OZ and everyone denounced Private Eye as a coterie of passé, repressed-gay, public-school twit-wits. But beyond the whispering gallery of the metropolis and despite W.H. Smug's efforts, the papers were connecting with a readership who saw this great lithographic churning as a unified publishing effort in which they had a stake.

On a speaking tour in defence of the martyred OZ, I discovered Liverpudlian pensioners devoted to International Times, Barking Buddhists with a subscription to Socialist Worker, and Wigan shop stewards who collected Private

Eye. And although we would never admit it, *Private Eye*, in style, attitude and practical example, was the cardinal inspiration for the upsurge of unofficial journalism. When, fourteen years ago in *OZ*, we compiled the obligatory lampoon of *Private Eye*, it was even then a kind of homage. And in the great underground daze, the Greek Streeters themselves were in the throes of one of their radical phases – stimulated, at least in part, by their insolent juniors. Writing in 1971, on the magazine's tenth anniversary, Richard Ingrams angrily denied that the *Eye* had "become part of the Establishment" and announced that "the history of *Private Eye* as a journal of investigation is only just beginning."

Something went terribly wrong. We thought we were heading for the millennium and we got Margaret Thatcher, the Mini Metro and the Boomtown Rats instead. Alas we are not celebrating the 382nd issue of *Ink* or the ninth year of *Seven Days*. The radical survivors of that publishing era are pallid and predictable versions of their younger selves. Publishing economics now make independent new ventures virtually impossible. And it's not at all clear, apart from the shareholders of Pressdram Ltd, that the rest of us have a great deal to cheer in the 500th issue of Lord Gnome's organ, now officially a Great British Institution. As with certain drugs, what starts as a thrill ends up just a habit. *Private Eye's* nonsense writing is still addictively funny, although for years now it has been parodying itself. But the complicated snobberies and sneers, the intramedia bickering and tittering, the peculiar cannibalistic style has become somewhat dated: more mimic than satiric, all bite and no sting.

Nor has slim, teetotal, ex-Trot Martin Tomkinson, who succeeded Paul Foot's initiation "of *Private Eye* as a journal of investigation" etc. etc., proved an unmitigated success. Despite strong material on the extreme right, certain mysteriously unapprehended north London crimes and the Long March of the Pornographers down Old Compton Street, his columns are often turgid, ill-written and widely unread (but the Foot's own Rantzen-Esquire *Daily Mirror* page is not a lot better).

Even the lovable Auberon Waugh, sadly minus Nicholas Bentley's suitably olde worlde illustrations, seems to be going a bit soft. Waugh once seemed to have the makings of a decent little neo-fascist, but now he's settled into the usual potty Tory anarchist whose lonely loathing for the rest of the world is somewhat pitiable. (Although to accuse him of being a xenophobe or a sexual chauvinist is about as profound as accusing the Eiffel Tower of being in Paris.)

Nevertheless, my final loss of sympathy with Lord Gnome has been over their anti-gay libel programme, in particular a spectacularly inaccurate sexual allegation about an East London clergyman. This false information was probably fed to Greek Street by an extremely right-wing ecclesiastical body. It was certainly gleefully reprinted and redistributed by them. The cleric concerned just happened to have taken an exceptionally active and public stand against the local racist and fascist groups, who took great comfort in the *Eye's* little effort. The importance of factual accuracy is often overrated, especially in relation to the powerful. But that sort of malicious inaccuracy, malevolent innuendo and political ineptness is not easily explained or forgiven. Indeed, *Eye* seems to regard its misogyny and homophobia as evidence of its integrity. It would be pathetic if it wasn't so near to pathology.

Private Eye was not always so politically daft. The ungainly and self-deprecating Ingrams once confessed that the "satire movement has been working with Wilson to undermine the fuddy-duddies", and *Private Eye's* anti-Tory wrath in the days of Harold Macmillan and Sir Alec Douglas-Home was wondrous to behold: "We did everything short of assassination." But it is twenty years on, Wilson is long gone and we are delivered, via Callaghan's sordid interregnum, to the mercies, and they are few, of the Finchley Phantom. Now we really do need to know, as Claud Cockburn says, "where to put the razor blades in the potato".

Yet the rebels of Greek Street are giving Mrs T a curiously easy ride, indeed they have some responsibility for the passion for reaction which brought her to power. The *Eye's* attitude is one of bemused resignation rather than indignation. (The "Dear Bill" column works so brilliantly because, among other things, it is a joke at the expense of Ingrams and Wells's own Denis Thatcherist political attitudes.)

Christopher Booker is more and more like a drag Whitehouse and the *Eye* staff seem to have heeded Comrade Waugh's entreaty to "learn to love the system for the beautiful, incredibly complex thing that it is." For the *Eye* is now part of that beautiful complexity – an inbuilt compensation device, an upper-class elite within the elite of the upper classes, mirroring their exclusivity, mocking their excesses but knocking their opponents, us odious Sparts, boring brothers and uppity slags. All that remains in the traditional sequence of events is the final conversion to some species of High Anglican piety as espoused by "the guru" Muggeridge.

There remains one snag in this ascension to the satiric calvary. It is based on a lie. The system is not beautiful. It is run by a small number of people for their own good and therefore chaotically. It is not efficient or organised or practical. Nor is it eternal. It depends on the passive loyalty of a large number of people who could change sides quite quickly. The *Eye* can be inspiring because it can cut through the system's protective assumptions and pretensions, and wound it more intimately than the broad blows of political analysis. But unless the satirical rapier is guided by some analysis, it is merely wounding, often of innocent parties. It also becomes rather dull, both for its authors who find themselves welcome at the table whose corrupting hospitality they once despised, and for the readers hooked on its awesome predictability. Yet it was once possessed of a cutting edge we sorely need to recover.

In 1963, a less respectable *Eye* went into electoral battle under the Spartish slogan "Protest. Death to the Tories." Where is that banner now that we really need it?

Time Out, 1981

Urban Visions

Review of *Inside the Inner City*, by Paul Harrison[180]

The sociology of the inner city is beautifully simple; it is a sink into which the least able of the modern working class have sunk. Those who have got on, have got out. Those who remain, in a resentful proximity, have been reduced to a state of Giro dependence.[181] These pensioners of an ungenerous state are apt to vent their frustration in unacceptable forms: petty crime, vandalism, riots and reselection meetings. The only growth industries are video rentals, takeaway tandooris and winding up documentary film crews, and the most genuine job creation scheme has been in descriptive sociology, unfortunately a passing trade.

Readers of this journal will be connoisseurs of both the inner-city "colour" pieces ("Esme pulled laconically on her Red Stripe. She is fifteen and eligible for Youth Training in Washing Up.") and the complex political mathematics being played out between the institutions of Thatcherite centralisation and the socialist city councils. Indeed, a satisfactory account of both the flavour and the facts about the crisis of the modern inner city would require the skills of a Mayhew and an Engels.

Having admired early extracts from this book in *New Society* – the account of the Hackney Council direct labour bonus scheme (an unpromising subject) is a masterpiece of political economy – I expected great things. But the

---

180 Paul Harrison, *Inside the Inner City* (Penguin, 1983)
181 Giro is short for Girocheque, associated in the UK with welfare dependence.

speed with which it has made Hackney an object of pity in *Guardian* editorials and the Labour leadership race should have sounded an alarm. *Inside the Inner City* is a brilliant disappointment; less well researched than it would like to think, politically fatalistic and too often inaccurate.

In taking issue with Harrison, it is important to be clear where the disagreements lie. The contrast in basic living standards — diet, living space, education and health — between the inner cities and what is taken for granted in suburban England (the view from the Inter-Cities, so to speak) is vast. And he is absolutely right that the combined pressures of long-term unemployment, weak unionism, bad housing, low-expectation schooling and belligerent policing don't just add up but act to multiply each other's negative effect, so that an appeal to self-help is not only ineffective but insulting. If the conscience of modern monetarism was amendable to feeling, the remorseless evidence of this study would change history. For things are, behind the camou-flage of a now past affluence's colour TVs and concrete, once again the dreadful city of the night.

Indeed in some respects things are even worse than this book's grim picture: the schools have started to ooze asbes-tos, the carnage of the HGVs has, literally, accelerated into the front rooms, and alcoholism, that liquid correlative of inflation and depression, is epidemic. So one has little sym-pathy for Hackney hoorays who write for the *Times* about how spiffingly multiracial the place is. The problem is, as someone quoted in the book remarked to me after reading it, that Harrison makes it "almost too awful to be taken seriously".

For the weakness of this book's vision is its one-sidedness and its systematic exclusion of any evidence which would detract from Hackney-as-pathology; "an alien world"; "the indescribable"; "a breaker's yard"; "the dark side of a whole society"; "a motley"; "a bubo of plague"; "a Slough of Despond"; "an overcrowded cage". And to sustain this perspective, a reporter of exceptional craft is frequently reduced to journalistic jerry-building.

The section on health, for example, which could have been brilliant, instead brandishes a selection of facts of different value and vintage with some vox pop testimony from a women's health group whose dutifully reported assertions about travelling times to hospitals and inaccessible chemists are clearly unreliable. There is neither account nor interview with either patients or staff at hospitals or health centres, nor any serious analysis of changes in morbidity (Hackney's infant mortality has improved quite dramatically over the last five years).

Still more important, there is barely a mention of the quite fierce local campaigns against the hospital cuts which include some of the most effective strike action in NUPE's history. The net result is a picture of moronic passivity all the worse because it is obviously well intentioned.

And so it goes. Infant schools are snap-judged when karate chops are spotted in the playground; they, not the improving efforts of the parents and staff, are allowed to set the tone. The Labour Party is reduced to a snapshot of an ex-MP's surgery with only passing mention of the politics of the current council, far less the quite extensive and long-standing influence of the independent left or the relatively large Communist Party. The only type of community activity surveyed, and this condescendingly, are tenants' associations; there is no mention of community centres or rights offices or publishing projects or street festivals.

Organised racism has mysteriously subsided, notes Harrison, but there is no suggestion that the ordinary people of Hackney, black and white – might have played any part in it. And trade unionism apparently died at the sit-in at the Staffa engineering works, which Harrison describes, and subsequently merits less attention than shit in the lifts.

Eventually the effort becomes almost comic. Hackney is denounced for lack of parks and museums (with which it is relatively well provided), the shortage of late-night chemists is cited as a serious cause of ill health (whereas people cross London to the Amhurst Road late-nighter), a Rock Against Racism event is cited as evidence of black criminality (but was in reality a rain-soaked vindication of the organisers' slogan "Unity Inna Community"), London Fields becomes a muggers' run (league cricket and landscape gardening have been the main activities this summer), and Holly Street is slated as a disaster for kids (in fact the day nursery is the estate's big success story).

These omissions and errors of emphasis do not alter the force of Harrison's argument that Hackney is "one of the two or three contenders for the title of the Most Awful Place in Britain". But they obscure and deny all the evidence that new political identity is being forged out of the adversities of the modern inner city.

New Society, 8 September 1983

History Without its Aitches

Review of *East End 1888*, by William J. Fishman[182]

Magistrates and Tory MPs fulminate about falling moral standards while the would-be-employed have to fight one another for work. Welfare managers boast about their "efficiency" savings and buck-passing schemes for "internal markets" while the working poor lack fresh food, sound education and clean air. Newly arrived immigrants with their large families and language difficulties are harassed by xenophobic locals and exploited by co-religionists. The royals go walky-talky and are deeply shocked. The large employers attempt to break organisations with bribed non-union labour but are fought by rank-and-file ingenuity and socialist conviction. And in the face of flaunted wealth and moralistic hypocrisy, the unrespectable working class turns, not to the tenets of revolutionary socialism – though some did – but to crime, drink, cheap entertainment and stylish clothes, spending Sunday mornings recovering from a collective hangover which stretches from Aldgate to Poplar.

Plus ça change indeed. For this is not the Giroland E14 of today with its stingy doles, flashy discos and bashed-up Bangladeshis but the labouring poor of Tower Hamlets a century ago, recreated in all its conflict, complexity and indecent inhumanity by Professor Fishman. The doyen of the historians of the Jewish ghetto in Whitechapel here covers the whole of Tower Hamlets: Jew and gentile, Salvationist and anarchist, do-gooder and do-badder over twelve months of the turbulent year of 1888 when the match girls went on strike, the Ripper struck and the

---

182 William J. Fishman, *East End 1888* (Duckworth, 1988)

parliamentary commissions on sweated labour and immigration took their evidence. And he has produced a captivating book, alive with detail, humour, local knowledge and, above all, contemporary relevance.

At first appearance, it is social history of the conventional sort, taken by subject – "Housing, health and sanitation", "Women and children", and "Leisure" – rich in source material, including royal commissions and contemporary fiction, and leavened by fine-combed local and socialist newspaper reports. Indeed the very wealth of detail, compressed into the span of a single year, threatens indigestibility. But the unconventional Yiddish-anarchist-humanist culture the author imbibed as a Stepney child works its insidious magic. And as the book progresses, a subtle social geography emerges: of the polarity between the Anglo-Irish dockland and the immigrant ghettos of Whitechapel, an axis which still shapes the borough; of the division of respectable Bow and Mile End old town from the "islands" of Wapping and the Isle of Dogs by railway expansion and sanitary clearance and of the dire rookeries and hovels of Whitechapel, awaiting, as always, "redevelopment".

A sense of political crisis builds up, too: of worsening poverty, overcrowding and unemployment driving the desperate towards defiance (120,000 had marched in May 1887 at the funeral of Alfred Linnell, killed by the police on an unemployed march), of new unionism and classical Fabianism, both about to emerge, and of the sharp intellectual and practical competition between socialists, evangelical Christians and Tory John Bulls for the soul of working-class London. Unobtrusively, Fishman's calendar acquaints us with all the elements which make comprehensible the otherwise unimaginable upsurge of the great 1889 dock strike.

This being East London, the individual characters in the social drama are larger than life: toothless sword swallowers, autodidactic tally clerks, drunken public vaccinators, embezzling vestrymen, mothers of four dying unattended of breast cancer, poor law inmates smuggling out reports of the master's cruelty, "chirrupers" demanding money with menaces from music hall artistes and even Charrington, the brewer-turned-temperance-fanatic and scourge of prostitution whose portrait was said to hang in every brothel in East London.

But this is not a picaresque guide (there is mercifully little about the Ripper), and Fishman's judgements on the leading figures are sober and acute. He is intriguing on the popularity of Booth the Salvationist with his Irish gab, love of the dramatic and practicality (the Salvation Army hostels, then as now, were clean and warm). And he is scathing about the volte-faces of the Chief Rabbi (then as now an old reactionary). And while Fishman enjoys teasing the socialists and feminists, he is no mere humanist but emphatically and unsentimentally on the side of the workers whenever and wherever they come into conflict with the powers that be.

This is most moving in his intricate account of the grim anti-palliatives of the Poor Law system, but it is also evident in his attention to the exact mechanisms of the sweating system and his careful separation of the adjacent but not identical issues of immigration and "undercutting".

The system, which still operates, is not simply about the guarantee of cheap products and cheap labour but, as a contemporary issue of the Socialist League's *Commonwealth* argued, concerns the inner-city landlords, the large clothing distribution chains and the "investing capitalist" as much as the overseers of the outworkers. And would be solved only when, in Fishman's words, "the troglodytes hitherto entombed in their cellars came up for air and smelt battle."

Best of all is his treatment of the match girl strike, beloved in socialist legend but often poorly understood. This vindicates the courage of the girls, asserts the importance of "middle-class interlopers", socialist organisers like Annie

Besant and Eleanor Marx, but places the main emphasis on solidarity, first between employees and then with other workplaces.

Benefit courses, priests' letters to the *Times* and consumer boycotts were all very well but what won the dispute was active solidarity and the equivalent of secondary picketing. Against the New Realists of the day, solidarity between disputes was central in this period, perhaps most importantly between the Tilbury and West India dockers. It, above all, was the vector in the making of the East London working class. The potential of working-class power, if organised, pervades this wonderful book and only an emeritus professor at Oxford University (Richard Cobb in his characteristically perverse introduction) could find it hearteningly unrevolutionary. It will certainly cheer those conditioned by accounts of East London labour *à la* Stedman Jones even to read of meetings held to oppose the Highland Clearances and to barrack clan hierarchies.

This is history without its aitches, full of low-life wisdom and sharp observation as well as intricate scholarship. Without mentioning it once, it is a sustained attack on the present government's political philosophy. And so ironically, it is a very Victorian book: enjoyable as well as edifying.

New Society, 1988

Strife in a Cold Climate – East End

Like John Major, the TV soaps took a long time to notice the recession. Some still haven't or think, laughably, that it is going to be dispelled by a fourth-term feel-good factor. But it hit the pseudo neorealists who write *EastEnders* with a fury about three months ago and now there's hardly an Albert Square regular who isn't on hard times.

Frank Butcher, the series' entrepreneur par excellence, has had to sell the B & B to pay back tax and has ended up homeless. Rachel, the token progressive, has had her women's study course closed and now sweeps the "caff".

Meanwhile, the Queen Vic is deserted at midday (lunchtime is indeed an accurate barometer of East End affluence) and the bar staff connive to look busy to avoid their P45s. As for the Green Shoots of Recovery, Ian Beale is virtually the only young person in the soap who isn't squatting, living in an overcrowded house or in trouble with the police. And he has only prospered by becoming a vicious bastard. (At least Den Watts was an attractive vicious bastard.)

The older, more interesting characters have always been broke, but nowadays everyone is on their uppers. Like the good TV cockneys they are, they keep on being relentlessly chirpy down the convivial "caff". Of course, even in a "progressive" soap, no one is permitted to discuss politics in anything but personal terms, so no demonstrations, riots or party political rows. But with all the limitations of its form, *EastEnders* is probably giving a more realistic picture of the economy than that transmitted by Norman Lamont.

Even before the Canary Wharf debacle, the economy of inner East London had been devastated by the closure of the docks and the riverside industries that had dominated local employment. The odd sweeping and security jobs at London City Airport and the printing presses have done nothing to replace the jobs developers demolished in the seventies. But skilled workers kept going through the 1980s by migrating to big construction projects – the Channel Tunnel, Disneyland and Kuwait – as subcontractors. And other people made a living at the bottom end of the capital's service and tourist economy. Now the big projects are themselves in crisis and there are no new starts west of Hong Kong. The service sector, most notably banking and catering, is shedding staff. And the NHS and local authorities look set for further job losses to pay for their pre-election cushioning.

The effect of a jump in unemployment of this magnitude on an already borderline local economy produces collateral damage surprisingly close to that in the *EastEnders* plots. Pubs, in the East End of all places, are boarded up. The Roman Road clothes shops have their leases up for auction. Brick Lane's Sunday market has got still more desperate, with the section where pensioners wait all morning to sell two or three items for pence having doubled over the past eighteen months. The area's cheap supermarkets advertise a depressing but epidemiologically accurate staple diet in their windows of Special Brew, oven-ready chips, Strongbow cider and Pampers.

In our antenatal clinic, cases of under-sixteen pregnancies, marital violence and teenage homelessness have increased noticeably. When local authority housing stock was expanding, it was not too difficult for a young mother to find a flat somewhere once she had delivered. Now, they are all sent with their babies for a qualifying purgatory in some grim hotel. We GPs regularly get phoned at night by desperate teenage mothers with sick babies in hotel rooms miles from us – or from anyone else they know. Families in poverty and distress who have been temporarily put up in grim emergency accommodation are offered one chance at rehousing. If they refuse, they are evicted and on the street again.

Homelessness is the most extreme form of poverty and it's more pronounced than ever in the East End now. The semi-permanent fog of fumes from the A11 and A13 is mixed with dust from the new and hideously expensive Limehouse Link motorway, causing an increase in consultations for eye, throat and respiratory ailments. Yet, given the slow-motion collapse of Olympia and York, both the link and the Jubilee Line Extension will be rendered pointless.

Just think what the level of investment could have achieved if it had been spread over East London instead of pandering to development megalomania. A tube extension to Hackney would have gone where real people live and work, not to a half-empty monument to the Thatcher years. Some housing could have been built, appropriate to the descendants of those who built and worked the docks and endured the Blitz – as well as the more recent refugees, immigrants and exiles who have joined them.

The impact of prolonged high levels of unemployment goes even deeper than poverty and homelessness. It creates a sense of despondency, worthlessness and eventually physical ill health in individuals, and despair in communities. Although police racism was the spark in Los Angeles, the fuel was the recent increase in unemployment in the defence-related manufacturing industries whose previous density and momentum was unique to Southern California.

It is unemployment, much more than inflation, which destroys working-class communities and organisations and generates ill health. Unemployment erodes rank-and-file trade unionism – which has been a progressive force in East London for a century. When Marie Jahoda carried out her pioneering sociological studies on the Austrian village of Marienthal, she showed that loss of self-esteem was only repaired by work; handouts did nothing. And work, we should remember, was supplied by Hitler, together with soup kitchens, warm uniforms and conscription.

In that sense, at least, the Third Reich was just a pioneer of the permanent arms economy of the modern military industrial complex. Our post-cold-war market economies are turning out to be high-unemployment economies – they are bound to be if the market in the East, the West and the developing world is to operate untrammelled.

Unemployed people, most noticeably young single mothers, also seem to lose, or never acquire, confidence in dealing with health matters. They are more likely to consult doctors over minor complaints that they are perfectly capable of dealing with themselves. There is well-documented evidence of the increased incidence of mental illness, especially depression and suicide, among the unemployed (suicide remains a significant cause of male premature death in the East End). And despite technical difficulties and lack of a government interest in funding research, there is now impressive evidence of a positive correlation between unemployment and physical pathology,

The NHS in London faces inevitable shrinkage, despite the efforts and protests of those who work in it. But the numbers of those needing its help seems set to grow.

New Society, 1992

END

Another Last Exit

Anny Ash, Ben Bethell, Jesse Ash

The following text flows from conversations between Anny Ash, Ben Bethell and Jesse Ash, and is followed by two articles by David Widgery: "Last Exits", which muses on death in 1980, and "World Turned Upside Down", which gives a dissenters' vision of the future seen from 1991.[183]

Through these conversations it became clear that our childhood memories of Dave, his actions and what he stood for, were very much a combination of our own personal memories combined with the more public words and memories of others (family, media, friends etc.).

As a result, we wanted this polyphony to resonate in the text we made. Rather than speaking as a single narrator we tried to represent our conversations as best we could, with a collective voice, in order to talk with David about the past (obituaries) and the future (utopias).

*

You said, There was an aura, and I thought about how you make one of those. I thought, while listening through the music, that other people make it for you.

And we talked about other people's words. And how it was too loud to find your own. And I wondered if we could

---

183 Anny Ash is the daughter of David Widgery and Juliet Ash; Ben Bethell is the nephew of David Widgery; Jesse Ash is the stepson of David Widgery and son of Juliet Ash.

whisper instead, about your noise. If we could, we'd talk, about appetite and hope, and a genuine belief in something better. About how a personal struggle, confined, gathering words for later (some future better than that present) grew into a vivid opera.

Second-hand fossilised nervous energy. The magic flick of a spinning top, finger click and wrist into whirling balance who blinked, who made the magic snap.

Which reminds me...

That you said there's nothing to say, and that you didn't want to say it anyway.

And I agreed.

I thought about you making up words. Why not! (I think), but how can you cheat? (I thought). You once said you were the fastest reader in the world. Sitting on a beach I tested you and watched as you scanned the pages. I enjoyed the mystery of that. And now, in the future I see how you read, how you think and how you write. I remember your smile, eyes wrinkling through your happiness – half fun, half pride in your (our) games.

I want to hear as much as you want to tell, you said.

And so we talked about fear in the past. That giddiness, hysteria of tight hands clasped in feigned excitement. And about risk. The risk that takes a mind to find the places, people, colours and smells to make music. And we remembered how you listened. Head bent down inspecting the floor. Capturing every inch of that landscape. Stored and saved drone-like for more music.

The public you. The private you. In the future I see how you read.

Yes, I too love the idea of seeing how someone reads. I love the present tense of "read". Seeing how you think. Seeing how you write.

We remembered how you listened.

For half an hour? Forty minutes maybe?

You wrote about people exiting and you know we're writing about you, exited. We all remembered you and each memory was a different you, made in the telling. I won't tell you what I thought of you. Not here, but I'd imagine it wasn't your last exit. Even if you're not here. Your words are and we are.

You had so many heroes. You string them together singsong and I don't even know who they are, swallowed in a sentence of self-reference.

We raised our voices, told stories.

Had he heard this before?

Like we are simultaneously removing each other's complexly arranged costumes

and the trails tangle around ankles, trip us up, fog the mood.

We struggled. Some things we knew already, or knew from different angles. Or knew the feeling of it, had learnt the shape, from where the words were absent. That unworded way you learn something from how others fail to express it.

We meet again to discuss the future.

The energy, how we argued and wrote books and built theatres. You joined that list of people. We all will at some point, even the quiet ones. I'm not sure it's so important what they say after. Fandom. But talking about the future, I couldn't help feeling hopeful.

(Prescription: state authoritatively or as a rule that (an action or procedure) should be carried out.)

I thought about a child in hospital for weeks, months, years; thinking about a different kind of future. I wondered if you learned how to imagine from that bed.

Satirical visions, wide-ranging, searing, ironic, potent. Again we trip over words. Optimism and cynicism suck the life from each other, one snaps into the inversion of the other, like the sail of a boat turning inside out, the wooden boom switching in an instant.

Grand visions – building the future in the moment just like we tried to do, every day in how he treated patients, how he energised the world around him, how he nurtured us, how he pissed us off. A darkly brilliant, passionate, creative unfathomable dad-uncle-brother-son, a tireless activist and intellectual – around him the future seemed to be the present moment unfrozen – potential unfolded – daily, minute by minute, decisions, mistakes, choices – principles and struggles manifested in a swirl of action.

Laugh at what's coming, read the books, learn what people think is round the corner and buy a ticket, join the circus. It's happening. It is what is before us. If you walked in today you wouldn't recognise it and you'd love it. Your Amstrad floppy discs might be redundant and you'd be disappointed you missed the Olympic NHS carnival.

Last Exits

Birth, death? Yes, these are facts of nature,
universal facts. But if one removes history
from them, there is nothing more to be
said about them; any comment about them
becomes merely tautological!

Roland Barthes[184]

... That corpse you planted last year in your garden,
Has it begun to sprout? Will it bloom,
this year?

T.S. Eliot[185]

Secular Grieving

The way some people die is impossible to forget. Because
their dying says so much about what it is to live. One such
death was of a friend and a revolutionary who was an engineering shop steward in Ford's Dagenham plant. He died
young, of a long and intricately painful muscle-wasting
disease. It was the funeral which is the hardest to forget,
although, as these things go, it was a very decent ceremony.

Our secular grieving – rightly rejecting the embellish-
ments of religion and ritual – had somehow ended up
cheating itself. Our last offices, so stripped of ceremony,
were almost unbearably bare. If only we could have painted
the town red, hurled manifestos, cried and keened together

---

184 Roland Barthes, "The Great Family of Man", *Mythologies*
   (Editions du Seuil (French), 1957)
185 T.S. Eliot, "The Waste Land" (Horace Liveright, 1922)

and dared to look his death defiantly in the eye. But we had "Nothing to kill or die for and no religion too".[186] Trying to face death without religious or mystic belief is hard to do.

Mumbled Shelley for Brian Jones, over hasty grave for Jim Morrison, circuses for Hendrix and Joplin, bugger-all for Lennon, our generation's incompetence with death (and associated proclivity for suicide) has become all the more apparent in this year's grim reaping. What was truly tragic about John Lennon's end was that we lost not only his life but his death too. Death as brisk merchandising, voyeurism, masquerades of grief, unspeakable oiks who first-met-John, damn Yankees with their habitual shallowness and finally in Yoko Ono's truly appalling open letter of blessing, death as performance art and spirit possession. And still, literally thousands of people who still privately mourn but are unable (except Liverpool with its traditions of solidarity) to publicly grieve. What are we to make of the clarion of silence over the grave loss of the dramatist David Mercer (not as important to the *Sunday Times*, that watchdog of our cultural snobberies, as Yootha Joyce)? And then with Mercer so numbingly written off, who is going to grieve General Echo, teenage dub-genius, so casually offed in Kingston last month? General Who?

How we mourn, or how we seem incapable of it, is a most telling indicator of our culture's present depth ... or rather, shallowness. And this patter of radical premature deaths which, hastened by political assassination (Walter Rodney) and right-wing random terror (Bologna, Paris, Marseilles, Deptford), threatens to become a deadly drizzle and to prefigure a larger and more ominous catastrophe. As long as we are unable to come to terms with it – or even to attempt an estimation of what we have lost – we will be unable to refill that sense of cultural emptiness which has become almost constant. Our refusal of faith and dislike of "leaders"

---

186 "Imagine", *Imagine*, John Lennon, 1971

threatens, then, to become a kind of negligence and leads into another very English vice: the failure to cherish genius until it is safely dead ... preferably somewhere overseas. So, however unable or unwilling to mourn, we ought, for our own sakes, to attempt to place a marker on their last exits. A loss unmarked, extinguishes hope.

The Other Side Died

In fact the other side died too in plenty, usually in their well-fed eighties. 1980 was remarkable for the departure of some of the giants of conservative English popular culture. Billy Butlin, inventor of the holiday camp, that strange package of exhilaration and regimentation, the man who understood that leisure could be merchandised just like everything else. Alfred Hitchcock, that most British of film directors, a High Tory Buñuel, the lugubrious connoisseur of lower-middle-class, high anxiety, of suburban lewdness and domesticated horror whose fifty-three perfectly crafted, intellectually vapid and emotionally perverse movies are the final squirming tribute to what used to be the British Film Industry. And Mantovani and Gracie Fields, pre-rock-and-roll pop stars, so versed in arts of snobbery, so careful to live long and die rich. Perhaps, Cecil Beaton, that most wonderfully wasted of talents.

The Intellectual Rock Face

Lying beside them in a 1980s mass grave but from the opposite political pole are some of the shapers of post-war European cultural and sexual radicalism. Marcuse and Fromm, Sartre, Piaget, Barthes. And alas poor Mrs Althusser. When adding their demises together it is impossible not to feel that a whole slab has fallen from the intellectual rock face. Sartre, *primus inter pares*, and perhaps the most exceptional of post-war intellectuals, was mourned, in the city in which he was born, lived and died, in what was, for once, a beautiful burial. It is customary to see his importance in his (most un-English) insistence on merging the forms of literature, politics and art, and his mastery of intellectual versatility grasping the idioms of formal philosophy, literary criticism, novels, short stories, essays, autobiography and film script. But what is more permanently inspiring is that, with such prodigious gifts for nuance and subtlety, he conducted a lifetime of practical political commitments, with all the imperfections and compromises this implies. Not a commitment to the comfortable platitudes of party and dogma but a remorselessly, self-examining loyalty to the underdogs, the oppressed and the struggling. What bourgeois and Stalinist critics call fickle and inconsistent mark, by and large, a political career of singular honesty. He was able to campaign for Algerian independence and yet to openly criticise the Algerian revolutionaries for failing to develop a genuinely socialist society. He was able to support and street-sell the Mao-Spontex *Cause du Peuple* while making penetrating criticism of romantic Sinophilia. Even at his most bafflingly verbose, there is, in his commitment and effort at continuity between private and public life, between his artistry and his politics, that which anticipates and survives the now-trite slogan, "The personal is political." A striving at consistency and political honour which needs to be constantly recovered and reattempted.

It was present too in the penetrating gleam and silvery gaze of Herbert Marcuse whose death in 1979 was so ignorantly obituarised and whose last writings on aesthetics and sexuality brought the preoccupations of his earlier theoretical work into the present tense. And Erich Fromm, who died in March 1980, was a philosopher of liberation in a world of repressive empiricism and mass efficiency. His laconic accounts of the insane competitiveness, crazed commodity-mongering and inner hopelessness of Cold War Amerika became the clichés of the yippies and the growth movement. The use of psychoanalytic metaphors for political analysis was done to death by "me-generation Marxism". But for Fromm and Sartre and Marcuse, to explore the politics of the subjective and to extol the private rebellions of the psyche was an act of considerable political perception in the midst of the cold war's false dualities. And even that obnoxious old goat Miller popularised a kind of subversive pantheism against the air-conditioned nightmare which, as with Lawrence, far outweighs his rampant and pathetic chauvinism.

English Subjectivity

The post-war upsurge of English subjectivity was sandwiched between the European theoreticians of Paris and Frankfurt and the empirical radicalism of the North American underground in some sarcastic, satiric, sharp-styled, hard-edged, class-conscious, male-dominated, surreal socialism just about personified by Lennon and the crazy practicality of "Imagine", that twentieth-century version of Marx's *Theses on Feuerbach*.[187]

In the English sixties, the blocked-up channels of establishment art and politics diverted the creative flow to irrigate the fields of theatre, rock music, the visual arts and fashion (as it does again in the eighties ... now as farce). The sixties tended to produce intellectual entrepreneurs rather than philosophical gurus. In publishing it was the time of Tony Godwin, in theatre and journalism that of Clive Goodwin ... now both prematurely and tragically (how can one stop using these words) dead. In both resisting and inspiring this popularisation, Kenneth Tynan was a critical catalyst. "I'm beginning, I'm beginning!" cries Beatie exultantly at the end of *Roots*, which Arnold Wesker wrote when he was

---

187 Karl Marx's "Theses on Feuerbach" comprises philosophical notes Marx made whilst outlining the first chapter of his and Friedrich Engels's book, *The German Ideology* (1845–6).

twenty-seven.[188] And the best of Tynan's critical journalism was saying just that, not for himself but for that remarkable upsurge in English theatre which started at the end of the fifties and for which he was chief advocate, enthusiast and publicist. We know where it ended for him: first the National Theatre's lamentable imports, revivals and overpriced open sandwiches, then emphysema in LA and those sad, staid theatre profiles for the *New Yorker*.

There was a time when he seemed to be swinging towards some sort of idiosyncratic Marxism; he praised Trotsky when that much-maligned man was still in the political doghouse and was always talking about a "big book" on Reich. Gore Vidal claims that he preached unimpeached Marxism so ardently in New York that an editor of the once-Trotskyist-now-Republican *Partisan Review* told him: "Mr Tynan, our arguments are so old that I've forgotten the answers to them." In 1964 he wrote, "I have become aware that art, ethics, politics and economics were inseparable from one another; and that no theatre could sanely flourish unless there was an umbilical connection between what was happening on the stage and what was happening in the world." But as is less common in a left-wing intellectual, he had great descriptive exuberance, considerable ability as a hustler and a gift for experiencing instead of explaining.

Tynan's good behaviour in late life guaranteed him some sort of official recognition after his death. David Mercer, the playwright who struggled to hold true and to work through many of the ideas which had been simply attitudes in Tynan's work was, bar a sordid Workers Revolutionary Party rally and a free RSC reading on the night of the CND mega-march, rewarded with virtual silence when he died at the typewriter, of a heart attack,

---

188 *Roots*, Arnold Wesker (1958); This is the second play in *The Wesker Trilogy*.

at the absurdly early age of fifty-two. Bitter, verbally ferocious and famous for his drunkenness, Mercer's later works became increasingly elliptic and allegorically remote (as are the current works of his only equal, Dennis Potter). But his debut as a TV dramatist, with *The Generations* trilogy, redefined the limits of what was artistically possible on television as well as providing an account of the rise and fall of early sixties radicalism ten times more astringent and enduring than the sum total of the Not-So-Angry-Young-Man-After-All stuff.[189] Although the plays appear to have been wiped by the BBC, they stand as a good candidate for the first TV revival of itself. "There are people in every generation,' says the anti-hero Colin, miraculously played by the young Tony Garnett in a passage that might have been written for John Lennon, "who act out some of its hopes and needs. The subjective reasons for their actions hardly matter. In some ways they define a generation to itself. In times of violent or radical change such people, either as individuals or a group, can be decisive. In times of stagnation what are they? Articulate phantoms."

The Spirit of Suicide

Articulate phantoms seem, too, to perfectly conjure up the spirit of the suicides which brought English rock and roll so dolefully into the eighties. Ian Curtis's self-hanging at just the time Joy Division's awesome (and very un-suicidal) music was sweeping to mass esteem. The loss of Malcolm Owen, Roman-like in his death-bath (in that heroin addiction is a species of slow-motion suicide). Malcolm, whose intelligence, lyrical fury and sense of political solidarity had

---

189 *The Generations* trilogy comprises *Where the Difference Begins* (1961), *A Climate of Fear* (1962) and *The Birth of a Private Man* (1963). All three TV plays were written by David Mercer and directed by Don Taylor.

far more to do with punk than any vicious mock-martyr. Articulate phantoms: the phrase may say something truthfully about the suicides of the novelist Jacky Gillott and the film critic Jan Dawson.

There is a painful parallel in the wave of suicides which swept the European socialist movement immediately prior to the First War and perhaps to the nihilist bombings that accompanied them. The link is nothing so simple as despair – rather, that lethal combination of a well-informed political foreboding and a profound sense of political powerlessness and personal isolation. The socialists killed themselves not because they knew world war was imminent but because they realised the socialist parties were going to do nothing to stop it. As we now move from a post-war to a pre-war era, as Loamshire (Tynan's synonym for British middle-class philistinism) takes its revenge and as a Great Fear begins to settle over the culture of the Arts Council, the BBC and the better bookshops, it is sometimes impossible not to feel desperate.

But to indulge and act out that despair instead of understanding its causes and therefore its collective remedy, is itself a kind of death; the little murder of militant indifference, the individualism which sees suicide as painless, just another trip that's cool too, the ultimate art game. That is to admit Thatcherism to the soul, to embrace the vision of life as a jungle where we fight each other or perish and in which death is the just reward for failing to stay alive. It is to fail to realise death is the sting and so dishonours those who have fought to stay alive, whether they are C.L.R. James or Bernadette McAliskey or Keith Richards. It is to show a gross self-indulgence of the spirit in the face of pressure, which is still quite minor when set against the story so far in this Century of Blood.

Mercer used a survivor of Stalinism, Jurek, to put Colin's wonderfully articulate but somewhat phantom suffering into emotional perspective in a way which is now more profound than when it was first written twenty years ago. "Jurek," says a woman character, "has had to fight too, you know. For truth and honesty. For what communism should mean. He's been doing it all his life. He's tired. But he goes on. What stops you, except your own preoccupation with your sense of defeat? You can't afford it. It's a luxury."

ZG, 1981

World Turned Upside Down: A Dissenter's View of the Future

It was a solemn moment at Millennium Hall (as the main square of the Canary Wharf complex had been renamed when roofed over after the Second Great Insurrection of 1998). The delegate from the Seattle Convention of the Western Republics, Citizen Prairie Gates, had just finished speaking of the historical links between the American Revolution and the new Republican Federation of North East European Islands.

> We in Amerika, in honouring the spirit of Tom Paine, send greetings to the descendants of Citizen Connolly, Citizen Larkin and Citizen Pankhurst. We remember the British cotton workers who supported the struggle against slavery and we salute the inventors of regicide, hunger strikes, civil disobedience and the reggae-punk rock fusion.

Her words, transmitted simultaneously to two thousand open-air gatherings celebrating Year One of the twenty-first century, were replied to by Citizen Devlin, the president of the federation, live from Dublin. "It was only your efforts in returning North America to its revolutionary origins and the true values of its dissenting pioneers," she asserted, "that has enabled us northern Europeans to at last shape our own destinies free from Nato, the multinationals and junk TV. Neither the Hang Seng index nor the Bundesbank but international Winstanleyism."

There was spontaneous singing of "Jerusalem" and "Anarchy in the UK" at the London meeting, which included veterans from the Second Great Anti-Fascist War in the Urals in the mid-nineties in which Geordie, Belfast and Scandinavian volunteers had been so important, representatives of what had once been called the Third World on their way to Dublin to sign fomal cancellation of their entire debts, and delegations of Central African health workers who had announced earlier that day the eradication of new cases of AIDS worldwide through the "San Francisco-Lusaka Project" into which the military budget of the old USA had been channelled.[190]

Events in the mid-nineties had been almost too rapid to comprehend. Eastern Europe, with market theory utterly discredited and the Wars of the Yeltsin Succession finally over, had successfully refederated under a highly efficient system of workers' and producers' control known as the Kropotkin Plan. The Pan-American Bank Collapse of 1995 and the subsequent Gun Wars had led to the disintegration of the USA into a series of pacifist self-governing states without a national leadership except by the anarcho-syndicalist convention in the north-west, which had close connections with People's Canada, now the main non-dominant force in the region.

The successful workers' insurrections in Shanghai, Rio and Seoul had seemed curiously like 1917, with occupied factories, flags and mass meetings. Be Juen, "the Taiwan Lenin", a gay telecom engineer who had chaired the first Disembodied Soviet of South East Asia, called himself a "post-electronic Bolshevik". The Pacific Rim was now dominated intellectually by radical Gnosticism.

In Britain capitalism didn't so much collapse as just

---

190 "Jerusalem" was originally written as a poem by William Blake in 1804; the lyrics were added to music written by Hubert Parry in 1916.

"Anarchy in the UK", *Never Mind the Bollocks, Here's the Sex Pistols*, Sex Pistols, 1977 grind to a halt. Major, despite halting the Channel Tunnel, abandoning the NHS "reforms" and pledging himself to personally reintroduce the welfare state, had not lasted long. The Smith-Ashdown coalition was unable to cope with the expectations of a surge tide of long-suppressed public resentment. After decades when the British government had praised dissent everywhere else in the world, the people of UKania themselves became a byword for revolt: there were mass teach-ins on transport, and sacked soldiers organised forces' parliaments while poets and jazzers rebelled.

"Children of Albion" demanded excellence and imagination in education; becalmed commuters held incessant intemperate marches between the few remaining nuclear installations. After the General Council of the TUC joined the Royal National Government of 1996, and with the success of the subsequent strike wave headed by NHS workers, rank-and-file trade unionism got out of its coffin and started to tango. After the granting of Charter 88 and a series of increasingly incomprehensible elections whose voting system was only understood by *Guardian* readers, most people decided not to bother. A new "People's Charter" was set up to demand the right not to have a parliament at Westminster, now synonymous with the Old Corruption.

Whatever else he was wrong about, Marx turned out to be right about economics. No longer stabilised by massive arms spending, the world economy imploded, the banks folded and workers simply took over their places of work and ran themselves, out of convenience as much as conviction. The transnational networks organising this new system called themselves Winstanleys rather than Workers' Councils, and their leading theorists claimed to be inspired by the newly discovered philosophical writings of the young George Bernard Shaw. The Great Dissent had started when disgruntled Thames TV workers put their pirate station at the disposal of the networks of Winstanley Committees and the old *Sun*, now renamed by its journalist-printer collective the *Unstamped*, succeeded in, as its motto put it, "Making striking sexy again". Now that the collapsed school and university system no longer taught compulsory Wollstonecraft, Milton, Woolf or Orwell, these writers became immensely popular among the young and were set to rap and rock music.

In fact, the Harold Wilson-King Charles Royal National Government's final collapse was not in revulsion at the hated Lord Hattersley's brutal repression (rioters had their hands cut off by privatised surgeons). The real damage was done by the Swuppies, an elite cadre of disgruntled City dwellers who had joined the SWP and spent their time sabotaging what was left of the international stock market by making bogus loans and siphoning payments into workers' groups. Curiously the Swuppies, while intensely loyal to the general line of SWP philosopher Tony Cliff, also claimed loyalty to the cosmic re-embodiment of the Levellers.

In some ways it was suprisingly peaceful. When the Thatcher putschists ordered the air force to bomb the Festival Hall, where the people's parliament had been established after the Second Dissolution, its officers declined. The police found the sheer size of the processions during the Great Dissent impossible to intimidate. The information of the Secret Service was much inferior to the dissenting parties, and King Charles, before his execution, confessed himself amazed that "modern states are so dependent on a human bureaucracy whose loyalties can change abruptly."

Many leading industrialists and bankers recounted that what had amazed them had been that in the early nineties they had been able to conceal for so long the terminal disintegration of the international economic system.

"The Soviet collapse was meant to save us but then Eastern Europe realised the market didn't work either," said Rupert Murdoch in his suicide note. The words of Paul Reichmann, Canary Wharf's progenitor, when his creation was taken over as a Tatlin Tower of NE Europe were a good epitaph for the end of century: "Hell, what took you so long?"

The Guardian, 19 November 1991

CONTRIBUTORS

Editors

Juliet Ash was a lecturer in the history of design in a number of art and design schools, and from 2001 to 2014 she was a tutor in dress/textiles design history at the Royal College of Art, London. She is author of *Dress Behind Bars: Prison Clothing as Criminality*, co-editor with Elizabeth Wilson of *Chic Thrills: A Fashion Reader*, and has written a number of published articles on the history and theory of dress. She is the widow of David Widgery.

Nigel Fountain has written for the *Guardian, Observer, Sunday Times, New Statesman, Oldie, Listener, London Magazine, Socialist Worker, History Today, New Society* and *OZ*. He was a *Guardian* commissioning obituaries editor (1994-2009), *City Limits* magazine co-editor (1982-87) and a *Time Out* assistant editor (1980-81). His books include *Days Like These; Underground: The London Alternative Press 1966 – 74; Lost Empires;* and *When the Lamps Went Out: Reporting the Great War 1914 – 1918*. His friendship with David Widgery began in the 1960s.

David Renton is a barrister and the author of *Fascism, theory and practice: Fascism, Anti-Fascism and the 1940s, Dissident Marxism* (including a chapter on David Widgery), *When We Touched the Sky: The ANL 1977 – 1981,* and *Colour Blind?: Race & Migration in North East England*. He has also written histories of the British Communist Party and biographies of Leon Trotsky and C.L.R. James.

Section Introduction Contributors

Anthony Barnett is the founder of openDemocracy. He was the first director of Charter88 from 1988 to 1995 and co-director of the Convention of Modern Liberty from 2008 to 2009. He worked on *Beating Time* with David Widgery in the publishing imprint Tigerstripes in the mid-1980s. He was on the early editorial committee of *New Left Review*. Anthony's books include *Iron Britannia: Time to take the Great out of Britain*, on the Falklands War, now republished by Faber Finds, and this year, *Blimey, it could be Brexit!* published on openDemocracy.

Anna Livingstone has been a GP since 1983 at Gill Street Health Centre in Limehouse, the same practice as David Widgery. She follows the nineteenth-century physician Virchow's view that "medicine is a social science and politics is nothing but medicine writ large." She is a socialist and a feminist and active in UNITE/Medical Practitioners Union and the BMA, and is secretary of Tower Hamlets Keep Our NHS Public.

Kambiz Boomla has been a GP in Tower Hamlets from 1982, and worked closely with David Widgery. He is a member of the Socialist Workers Party, and was for many years chair of the City and East London Local Medical Committee. He is currently a clinical senior lecturer at Queen Mary University of London attached to Barts and the London Medical School. He has written articles for *Pulse Today* and has been interviewed on BBC Radio 4 about health issues.

Ruth Gregory was a key London activist and designer in the collective movement Rock Against Racism, when David Widgery was writing and working for RAR. They collaborated on the RARzine *Temporary Hoarding* from

1976 to 81, the Save Bethnal Green Hospital campaign in 1979, and his book *Beating Time*, along with Andy Dark, in 1986. Her work and collected archive from her RAR days formed half of the exhibition: *A Riot of Our Own* at Chelsea Space, 2008 and the *East End Film Festival*, 2010.

Tony Gould served in the British military, then studied English at Cambridge. He has worked as a BBC radio producer and as literary editor of *New Society* and the *New Statesman*. It was in this capacity that he commissioned David Widgery to write reviews and articles. Tony Gould's books include *A Summer Plague: Polio and Its Survivors* and *Inside Outsider: The Life and Times of Colin MacInnes*, winner of the 1984 PEN Silver Pen award.

Sheila Rowbotham, who helped to start the women's liberation movement in Britain, was influenced by the ideas of "history from below" associated with the history workshops held at Ruskin College, Oxford. She met David Widgery after he wrote to her enthusiastically about her early pamphlet, *Women's Liberation and the New Politics*. She has written widely on the history of feminism and radical social movements; her most recent books are *Edward Carpenter: A Life of Liberty and Love, Dreamers of a New Day* and *Rebel Crossings: New Women, Free Lovers and Radicals in Britain and the United States*.

Michael Rosen is a children's writer and author. He was Children's Laureate from 2007 to 2009. Michael co-edited with David Widgery *The Chatto Book of Dissent*. He writes a regular column on education for the *Guardian* and is a prizewinning broadcaster, presenting a range of documentary features on British radio as well as BBC Radio 4's regular series about language, *Word of Mouth*. He is Professor of Children's Literature at Goldsmiths, University of London.

Anny Ash is a Macmillan social prescriber at the Bromley by Bow Centre in East London and has worked for a number of charity organisations including as head of youth services at Body & Soul. She has co-written a published case study research paper on "Broken Homes and Violent Streets" for the journal *Mental Health and Social Inclusion.* She is David Widgery's daughter.

Jesse Ash is an exhibiting artist who is represented by the Rome art gallery Monitor. He has shown his work in a number of countries, including Italy, the US, Brazil, the UK, France, Brussels, Germany and Puerto Rico. His written texts include contributions in *UOVO* contemporary art magazine and *F.R. David,* edited by Will Holder, and he has co-presented a radio programme. Jesse teaches at Central Saint Martins college and Wimbledon College of Arts (London). He is David Widgery's stepson.

Ben Bethell runs a dance hall and reggae sound system called the Heatwave. Ben has a degree in social and cultural studies from Goldsmiths. He is David Widgery's nephew.

SELECTED BIBLIOGRAPHY

Articles, Chapters, Essays, Letters

Allan Flanders, *Steel Review* (July 1966)

Alexandra Kollontai, "Sexual Relations and the Class Struggle" (1921)

Boris Arvatov, "Materialised Utopia", *Lef* 1 (1923)

Christopher Caudwell, "Love: a Study in Changing Values", *Studies in a Dying Culture* (Lane, 1938)

Dziga Vertov, "Film Directors: A Revolution" (Russian essay, 1923)

Friedrich Engels, "The Book of Revelation" (1883)

George Orwell, "Looking Back on the Spanish War" (est. 1942)

Jack Kerouac, "Statement on Poetics", *The New American Poetry: 1945–1960*, ed. Donald Allen (Grove Press, 1960)

James Baldwin, "An Open Letter to My Sister, Miss Angela Davis", 19 November 1970 (published in *New York Review of Books* 7 January 1971 (Volume 15, Number 12))

James Baldwin, "The Black Boy Looks at the White Boy Norman Mailer", *Esquire* (May 1961)

James Baldwin, "The Preservation of Innocence", *Zero* 1.2 (1949)

Karl Marx, "Human Requirements and Division of Labour Under the Rule of Private Property", *Economic and Philosophic Manuscripts of 1844* (1932)

Karl Marx, "The Power of Money", *Economic and Philosophic Manuscripts of 1844* (1932)

Kate Millett, *Sexual Politics* (Doubleday, 1968)

Leon Trotsky, "Against Bureaucracy, Progressive and Unprogressive", *Problems of Life* (Methuen, 1924)

Norman Mailer, "The Prisoner of Sex", Harper's Magazine (March 1971)

Olive Schreiner, *Woman and Labour* (T.F. Unwin, 1911)

Peter Sedgwick, "Natural Science and Human Theory: A Critique of Herbert Marcuse", *The Socialist Register* (1966)

Roland Barthes, "The Great Family of Man", *Mythologies* (Editions du Seuil (French), 1957)

Ted Berrigan, "Jack Kerouac, The Art of Fiction No. 41", *The Paris Review* (Issue 43, Summer 1968)

Walter Benjamin, "The Work of Art in the Age of Mechanical Reproduction" (German essay, 1935)

William Blake, "Annotations to Lavater's *Aphorisms on Man*", London 1788

William Blake, "Letter to Mr John Flaxman, Buckingham Street, Fitzroy Square", 12 September 1800

Books

Arts Council of Great Britain, *Art in Revolution: Soviet Art and Design Since 1917* (Arts Council of Great Britain, 1971)

Billie Holiday and William Duffy, *Lady Sings the Blues* (Doubleday, 1956)

Bertrand Russell, *Appeal to the American Conscience* (Bertrand Russell Peace Foundation, 1966)

Charles Dickens, *David Copperfield* (Bradbury & Evans, 1850)

C.L.R. James, *Notes on Dialectics* (Lawrence Hill & Co., 1980)

C.L.R. James, *The Black Jacobins* (Dial Press, 1935)

C.L.R. James, *The Future in the Present* (Allison & Busby, 1977)

David Cooper, *The Death of the Family* (Vintage, 1971)

David V. Erdman, *Blake: Prophet Against Empire* (Princeton UP: 1954)

David Widgery, *Beating Time* (Chatto & Windus, 1986)

David Widgery, *Preserving Disorder* (Pluto Press, 1989)

David Widgery, *Some Lives!: A GP's East End* (Sinclair-Stevenson, 1991)

David Widgery, *The Left in Britain, 1956-68* (Penguin, 1976)

Don Milligan, *The Politics of Homosexuality* (Pluto Press, 1973)

Dora Russell, *The Right to be Happy* (Harper & Brothers, 1927)

Dora Russell, *The Tamarisk Tree* (Elek/Pemberton, 1975)

Edward Carpenter, *Love's Coming of Age: A Series of Papers on the Relations of the Sexes* (Labour Press, 1896)

Eldridge Cleaver, *Soul on Ice* (Ramparts Press, 1968).

Elizabeth Crawford, *The Women's Suffrage Movement: A Reference Guide 1866–1928* (UCL Press, 1999)

Friedrich Engels, *The Origin of the Family, Private Property and the State: In Light of the Researches of Lewis H. Morgan* (Verlag der Schweizerischen Volksbuchhandlung (German), 1884)

George Orwell, *The Road to Wigan Pier* (Victor Gollancz, 1937)

Herbert Marshall, *Mayakovsky and his Poetry* (Pilot Press, 1942)

Jack Kerouac, *Big Sur* (Farrar, Straus and Cudahy, 1962)

Jack Kerouac, *Book of Dreams* (City Lights Books, 1961)

Jack Kerouac, *Desolation Angels* (Coward-McCann, 1965)

Jack Kerouac, *On the Road* (Viking Press, 1957)

Jack Kerouac, *Satori in Paris* (Grove Press, 1966)

Jack Kerouac, *The Subterraneans* (Grove Press, 1958)

Jack Kerouac, *Tristessa* (Avon, 1960)

James Baldwin, *Another Country* (Dial Press, 1962)

James Baldwin, *Autobiographical Notes* (Knopf, 1953)

James Baldwin, *Giovanni's Room* (Dial Press, 1956)

James Baldwin, *Nobody Knows My Name* (Dial Press, 1961)

James Baldwin, *Notes of a Native Son* (Beacon Press, 1955)

James Baldwin, *Tell Me How Long the Train's Been Gone* (Dial Press, 1968)

James Baldwin, *The Fire Next Time* (Dial Press, 1963)

James Connolly, *The Re-Conquest of Ireland* (1915)

John Berger, *About Looking* (Pantheon, 1980)

John Bunyan, *The Pilgrim's Progress from this World, to that Which Is to Come* (Two parts published in 1678 & 1684)

Karl Marx, *Capital: Critique of Political Economy*, three volumes (Verlag von Otto Meissner (German), 1867, 1885 & 1894)

Karl Marx, *The Eighteenth Brumaire of Louis Napoleon* (first appeared as an essay in the German magazine *Die Revolution* in 1852, but later published as a book)

Karl Marx, *Value, Price and Profit* (speech, 1865; book (German), S. Sonnenschein & Co., 1898)

Leon Trotsky, *The History of the Russian Revolution Volume 1: The Overthrow of Tzarism* (Granit (Russian), 1931)

Lisa Alther, *Kinflicks* (Knopf, 1976)

Martin Amis, *London Fields* (J. Cape, 1989)

Mayakovsky, ed. & trans. Herbert Marshall (Dobson Books, 1965)

Michael Horovitz, *Children of Albion: Poetry of the Underground in Britain* (Penguin, 1969)

Neal Cassady, *The First Third & Other Writings* (San Francisco City Lights Books, 1971)

Norman Mailer, *An American Dream* (Dial Press, 1965)

Norman Mailer, *Cannibals and Christians* (Dial Press, 1966)

Norman Mailer, *The Armies of the Night: History as a Novel, the Novel as History* (New American Library, 1968)

Norman Mailer, *The Prisoner of Sex* (Little, Brown, 1971)

Oswald Spengler, *The Decline of the West, or The Downfall of the Occident*, two volumes (Allen & Unwin, 1918 & 1922)

Patrick Hutt et al., *Confronting an Ill Society: David Widgery, General Practice, Idealism and the Chase for Change* (Radcliffe, 2005)

Paul Harrison, *Inside the Inner City* (Penguin, 1983)

Peter Fryer, *Hungarian Tragedy* (Dobson Books, 1956)

Richard Smith, *Unemployment and Health: A Disaster and a Challenge* (Oxford UP, 1987)

Rita Mae Brown, *Rubyfruit Jungle* (Daughters, 1973)

Robert A. Bone, *The Negro Novel in America* (Yale UP, 1958)

Sheila Rowbotham, *Hidden from History: 300 Years of Women's Oppression and the Fight Against It* (Pluto Press, 1973))

Sylvia Pankhurst, *The Suffragette Movement: An Intimate Account of Persons and Ideals* (Longmans, Green & Co, 1931)

The Chatto Book of Dissent, ed. David Widgery & Michael Rosen (Chatto & Windus, 1991)

The Writings of William Blake, III, ed. Edwin J. Ellis & William Butler Yeats (1893)

Thomas Okey, *A Basketful of Memories: An Autobiographical Sketch* (Dent, 1930)

Thomas Paine, *Rights of Man: Answer to Mr Burke's Attack on the French Revolution* (J.S. Jordan, 1791)

Tom Wolfe, *The Electric Kool-aid Acid Test* (Farrar, Straus and Giroux, 1968)

Victor Serge, *Destiny of a Revolution*, trans. Max Shachtman (Jarrolds, 1937)

Victor Serge, *Memoirs of a Revolutionary, 1901–1941*, trans. Peter Sedgwick (Oxford UP, 1963)

Victor Serge, *Year One of the Russian Revolution*, trans. Peter Sedgwick (Allen Lane, 1972)

Walt Whitman, *Leaves of Grass* (Walt Whitman, 1855)

William Blake, *America, a Prophecy* (William Blake, 1793)

William Blake, *Jerusalem, the Emanation of the Giant Albion* (William Blake, 1877)

William Blake, *The Marriage of Heaven and Hell* (William Blake, 1793)

William Carlos Williams, *In the American Grain* (New Directions, 1925)

William Carlos Williams, *Pictures from Brueghel and Other Poems: Collected Poems, 1950–1962* (J. Laughlin, 1962)

William Carlos Williams, *The Doctor Stories*, compiled by Robert Coles, MD (New Directions, 1984)

William J. Fishman, *East End 1888* (Duckworth, 1988)

William S. Burroughs, *Naked Lunch* (Olympia Press, 1959)

William Morris, *News from Nowhere or, An Epoch of Rest, Being Some Chapters from a Utopian Romance* (Reeves & Turner, 1890)

Films

Coma, dir. Michael Crichton, 1978

Doctor in the House, dir. Ralph Thomas, 1954

I'm All Right Jack, dir. John Boulting, 1959

Salt of the Earth, dir. Herbert J. Biberman, 1954

Sammy and Rosie Get Laid, dir. Stephen Frears, 1987

The Hospital, dir. Arthur Hiller, 1971

The Rocky Horror Picture Show, dir. Jim Sharman, 1975

The War Game, dir. Peter Watkins, 1965

Television

A Climate of Fear, dir. Don Taylor, 1962

"Cathy Come Home", *The Wednesday Play*, dir. Kenneth Loach, 1969

Crossroads, creators Hazel Adair & Peter Ling, 1964–1988

Dixon of Dock Green, creator Ted Willis, 1955–1976

It's That Man Again, creator Ted Kavanagh, 1939–1949

"The Big Flame", *The Wednesday Play*, dir. Kenneth Loach, 1969

The Birth of a Private Man, dir. Don Taylor, 1963

"The Rank and File", *Play for Today*, dir. Kenneth Loach, 1971

The Singing Detective, dir. Jon Amiel, 1986

The Sweeney, creator Ian Kennedy Martin, 1975–1978

Where the Difference Begins, dir. Don Taylor, 1961

Plays

Black Heroes in the Hall of Fame, Sandy Flip Fraser, 1987

Live Bed Show, Arthur Smith, 1989

Ma Rainey's Black Bottom, August Wilson, 1982

Mystery-Bouffe, Vladimir Mayakovsky, 1918

Pravda, David Hare and Howard Brenton, 1985

Ragamuffin, Amani Naphtali, 1988

Roots, Arnold Wesker, 1958

Salome, Oscar Wilde, 1893 in French (1894 in English)

The Bathhouse, Vladimir Mayakovsky, 1929 in Russian

The Bedbug, Vladimir Mayakovsky, 1928-9 in Russian

The Good Person of Szechwan, Bertolt Brecht, 1941 in German

The Long March, Sarmcol Workers Cooperative (SAWCO), 1986

The Pied Piper, Adrian Mitchell, 1987

The Rocky Horror Show, dir. Jim Sharman, 1973 (in London)

The Shaughraun, Dion Boucicault, 1874

Poems

George Orwell, "St Andrew's Day" (1935)

T.S. Eliot, "The Waste Land" (Horace Liveright, 1922)

Vladimir Mayakovsky, "A Cloud in Trousers" (1915)

Vladimir Mayakovsky, "An Order to the Art Army" (1918)

Vladimir Mayakovsky, "A Talk with Comrade Lenin" (1929)

Vladimir Mayakovsky, "At the Top of My Voice: First Prelude to a Poem on the Five Year Plan" (1930)

Vladimir Mayakovsky, "At the Top of My Voice: Unfinished Prelude to the Second Part of a Poem on the Five Year Plan" (1930)

Vladimir Mayakovsky, "Home!" (1925)

Vladimir Mayakovsky, "Lenin" (1924)

William Blake, "Jerusalem" (1804)

William Blake, "London", *Songs of Innocence and of Experience* (1794)

William Blake, "The Human Abstract", *Songs of Innocence and of Experience* (1794)

William Blake, "The Garden of Love", *Songs of Innocence and of Experience* (1794)

William Blake, "The School Boy", *Songs of Innocence and of Experience* (1794)

William Blake, "Vala, or The Four Zoas", *The Writings of William Blake*, III, ed. Edwin J. Ellis & William Butler Yeats (1893)

William Blake, "Visions of the Daughters of Albion" (1793)

William Carlos Williams, "Asphodel, That Greeny Flower", *Journey to Love* (Random House, 1965)

Radio

"Mrs Dale's Diary", *Light Programme* (BBC radio), 1967–1969

"Toytown", *Children's Hour* (BBC radio), creator Sydney Beaman, 1929–1960s; adapted for TV (ITV) in the 1970s

Songs, Albums

"Anarchy in the UK", *Never Mind the Bollocks, Here's the Sex Pistols*, Sex Pistols, 1977

Blonde on Blonde, Bob Dylan, 1966

"Fire in the Booth", *Knowledge Is Power Vol. 1*, Akala, 2012

"Imagine", *Imagine*, John Lennon, 1971

"Lover Man", *Lover Man (Oh, Where Can You Be?)* (single), Billie Holiday, 1945

"Song of the Streets (What Have We Got)", *Song of the Streets* (single), Sham 69, 1977

"Up Against the Wall", *Power in the Darkness*, Tom Robinson Band, 1978

"(White Man) In Hammersmith Palais", *(White Man) In Hammersmith Palais* (single), The Clash, 1978

"Young Woman's Blues", Bessie Smith, recorded 1926

"Strange Fruit", *Strange Fruit* (single), Billie Holiday, 1939